# SHOOT IT!

# SHOOT IT!

## HOLLYWOOD INC. AND THE
## RISING OF INDEPENDENT FILM

DAVID SPANER

ARSENAL PULP PRESS
VANCOUVER

ARSENAL PULP PRESS
Suite 101, 211 East Georgia St.
Vancouver, BC
Canada  V6A 1Z6
arsenalpulp.com

The publisher gratefully acknowledges the support of the Canada Council for the Arts and the British Columbia Arts Council for its publishing program, and the Government of Canada (through the Canada Book Fund) and the Government of British Columbia (through the Book Publishing Tax Credit Program) for its publishing activities.

Printed and bound in Canada
Cover design by Electra Design Group
Photograph on cover courtesy of Susan Seidelman
Editing by Susan Safyan

Library and Archives Canada Cataloguing in Publication:

Spaner, David
    Shoot it! : Hollywood Inc. and the rise of independent film / David Spaner.

Includes bibliographical references and index.
Also issued in electronic format.
ISBN 978-1-55152-408-5

    1. Independent films—History and criticism.  2. Motion picture industry—United States—History.  I. Title.

PN1993.5.A1S63 2011                    791.4309                    C2011-905445-0

*For the blacklisted, who endured with humor and dignity.*

"They'll rob you of your innocence, they will put you up for sale
The more that you will find success, the more that you will fail
So play the chords of love, my friend, play the chords of pain
If you want to keep your song, don't, don't, don't, don't play the chords of fame"
—Phil Ochs

# CONTENTS

Introduction   9

PART I: Why Are the Movies So Bad These Days?
*The Rise of Studio Film*

PART II: And Why Are They So Good?
*The Rise of Independent Film*

ON SEPTEMBER 15, 2010, while Mexican authorities were sparing no extravagance to celebrate the 200th anniversary of the country's independence, filmmaker Francisco Vargas assembled 850 photographers to create an "instantaneous" movie about Mexico City. They fanned out across town, word-renowned photographers and novices, to create *Nuestra Señora de Concreto* (*Our Lady of Concrete*), a loving portrait of their city and its people, but one with a question. "The unequal, uncertain, and violent reality we live in," says Vargas, "makes us ask ourselves if we really have something to celebrate."

‡

The better filmmakers have always had questions. The French New Wave's François Truffaut, for one, also always had an answer—No—whenever Hollywood studios came calling with offers. "He never really made a movie for commercial reasons," says his daughter Laura. These days there's even more reason to steer clear of the studios. "They don't care about the movie," notes Truffaut's other daughter, Eva. "They care about the products they sell." With ancillary profits from merchandising and home viewing, box office accounts for less than twenty percent of the bounty generated by a studio movie. There were early examples of commercial crossovers and product placement (the first film to win a best-picture Oscar, *Wings*, promoted Hershey's chocolates in 1927), but today's commercialism is so unbridled that the Writers Guild of America has complained that their members are being forced to write ad copy into their scripts. "The result is that tens of millions of viewers are sometimes being sold products without their knowledge, sold in opaque, subliminal ways and sold in violation of government regulations."[1] In *Cast Away* (2000), Tom Hanks isn't stranded on a desert island; he's stranded in a two-hour FedEx commercial. *I, Robot* (2004) wants to tell us that the distant future will have the same great commodities as today: Converse trainers, Ovaltine, Audi, FedEx, Dos Equis, and JVC. *Space Jam* (1996) star Michael Jordan *is* the film's product placement, along with everything he's ever dreamed of endorsing, from Wheaties to Nikes. The movie known at the time of writing as *James Bond 23* has reached new heights, deriving $45 million from product placements. "What disappointed me about *The Last Temptation of*

*Christ,"* notes the anarcho-punk Jello Biafra, "is here somebody spends $25 million of their own money to make a movie so violent and gory not even Tarantino could top it, but not one action figure. I want a Mel Gibson Jesus. That's the action figure I would be proud to display."

‡

Writing newspaper film reviews in the first decade of the twenty-first century, I was often faced with the question, *Why are the movies so bad these days?* It's a question, like so many regarding film, with an answer that mixes culture with politics. For instance, ask filmmaker Miranda July about the dearth of female directors and her answer combines her feminism and do-it-yourself cultural ethos. She says it goes back to the myth of the all-knowing, omnipotent director (passed down since the days of Cecil B. DeMille). "I don't come across whatever it takes to conceive of yourself as kind of a god-like creator much in women—and I know a lot of interesting, creative women," she says. "That's all a lie. You don't actually have to know. It's just that guys are raised to know that they can act in-charge, even without knowing. There's so much *not knowing* involved in making a film; it's actually about the act of going forth with doubt."

The studios of early Hollywood are now massive corporate entities with a devastating impact on the quality of movies and on local film cultures. The first half of this book follows the rise of this global studio system in the US and the resistance to it, from blacklisted writers to DIY filmmakers. There are also great movies being made in the new century, and the second half of the book looks at the talented, impassioned independent filmmaking that's rising everywhere to fill the quality void. Whether they're in Canada, England, France, Mexico, Romania, South Korea, or the US, independent filmmakers share similar values and hurdles—funding, distribution, exhibition. These filmmakers are determined to overcome all obstacles and just shoot it. Considered individually, they may seem isolated, but together they are the nucleus of an international independent movement.

Internationalism and globalization are as different as volunteering to fight fascism in Spain in 1937 and outsourcing Nike production to a non-union zone in China in 2007. Internationalism is about diverse local cultures joining to find common humanity across borders. "My nation is cinema, and my language is film," says Mexican filmmaker Alfonso Cuarón.[2] Globalization is about worldwide homogenization.

The globalization of culture has received less attention than the globalization of economies, but it is this conflict between internationalism and globalization, between the local and the global, that defines the difference between independents and studios. "The more local you are, the more universal and international you are," says filmmaker Jean Pierre Lefebvre who, as a young Montreal cinephile, fell in love with Italian neorealism. "What made Italian cinema universal? Because it always talked about Italian values. It showed landscapes, showed food, showed people with different attitudes." American folklorist Alan Lomax, writing in 1968, warned that "soon there will be nowhere to go and nothing worth staying at home for. Our western mass-production and communication systems are inadvertently destroying the languages, traditions, cuisines and creative styles that once gave every people and every locality a distinctive character—indeed their principal reason for living."[3]

While English is the studios' language of choice, no language at all is even better when you have a global target audience. So the studios have invented a new kind of silent picture—computerized effects, car crashes, and other action in place of dialogue—aimed at youthful, male moviegoers everywhere. It's no longer unusual for a studio movie to premiere overseas and draw most of its revenues outside North America. "I've found, dealing with studios, that decisions are made by their international sales departments," says Canadian filmmaker Don McKellar. Local culture falls prey to the globalization of culture because to survive (read: expand and dominate), corporate film, television, music, and publishing require a worldwide audience. While culture corporations like to speak of the "free flow of information," in their reality that means freedom for their products to reach a global audience without such nagging impediments as local cultures. So its noise drowns out local artists while its film industry benefits from local grants, tax breaks, anti-union legislation, and public financing of new roads and other infrastructure. It's the socialization of corporate costs alongside the privatization of cultural profits. The benefactors of this public largesse pull up stakes when not properly pampered. Besides running roughshod over other countries' filmmakers and cinemas, studio globalization means outsourcing Hollywood to the lowest bidder. Along with dictating which movies are seen, it determines where movies are made. Subsidizing corporate billionaires has become a way of life in today's film world.

Besides being nearly impossible to make a good movie within the

Hollywood studio system, producers everywhere else make bad imitations of bad American movies. "There are so many films that are made in Mexico that just follow this American recipe for making a romantic comedy or an action film," says Mexican filmmaker Mariana Chenillo. "Some of them turn out to be box-office successes, but most of them don't—and they look alike. They're just Hollywood wannabe films."

For France's Catherine Breillat, "What it's about is brainwashing, because it leads people to always want to watch the same thing, to go for series rather than innovation, repetition rather than creation, and sequels where you see a film and then the second, the third, the forth. People are always constantly ruminating on the same ideas, ruminating over the same material, like cows ruminating on shit."

‡

"Although the movies set out with only one purpose, to entertain, their unique power of suggestion soon made them the greatest selling force in the world," said Motion Picture Association of America president Eric Johnston in 1957. "Those who come out for the show will stay out to shop. What's more, they'll be in a mood for shopping."[4] But there were always those who didn't see it that way. In Europe, quotas were created in the 1920s to protect local filmmaking. French cinephiles launched cine-clubs, which screened non-commercial films. "To the public that loves and understands the cinemas, that foresees its destiny, there remains only a single means of battling this dictatorship of money: to band together," stated one Paris club's manifesto.[5]

From the beginnings of cinema, filmmakers have operated outside commercial confines. Depending on time and place, the kind of filmmaking celebrated in this book has been labeled "underground," "art-house," and sometimes nothing at all. The term "independent" is widely used from South Korea to Mexico, though its original definition—anything made outside the major Hollywood studios—is too widespread these days to mean much. A low-budget horror movie made for entirely commercial purposes, for example, has little in common with the films of England's Mike Leigh or Romania's New Wave. So "independent" in *Shoot It!* refers to movies made outside the studio system and with a non-commercial sensibility. Independent films are made by independent human beings who won't revamp their art because of a test screening or some whim of a financier or producer.

Most independent movies are director-driven and, in collaboration with actors and crew, express the filmmaker's personal vision. There are also collective-driven independents, such as the anarchist SIE Films of Barcelona, which made dozens of movies during the Spanish Revolution, or the North of England's Amber Films, which has produced movies since 1968. The filmmakers in this book have been deeply affected by the social and cultural upheavals of their times, from Depression-era street protests to punk rock. In the 1960s, France showed the exhilarating possibilities of film (the New Wave) and of society (Paris '68). Many filmmakers were touched by the counterculture, including Sally Potter, who was active in the London Film-Makers Co-op. "Working in the cooperative was very specific to that time; it was an integration of the process of working and the product," Potter says. "How people worked together was considered important, relevant. It wasn't just about putting a product out there. Every aspect of life was touched by that way of thinking—performance, theater, music, film, and politics—and women's politics—were all meeting and melting into each other."

There are independent-minded filmmakers who also work within the studio system. If the Coen brothers or Tim Burton can demand creative autonomy at a studio, good for them, but they are a rarefied handful; filmmakers from John Cassavetes to Gus Van Sant to Steven Soderbergh have been worked over by studio executives. "I couldn't conceive of working in the studio system, not for a split second," Mike Leigh says. "On various occasions, the studios have indicated they would do what other backers do for my films, which is to give us the money and fuck off. If they were to do that seriously, then fine. But pigs might fly. I wouldn't go there, because I don't know anybody who has not been fucked over by it."[6]

Despite Woody Allen's track record, he found himself facing increasingly intrusive American producers in the 2000s. "I've been very lucky and also a bit of a con man because I've spent my whole life in American films and always had complete artistic freedom," he told me. "No one read my scripts, no one had anything to say about casting. I always had final cut and I had always said—people said I was joking—the only thing standing between me and greatness is me. There was no excuse for me not to do great work. I could never blame it on anyone because I had all the freedom anyone could ever want, provided I work for my limited budget." That changed in the new century when his films didn't fare so well at the box office.

The film studios started to say, Look, we don't want to just be bankers: we don't want to just put the money in a brown paper bag and you give us the film. We'd like to know what's the film about or who's going to be in it … And I have been spoiled in decades of not working that way, and I don't think I could work that way, and I said, 'I would rather not do that.' So I found it hard to get financed because they wanted some input. I felt once you open that door, the input would never stop. So then all of a sudden London called.

Allen began his shooting tour of Europe, which "doesn't have film studios … I avoided that my whole life, and at the last second, when things were starting to encroach, managed to avoid it still by going to Europe. And artistically, it's been great for me."

‡

The protest pours down Hollywood Boulevard in support of the Writers Guild of America strike, stopping in front of Grauman's Chinese Theatre. "If the corporations make money on new media," Sandra Oh shouts from a makeshift stage, "the writers should too. *Share!*"

Alongside the Americans who churn out corporate brainwashing, there is another American cultural tradition from Woody Guthrie to Woody Allen, and there was a time when Hollywood progressives fought for creative input inside the studios, and unions went toe-to-toe with moguls. These activists were blacklisted and exiled, and the town would never entirely recover. During the WGA protest in 2007, Lelia Goldoni, who co-starred in John Cassavetes' first feature, *Shadows,* was in the streets for the striking writers. "I believe that all unions are threatened," says Goldoni. "The power structure really wants to get rid of all benefits to labor." Actress Kim Delaney, the daughter of a Philadelphia union organizer, is in the streets too. "I'm here in solidarity," she says. "However dark-hearted the moguls might have been, at the end of the day they loved making movies," the WGA's David Weiss tells me, "and I think that's absent from these corporations. That filters into the product. Now when I take a meeting, it's with somebody who's working for somebody who runs General Electric. It's a refrigerator manufacturer."

‡

As my interview with *Rebel Without a Cause* screenwriter Stewart Stern winds down, he shuffles papers in his Seattle waterfront home. "I can't write a commercial film, and I tried," Stern says. "My whole body would rebel." Finally, Stern finds his notes from a talk that director Wim Wenders delivered in Seattle. "The local cultures are being over-whelmed by the global, chiefly American one," he quotes Wenders. "It is all being replaced with fakes: fake stories, fake people, fake places. The division now is between films that tell stories and films that sell stories." I've brought a recording of Phil Ochs' "Jim Dean of Indiana" for Stern to hear. He listens intently, then opens his desk to a small matchbox containing a handful of corn seeds. "After the funeral, I went back to the farm where Jimmy grew up. Found these on the ground in the barn." He reaches into the box, offers me a seed from Jim Dean's farm.

I had mentioned to Stern that while directors are credited with in-venting independent cinema, Dean and other naturalistic actors from Italy, France, and the US in the 1950s and '60s provided the dose of raw reality that enabled the emergence of this new style of filmmaking. Many of the best character-driven filmmakers started as performers. Italian neorealist Vittorio De Sica, for example, utilized his experience as an actor to entice stunning performances from the non-professional actors he directed in *Bicycle Thieves* (1948). In France, New Wave au-teurs created an entirely new relationship with their actors, also often non-professionals, who had a casual, cool style that had little in com-mon with conventional movie stardom. "Brando and Dean and Paul Newman were far more influential to me than directors," says early Canadian independent Larry Kent, who wanted to be actor before turn-ing to directing. "Actors have to go in and, when they act, tell the truth. That's what I want to do as a filmmaker. And that's what I continue to do, so it is totally satisfying to make the film that you want to make."

‡

The various filmmaking communities described in this book are indica-tive of the independent world—rather than providing an encyclopedic view of it. Each of them represents a unique aspect of independent filmmaking and its relationship to the studios, but rebel cinema in the new century also thrives in many other countries, with filmmakers such as Finland's Aki Kaurismäki, Argentina's Lucrecia Martel, Austria's Michael Haneke, Japan's Nobuhiro Suwa, Switzerland's Ursula Meier, and Hong Kong's Wong Kar-wai as relentless as the best of the Romanian or French Waves. In the 1990s, Denmark's influential Dogme movement arrived, with its insistence that filmmaking is a no-frills collaborative art. There are also film industries entirely separate from Hollywood—such as Nollywood, whose small-budget DVDs sell on the streets of Nigeria, or Bollywood, whose big-budget musicals have a massive audience in India and beyond—but their focus is overwhelmingly commercial, and this book is about independent narrative filmmaking.

Of course, not every purely independent film is great cinema, but like Warner Bros. when it actually was the Warner brothers, independent filmmakers are more willing to take risks than today's business grads-turned-studio executives who always choose the safe route. And it is risk-taking that makes possible the movie that shatters expectations.

‡

The best movies bring characters to life. This book looks at the characters behind independent cinema, who have survived every attempt to absorb or marginalize their filmmaking. The movies are at another crossroads—with digital filmmaking and distribution in the wings—but there will always be a young filmmaker who comes along in Bucharest or Austin or Seoul and lights up a screen with the magic of Truffaut and Godard, Brando and Dean, Francisco Vargas and Miranda July. And he or she will know that film is too important to be reduced to commerce.

"Film is like breathing for me," Jean Pierre Lefebvre says.

> It's a vital need. I would never make a film for commercial reasons. I prefer not to do anything, not to shoot any film if it doesn't allow me to say what I really want to say. So I have to do other jobs. I teach a bit, and I always tell my students that ethics come first, because a beautiful war film makes war beautiful. There has to be an equation between the content and the form. If you make a beautiful film on fascism, well, it's very dangerous. A film on fascism has to hurt, otherwise you don't get the message through. I want only to make things that I love, for very precise reasons.

For the intractably independent director Charles Burnett, the drive to make movies is as strong and clear as the day he began in the early 1970s. "I stuck a camera in the middle of the street and just shot people."

‡

The quotes in *Shoot It!* that aren't footnoted are from interviews I conducted for this book: Bogdan Apetri, Katherine Quittner, Miranda July, Charles Burnett, Sarah Polley, Aaron Barzman, Whang Cheol-mean, Mike Leigh, Norma Barzman, Enrique Begne, Tom DiCillo, Jello Biafra, Serge Bozon, Catherine Breillat, Susan Seidelman, Rodrigo Plá, Julie Dash, Andrew Bujalski, Stewart Stern, Seymour Cassel, Park Chan-wook, Mariana Chenillo, Alex Cox, Francisco Vargas, Claire Denis, Laura Truffaut, Kim Jong-guk, Jennifer Beals, Gus Van Sant, Seo Won-tae, Cristi Puiu, Atom Egoyan, Sam Fleischner, Declan Recks, Tanya Frederick, David Weiss, Jack Garfein, John Sayles, Lelia Goldoni, Catherine Hardwicke, Mary Harron, Nicole Holofcener, Walter Bernstein, Jun Hyung-min, Henry Jaglom, Kim Ji-hyen, Larry Kent, Sloane Klevin, Brett Morgen, Rodrigo Ortuzar, Mila Bays, Barbara Williams, Woody Allen, Jean Pierre Lefebvre, Ken Loach, Virginia Madsen, Daniel Mays, Don McKellar, F.J. Ossang, Kim Delaney, Francois Ozon, Yim Phil-sung, Corneliu Porumboiu, Sally Potter, Carlos Reygadas, Simona Paduretu, Axelle Ropert, Zenide Ruxandra, Kim Sam-ryeok, Lee Sang-woo, Nancy Savoca, Tom Scholte, Bruce Sweeney, Kim Tai-sik, Eva Truffaut, Thomas Schmitt, Lili Taylor. I thank them all.

Special gratitude to those who supplied photographs: Susan Seidelman, Norma Barzman, Axelle Ropert, Francisco Vargas, Stewart Stern, Mariana Chenillo, Julie Dash, Henry Jaglom, Nicole Holofcener, Bruce Sweeney, Larry Kent, Andrew Bujalski, and Ruxandra Zenide.

I thank the many people who helped out one way or another with this book, including Catherine Bloch, Jose Alberto Rodriguez, Willow Johnson, Karen Spaner, Justine Shapiro, Wonjo Jeong, Carolyn Soltau, Fabienne Lips-Dumas, Jon Fleming, Lindsey Hunnewell, Adena Altman, Sloane Klevin, Leonard Schein, Ari Brickman, and so many others who help facilitate interviews. Much appreciation also for the invaluable assistance provided by everyone at L.A.'s Margaret Herrick Library and the Vancouver International Film Festival. Finally, I'm grateful for the insight and support from my colleagues at Arsenal Pulp Press: Susan Safyan, Brian Lam, Cynara Geissler, and Shyla Seller.

# PART I

*Why Are the Movies So Bad These Days?*
*The Rise of Studio Film*

## CHAPTER ONE

## *Class War in the Valley*

THE STREET IS FILLED with bloody hand-to-hand combat and choked with teargas.

The night before, October 4, 1945, at a mass meeting of the striking Conference of Studio Unions at the Hollywood Legion Stadium, one CSU member had stirred fellow film workers when he stood up to propose: "If we had 1,000 pickets at Warners in the morning they couldn't open the studio. Let's do it."[1]

At five a.m., the first pickets arrive at Warner Bros. studio in Burbank. By seven a.m., 750 are on the line. A cop tries to drive through the pickets and his car is overturned. Moments later two scab cars trying to cross are overturned. As morning breaks, there are sporadic fights between strikers and the crowd that has formed across the street—a collection of scabs, mobbed-up toughs, and members of the non-striking IATSE union. The anti-union crowd is bolstered by police from four detachments and a riot squad with steel helmets, gas masks, and clubs.

The picket line holds. Warner Bros., as predicted, is shut down. But something that might seem almost inconceivable in the early twenty-first century is about to break out—class war in the San Fernando Valley.

Shortly after noon, firemen perched on towers turn two high-pressure hoses on the pickets below, then the police hurl gas bombs. The pickets quickly build barricades out of studio tables and fire back with unspent teargas bombs, bricks, bottles, rocks and, adding a California twist, oranges.

The pickets are stormed from two fronts: police from inside the studio and the anti-striker crowd from across the street, "armed with chains, bolts, hammers, six-inch pipes, brass knuckles, wooden mallets and battery cables." A picket is stabbed in the face, another struck in the eye with a teargas bomb; many are stoned, clubbed, and badly cut up. But the pickets fight back. One union man "sidestepped a blow aimed at his throat by a man wielding a screwdriver. He felled the man with his fist, then stamped on the wrist of his assailant."[2] Finally, a passage is "pierced" for the strikebreaking workers.

Immediately following the battle, a superior court judge orders that pickets be limited to eighteen, and CSU president Herbert Sorrell is

*Union firebrand Herbert Sorrell puts everything on the line in 1946. Photofest.*

charged with rioting. But day after day, the mass picketing continues. On October 9 at three-thirty a.m., pickets arrive at Warner Bros. Two hours later, 200 riot police appear, this time with submachine guns and side arms along with their truncheons. The picketers are surrounded, and 307 are loaded onto buses and vans, charged with rioting and disobeying the anti-picketing court injunction. Jack Warner and other executives watch from a soundstage rooftop, as though viewing the storming of the Winter Palace during the Russian Revolution.

It wasn't too much for the studio brass to link a Russian revolution at the gates of Warner Bros. with the notion gaining ground in Washington that "reds" had a hold on Hollywood. The CSU strike of 1945–46, a street fight between movie workers and studios, would change Hollywood; its reverberations are still felt. Besides being a turning point in the strike, the Warners' war would prove to be a turning point in studio history. It was a catalyst for the studio bosses to embrace the blacklist and join with Washington in exiling the Hollywood left. It was a clash that had been brewing since the first days of Hollywood.

‡

Stewart Stern would go on to write movies, including *Rebel Without a Cause* (1955), but on a summer night in 1931 he was an eight-year-old awakened by thunderous sounds outside the bedroom. "I didn't know where I was, so I felt my way out of the room and found this door that was studded with great big nails and a huge doorknob that I had to contend with," he says. "I opened it up and looked down, and I was looking over a balcony rail into a medieval dining room. Far, far away I saw this shape. It turned and started toward me. This was the biggest fright that I have ever had in my life—this face—I thought I was dreaming. I just began to scream. It was one of the first screenings of *Frankenstein*."

The Stern family lived in Manhattan, but on this weekend they were visiting their friends the Katzes at their large home in suburban New City. Sam Katz was the right hand of Paramount Studios' owner Adolph Zukor. That sudden image of Frankenstein would always stay with Stern. "That was my introduction to the monster, and I internalized him. I made an incredible Frankenstein get-up with the head and everything, and every Halloween I'd go out to the beach and just walk. Every once in a while I'd stop, look up at all these Malibu houses, and I'd just—" Stern lets out a harrowing Frankenstein cry. Then he laughs.

Stern's grandmother came from Hungary to the Dakota territories, homesteaded in a sod house, and gave birth to ten children. His mother, Frances, grew up in Chicago, where the family had moved; she loved the theater and always wanted to be an actress. His father, Emanuel Stern, was a doctor who started the first health insurance and medical department at a studio. "He had the hospital built on the Paramount lot in California, and it's still functioning I believe." And Frances's older sister Lottie had a suitor—Adoph Zukor.

The first hint of Zukor's ingenuity came when he was a young furriers assistant. "Women at that time would wear a whole fox around their neck," explains Stern, and "he invented that embroidered sprung lower jaw so that it could bite its own tail." Zukor would go on to invent the Hollywood studio system. He operated theaters in New York State for nearly a decade before launching Famous Players in 1912 to distribute the French film *Les Amours de la reine Élisabeth*. "When Uncle Adolph bought the rights to *Queen Elizabeth* with Sarah Bernhardt, he screened it at Broadway houses," Stern says. "Any day that there wasn't a matinee, he was able to put it on in the legitimate houses." Just as the American independent filmmakers who would emerge at mid-twentieth century were heavily influenced by the French New Wave, Zukor and other American independent producers who pioneered the Hollywood system early in the century were influenced by film developments in France. Formed in 1896, the French studio Société Pathé Frères was the world's largest film company, producing and distributing silent pictures and owning 200 theaters from Paris to Japan to New York. Pathé also set up production facilities in London and Fort Lee, New Jersey. And there were other major French filmmakers: Gaumont, the Lumière brothers, and Georges Méliès.

In the US, by the beginning of the twentieth century, there were small production companies established in New York and New Jersey, but it wasn't until 1908 that a company with a reach rivaling Pathé was formed: the Motion Picture Patents Company (also known as "The Trust"). Several early producers, including the Edison Film Manufacturing Company and the Biograph Company, shelved feuds and litigation and joined forces to form the MPPC. Producers, distributors, and exhibitors were invited, for a license fee, to join this trust, which would set prices and control distribution and production. The MPPC established the General Film Company to produce movies, and it dealt harshly with those who wouldn't ante up for this license—independents, they called themselves. The MPPC refused to screen their films at theaters that showed unlicensed films, so some of the independents left the East Coast for Los Angeles to escape its grasp. A group of independent producers—including Carl Laemmle of the Independent Motion Picture Company and Harry Aitken of Majestic Films—formed the Motion Picture Distributing and Sales Company to do battle with the MPPC.

"Is the independent market controlled by a trust too?" asked an ad, purchased by the frustrated independent Revier Films in a 1911 issue of *Moving Picture World*. "Don't be bamboozled by the cry of independence and business freedom. If you are going to be independent, do it right, and demand Revier Films ... Take for instance our release of Jan. 4th, *For Better or for Worse*. Tell your exchange you 'must' have this film, there is no earthly reason why he can't give it to you unless he is taking orders from 'Trust No. 2.'"[3]

Early on, the independent producers sold their films directly to theaters or distributors. In 1914, William Hodkinson came up with the idea of the distributor providing a cash advance to the producer to help finance the film in return for rights to the movie. Hodkinson called his distribution company Paramount Pictures, and signed on several independent producers, including Zukor and his friend Jesse Lasky. After drawing crowds to *Queen Elizabeth*, Zukor had co-produced *The Prisoner of Zenda* (1913), "the first long picture made in this country."[4]

Zukor soon wanted out of the arrangement with Paramount, feeling it unfairly favored Hodkinson, but he was denied. Within a year Zukor and Lasky held the majority of Paramount stocks and ousted Hodkinson. Combining Paramount's distribution with Zukor and Lasky's history in theater ownership and production provided the three-armed, vertically structured template for the studio system. The new studio system would have a few additional defining traits. Sarah Bernhardt had shown Zukor that stars attract audiences, so he was determined to create a system driven by celebrated movie actors. He also initiated block booking, the distribution system that forced theaters wanting one of Paramount's "A pictures" starring, say, Mary Pickford, to also purchase several of its "B pictures." And studio movies would be made with assembly-line precision.

In the 1920s, Stern's "Uncle Adolph" still had a studio on Long Island, as everything film-related hadn't yet moved from New York to Hollywood. "There was an overlap. They made *Dr. Jekyll and Mr. Hyde* (1920) at the Long Island studio, and they made *Peter Pan*, in 1924, at the Hollywood studio."

‡

The first runaway movie production ran away *to* Hollywood. Fleeing the more expensive, heavily unionized East Coast, where the early film industry was dominated by the MPPC, the moguls-to-be, like earlier pioneers, made their way across the continent. While the bulk of film financing remained in the east, by 1915 most production was in L.A. where you could shoot year-round. A parade of early independent producers moved west to form companies along the lines of Zukor's Paramount. There was Marcus Loew and Louis B. Mayer at Metro-Goldwyn-Mayer, William Fox (20th Century Fox), Carl Laemmle (Universal), Joseph Schenck (United Artists), Harry Cohn (Columbia), and Harry, Albert, Sam, and—mostly—Jack Warner (Warner Bros.).

The Warner brothers started out as small-time theater owners who ran headlong into the Trust, so they became independents. By 1920, the brothers had set up shop in L.A. and incorporated the name Warner Bros. Pictures. In 1924, an article in *Moving Picture World* said that Warner Bros.' "history is virtually the history of the independent market."[5] Jack, in the lab, and Harry, as a producer, had worked at Laemmle's Independent Motion Picture Company, which would evolve into Universal Studios. Laemmle had been a Chicago-based theater owner/

distributor whose exhibitors had drawn heat from the original trust. "The trust is threatening exhibitors with 'fines and calamities' for running my films," he told his customers. "If anyone comes into your place and tries to scare you with any sort of bluff, hand him one swift, speedy kick in the seating capacity and I'll pay the damages."[6]

• While continuing to do battle with each other for audiences, the studios, when they found it beneficial, would make common cause through the Motion Picture Producers and Distributors of America, formed by the eight big studios in 1922. By the time Zukor's exhibition, distribution, and production model had entrenched studio power in the US, the MPPDA—also known as the Hays Office for its president Will Hays, a former chairman of the Republican National Committee—was already turning its attention to the world. The studios were pioneering what would come to be known as globalization. As the 1920s got under way, Zukor wrote in *Moving Picture World*: "The prospects for the foreign business of [Paramount has never been] better. Contracts signed to date and those in the process of being worked out give every assurance that the next few months will be a record breaker in the foreign field. Reports received from our various offices and agencies indicate a greatly increased demand for Paramount productions."[7]

As the rest of the world ceded a goodly portion of their movie market to the studios—with their capacity to provide a steady supply of features, shorts, and newsreels—the studios established foreign versions of their distribution and exhibition system, working together through their MPPDA. France had dominated world screens in the first two decades of cinema, with no more regard for local cultures than Hollywood studios would later show. But by the end of World War I, France's Charles Pathé was ready to refocus from production to distribution and exhibition. "In the future, it became necessary to recognize that … the United States, with its boundless possibilities, would take possession of the global market probably forever," he said.[8] Europe's production companies didn't lose ground to Hollywood's moguls for lack of trying, but the continent's economy was in disarray following the war, just as the US studios were refining their system with its massive infrastructure. It was difficult to compete with a studio system sitting in the world's largest domestic market—their movies made a profit before even leaving North America—with a star-studded vertical approach that provided the finances and glamor to entice the globe.

Hays said the "screen acts as a voiceless salesman for the goods it pictures."[9] The US government agreed. In 1918, congress passed the

Webb-Pomerene Act, making US industries exempt from domestic anti-trust laws in their overseas operations. The MPPDA would continue business as usual in most of the world regardless of later Supreme Court decisions to break up the studios' vertical integration.

In 1923 nearly ninety percent of films screened in Britain were made in Hollywood. "The bulk of picture-goers are Americanized to an extent that makes them regard the British film as a foreign film," complained London's *Daily Press* in 1927.[10] That year, parliament established a screen quota of twenty percent British content by 1935. Film production in the UK increased from thirty-four in 1926 to 228 in 1937.[11] Film quotas were the first act of resistance to the new global reach of the studios. Besides the UK, early quotas were established in Australia, Hungary, Brazil, Portugal, Germany, Italy, Austria, and France.

The Republican federal administrations of the 1920s abetted the studios' foreign policies—promoting their industry, monitoring film legislation, and negotiating to remove restrictions. The state department told its diplomats that if they noticed governments behaving "prejudicial to American motion picture interests, you are authorized ... to take informally appropriate steps calculated to protect the interests in question."[12] Hand in hand with these departments, the studios moved into action against the quotas being enacted in Europe. In response to a French quota requiring that for every three films imported into France, one domestic film had to be distributed, the MPPDA initiated a boycott. It refused to export studio films into France until the French government changed the ratio to seven to one. "There are few American industries that are more dependent on foreign markets than the motion picture industry; and there are still fewer industries in which American dominance of world markets has in the past been more dramatic and more complete," concluded the *Harvard Business Review* in 1930.[13]

‡

On the studios' home front, the MPPDA set out to construct a sin-free, sex-free Hollywood. A few silent stars were drawing screaming headlines, none more than comedian Roscoe "Fatty" Arbuckle. Although Arbuckle was acquitted of manslaughter charges, he alledgedly sexually assaulted aspiring actress Virginia Rappe at a party, resulting in her death; his movie career was over and an image of Hollywood debauchery began to spread, with religious groups and politicians increasingly anti-Hollywood. In 1922, for the first time, attendance at movie theaters was falling. Early Hollywood had operated with considerable abandon, releasing such titles as *Restless Sex* (1920), *Luring Lips* (1921), and *The Truth About Husbands* (1920). To diffuse censorious officials, Hays proclaimed a long list of unwelcome topics—studios made a "gentleman's agreement" to ignore sex, vice, nudity, passion, crime, drunkenness, vulgarity, and ridicule of religion or public officials. In 1924, the Hays Office rejected sixty-seven stories under consideration by the studios.[14]

After a decade of MPPDA discipline, the studios still allowed the occasional foray into bad behavior, such as Warner's *Baby Face* (1933), so Hays got even tougher, unveiling his Production Code Administration to regulate movies more tightly than the voluntary agreement. By 1934, the eight studios had to submit their scripts for approval, with infractions resulting in $25,000 fines and non-approved films being denied access to studio-controlled theaters. "Bad" activities could be depicted but only if accompanied by proper punishment. "Evil and good are never to be confused throughout the presentation," read the Code, whose definition of evil included profanity, abortion, homosexuality, and interracial sex.[15] Hays' staff, led by Joseph Breen, would review all studio scripts and delete anything contrary to code. Hollywood was mandated to produce a wholesome world, and unlike the later "studio indies," in which families are almost always dysfunctional, studio families during the code years were almost never dysfunctional.

Along with sexuality and its corollary sins, there was another bad behavior attracting studio attention: "bad" politics. Red-baiting started early on, with the Pinkerton agency even providing Universal with a report on the activities of the hobo-syndicalist Industrial Workers of the World (the Wobblies) in 1933 Hollywood. The Dies Committee—as Senator Martin Dies' early version of the House Un-American Activities Committee was known—produced a list of movie subversives in 1938 that included ten-year-old Shirley Temple. And during the 1941 animation strike, Walt Disney hinted at what was to come: "I believe you have been misled and misinformed about the real issues underlying the strike at the studio. I am positively convinced that Communist agitation, leadership and activities have brought about this strike, and have persuaded you to reject this fair and equitable settlement."[16] But the talking pictures were so popular—attracting some eighty-to-ninety million movie-goers each week in the late 1930s[17]—that the early reds-under-beds rhetoric found little traction with the public or the studio bosses.

‡

*Norma Barzman shortly after arriving in Los Angeles. Courtesy Norma Barzman.*

The day Norma Barzman arrived in Hollywood, her cousin, Screen Writers Guild activist Henry Myers, helped celebrate her twenty-first birthday by taking her to a movie. They drove up to a small, unadorned community hall. Inside, it was magic. "Henry opened the doors, and here and there I saw faces I knew," Barzman says. "I saw Gene Kelly and Lionel Stander, Edward G. Robinson and Betsy Blair. This was the Hollywood progressive community. I was enchanted. The movie was shown in a hall because in those days you couldn't show Soviet films in cinemas. Since it was my birthday, Henry and his friends took me to the Trocadero, the nightclub at the foot of Sunset Plaza Drive. "

Norma, who would become a screenwriter, sits across a table from me at Nate 'n Al's deli in Los Angeles, not far from the site of that birthday celebration, nearly seventy years later. She tells me about the long, round-about route between the Trocadero and Nate 'n Al's, much of it spent in exile. Born Norma Levor in Manhattan's Upper West Side, in 1930 she saw the movie that made her decide to be a writer. *Hot News* (1928) was an unusual picture for its time—written by a female screenwriter, Florence Ryerson, and starring Bebe Daniels as a very independent newspaper reporter.

In New York she would fall in love with the theater; her mother took her to everything from drawing-room comedies to Sherwin Anderson dramas to anything by the Group Theatre. "We saw every [Clifford] Odets play. And we didn't see it once; we saw it twice." Founded in 1931 by Lee Strasberg, Cheryl Crawford, and Harold Clurman, the Group produced incendiary dramas by progressive playwrights, most notably Odets, its performances rooted in Russian acting teacher

Constantin Stanislavski's method, which had actors draw on the depth of their own experiences and probe their characters lives to virtually become the roles they were portraying. Barzman was in the audience when the Group's first generation of method actors, writers, and directors—including Stella Adler, Frances Farmer, John Garfield, Elia Kazan, Sanford Meisner, Michael Gordon, Phoebe Brand, Morris Carnovsky, Lee J. Cobb, and Will Geer—brought characters to raw life in such plays such as Odets' *Golden Boy* and *Waiting for Lefty* and John Howard Lawson's *Success Story*.

‡

There were early union rumblings inside the film business. The Wobblies may be better known for their free-speech fights and militant strikes in immigrant mill towns in the Northeast, but they also were among the first to organize film workers. In 1911, they formed the Motion Picture Theater Workers of New York City and two years later organized 500 workers at the New Jersey Edison Company into the IWW. The next year, in L.A., the Wobblies organized extras at Universal and struck when the company refused a wage increase.[18] In 1916, the less radical American Federation of Labor tried to organize the film crafts—painters, carpenters, camera operators—into one union. In 1918, IATSE (International Alliance of Theatrical Stage Employees and Motion Picture Machine Operators), which included numerous crafts, staged the first film-industry strike after studios refused a wage increase and fired union members. In 1921, the studios unilaterally cut wages and locked out the unions.[19]

In 1927, studios finally came up with their answer to unionization: the Academy of Motion Picture Arts and Sciences. Now best known as the organization behind the Oscars, the academy was created as a company union "to promote industrial harmony."[20] Studios vowed to negotiate with film workers only through their in-house academy, but as Dorothy Parker noted: "Taking your grievances to the Academy is like trying to get laid in your mother's house. Somebody's always peeking through the parlor curtains."[21]

The same year the studios formed the Academy, they unveiled talking pictures. The first talkie, Warner Bros.' *The Jazz Singer* (1927), enthralled audiences. For the studios, new talkie technology meant windfall profits, but it also created problems, such as screenwriting and where to find it. Since it was a world without film studies programs, or even weekend screenwriting symposiums, the studios, desperate for dialogue, turned to New York. Street-smart writers and actors were lifted out of their own New York habitats and deposited poolside in Brentwood, and for the next two decades would contribute to everything from *Casablanca*'s (1942) dialogue to *The Wizard of Oz*'s (1939) lyrics. By and large, these new studio employees—including some who had worked with the Group and other agit-prop theater then so popular on the East Coast—were left-wing, with pro-union sensibilities, and weren't satisfied being represented by the studio's academy. Just as the working class in the northeastern US had been organized by waves of radicalized European immigrants, West Coast film unionization would be helped along by waves of newcomers from the northeast, often the children of those earlier immigrants. So the easterners converging on Hollywood solved one of the studio bosses' problems (a talkie talent pool), but often participated in another (unions). While the new East Coast transplants had a growing litany of concerns about the studios, they weren't about to remake Hollywood labor relations by themselves. And they were hardly alone in L.A.

Some confuse California's good looks with shallowness, but alongside L.A.'s emerging glitz, the place had a passion and a politic long before the New Yorkers showed up in the 1930s. Take 1911, for instance. During a wave of strikes and bombings, Socialist Party candidate Job Harriman lost a close race for mayor, and the Socialist Movie Theater opened in downtown L.A. "We want a theater that will portray working-class life without insulting us," said the theater's Frank Hillyard.[22] Early attempts at unionizing film workers continued when the industry crossed the continent; differences between the studios and their employees finally came to a head during the banking crisis of 1933. With Depression-era banks closing and customers losing their savings, the Roosevelt administration shut down the banking system (secure banks re-opened within a few days). Abruptly cut off from their instant cash, the studio response was a thirty to fifty percent pay cut for its workers. "Morale was already low," reported *Variety*, and this cut "seemed the last straw."[23] The New York newcomers were joined by many homegrown Hollywood workers who saw the cut as just the latest example of the studios' flagrant disregard for their unorganized employees. The Screen Actors Guild was organized; the Screen Directors Guild and Screen Cartoonists Guild followed. The new Screen Writers Guild had more to be concerned about than the cuts. The Big Eight studios (Warner Bros., MGM, 20th Century Fox, RKO, Columbia, Paramount,

Universal, and United Artists) announced they would give writers just one week's notice before termination and limit screen credits to two per picture. Studio executives could barely contain their contempt for the arrival of *actual* unionization—not company unionization. Fox's Darryl Zanuck, for example, told a delegation of screenwriters: "You put a picket line in front of my studio, and I'll mount a machine gun on the roof and mow you all down."[24]

‡

Not every independent wants to stay that way. Walt Disney started as an independent producer, but by 1941 was invited by the studios to their regular strategy sessions, having begun the long climb to major-studio status in 1937 with the release of the first animated feature, *Snow White and the Seven Dwarfs*. Made for a then-stratospheric $1.5 million, *Snow White* grossed a then-astonishing $8 million. Meanwhile, the Screen Cartoonists Guild was being born in secret meetings at the El Coyote Mexican restaurant. It quickly signed agreements with Warner Bros. and MGM, but Disney was a different story. Seeing more dollar signs than Uncle Scrooge, Disney was embarking on post-*Snow White* expansion, offering public shares that were quickly snapped up. Shortly after this, Disney proposed wage cuts.

Disney fired seventeen pro-union artists at the height of negotiations. That evening the new guild voted to strike, and the next morning Walt himself came face-to-face with a picket line when he showed up at the studio. (On one sign Pluto proclaimed: "I'd Rather Be a Dog Than a Scab."[25]) During the nine-week confrontation, the cartoonists were joined by Disney machinists, editors, actors, office employees, and film technicians. Printers refused to print the Mickey Mouse comic strip. The Technicolor Corporation wouldn't develop Disney footage. Finally, one morning Disney announced—to the shock of the cartoonists' negotiating team, including SCG president Art Babbitt and CSU president Herb Sorrell—that an end to the strike would be negotiated with IATSE president Willie Bioff, a non-participant in the conflict; the *Daily Variety* headline read "SCG Walks Out as Hoodlums Walk In."[26] Problems with IATSE went back to Chicago Local 2's request to the Capone mob to lend its muscle to an organizing drive. Soon the mob was on the local's executive board, whose president George Brown became head of all IATSE with his assistant Bioff dispatched to Hollywood. For a time, the studios enjoyed doing business with the accommodating

Brown and Bioff, and their union spread its muscle in Hollywood. But in 1941, the duo were convicted of extorting money from the studios. In exchange for not demanding wage increases and helping to defeat a 1937 strike by IATSE dissidents, Brown and Bioff received $50,000 a year from each major studio and $25,000 from smaller ones. After doing time, Bioff would be killed by a bomb planted in his car, while Brown would simply disappear.[27]

The strikers rejected Disney's settlement with IATSE. When Disney eventually backed down under coercion from his backers at the Bank of America, the workers were determined to continue their new-found solidarity with the CSU, and this played a critical role in the Disney cartoonists' victory. The CSU, abetted by collusion and dissension within IATSE, was quickly taking hold across the industry, adding electricians, carpenters, publicists, story analysts, office employees, set decorators, camera operators, costumers, and restaurant workers to its membership.

‡

Walter Bernstein would go on to write movies in Hollywood, but grew up 2,500 miles away, in Brooklyn, entranced by the adventure he could find in a movie house. "Cowboy movies, gangster movies, World War I movies—I loved those kind of movies," he said.

He was born in Brooklyn just after the war, his immigrant grandparents having made the move from Russia's Pale of Settlement to New York. As a son of the working class during the Depression, he was "saddened" by seeing "veterans of the World War I selling apples on the street corners, bread lines, and Hooverville. I didn't know anything about what the cause of it was; it just seemed to me a terrible thing that was happening."

Before starting college in 1936, he knew he would write, and his academic smarts won him six months at a school in Grenoble, France when he was just sixteen. "I remember riding my bicycle through the streets and workers in factories coming out, marching, and sit-down strikes. It was a pretty exciting time. My best friend there was going to Spain because there was going to be an alternative Olympics. I went home instead. And he went there and the war broke out."

Back in the States, Norma Barzman was following events in Spain. Just as the People's Olympiad—an alternative to the Olympics behind staged in Nazi Germany—was about to start, the elected leftist government of Spain was overthrown by fascist generals led by Francisco Franco and allied with Hitler and Mussolini. In response, Spain's workers and peasants rose, and the whole world watched the unfolding of the Spanish Civil War. It was the first rising against the fascism that was spreading across Europe, and volunteers from around the world made their way to Spain to join the good fight—not unlike Bernstein's cowboy heroes riding across a Brooklyn movie screen to clean up the West. Barzman knew some of the volunteers for Spain and her husband Ben "almost went."

Ben Barzman's family had come from Russia, part of the wave of immigration to North America to escape a series of *pogroms*, when sword-wielding Cossacks rode on horseback into Jewish villages to destroy homes and terrorize or kill villagers. Born in Toronto, Ben grew up in Vancouver, then moved to Portland, Oregon, where he wrote plays for the Federal Theater Project. One agit-prop production, *Labor Pains*, brought him to L.A., where he stayed to work in the movies.

"On October 31st, Halloween of 1942, I met Ben Barzman at a party at the Rossens," recalls Norma. Bob and Sue Rossen were pillars of the Hollywood left community.

> Sitting on a fuzzy white chair was a well-tanned guy with a moustache, very handsome, not very tall ... We got to talking, and I didn't like the condescending way that Ben had of talking about women when I said I wanted to direct. I kept getting more and more irritated, and by the time we got to the dessert I was so angry—this guy was attractive to me—I plopped a meringue pie on his face ...
>
> I knew he would call me, even though I knew how angry he was, and he did. He said, 'I might cook something you like.' And I said, 'Can I bring a dessert? Oh, not a dessert. I'll bring wine.' He had a little apartment on Vista. We had dinner and we went to bed and we stayed in bed for about three weeks.

‡

During World War II, there had been a "no-strike pledge" among unions as part of the united front against fascism, and near the end of the war, many union members were anxious to make up for lost picket lines. Having established its unions in the 1930s, Hollywood wasn't immune to the new mood. The events that would lead to the battle of Warner Bros. began in March 1945 when the CSU walked out in a jurisdictional dispute with IATSE over the issue of which union represented seventy-seven set decorators. Although the National War Labor Board had recognized the CSU as the set-decorators' representative, the studios refused to abide by the decision, and IATSE instructed its members to cross the CSU picket lines. "We shall remain on strike until the producers obey the board order," said the CSU's Sorrell.[28] While Sorrell wasn't much for the ideological wrangling of the day, he was a proud product of the militancy of his times, a working stiff with a two-fisted approach to picket-line etiquette. ("I love to hear the cracking of bones on a scab's legs,"[29] noted the quotable Sorrell, who was active in the Painters Union, organized cartoonists and screen office workers, and in 1941, co-founded the CSU as a progressive, democratic alternative to IATSE.)

The CSU was an umbrella organization for nine guilds, and when the set decorators walked, it opened the floodgates. Soon 15,000 CSU workers joined the walkout—everyone from electrical workers to office employees—and a unique combination of militancy and theatricality set in. When picketing spread to studio-owned theaters, creative protestors outside a New York screening of *Lady on a Train* (1945) gave away the ending to keep movie-goers from seeing the film. "Save your money. We'll tell you all about it," their leaflet said. "Don't be fooled by Dan Duryea—Ralph Bellamy did it. He's the killer. And David Bruce gets the girl."[30]

The War Labor Board ordered an "immediate end" to the strike. The CSU, an American Federation of Labor affiliate, was also instructed to end the strike by AFL president William Green, who denounced it as a violation of the no-strike pledge. "I officially disavow your strike," Green telegrammed Sorrell. "I call upon you and your associates to cease and desist from using the name of American Federation of Labor in any way in connection with your strike."[31] Sorrell telegrammed back: "We pay our per-capita tax to the AF of L and are bona fide AF of L unions, but we also are an autonomous and democratic group, and feel that we know what is best for our membership ... The strike goes on."[32]

As IATSE crossed picket lines to work, CSU strikers issued an open letter: "The IATSE is no longer a union. It is a strike-breaking, scab-herding agency!"[33] Within IATSE, there was increasing division over the strike. Although IATSE leader Richard Walsh told his membership to cross the line, L.A.'s IATSE Local 44 voted to support the strike. "It's a protest of the rank and file members against the dictatorial methods of the international officers," said rebel leader Irwin Hentschel.[34] Two more IATSE locals refused to cross, and the union's insurgents convened a meeting attended by 1,500. "Thousands of IA workers refused to cross picket lines, even in the face of threats of fines and having cards revoked," reported *Variety*.[35] IATSE would eventually expel eight members for siding with the CSU, including Hentschel.

Enough IATSE members and others crossed the lines for studios to continue some production. The Screen Actors Guild was divided. While Katharine Hepburn, Charlie Chaplin, Edward G. Robinson, and others spoke out for the CSU, much of the guild's leadership coalesced around future SAG president Ronald Reagan's support for IATSE and his ongoing attacks on Sorrell and company. Others were resolute, including the cast of David Selznick's epic *Duel in the Sun* (1946). "Jennifer Jones, leading lady in the $4,000,000 spectacle, walked out when she saw the pickets. Lillian Gish walked past the studio waving to the pickets when she saw the line. Other players—Gregory Peck, Lionel Barrymore, Walter Huston, Charles Bickford ... did not show up at all."[36] The Carpenters Union, the International Brotherhood of Electrical Workers, and the International Association of Machinists respected the growing picket lines, and while the AFL provided no help for the strikers, the L.A. branch of the rival union federation, the Congress of Industrial Organizations, voted to support the strike and join picket lines.

As the strike continued, the rioting at studios became a recurring headline. At RKO, there were fistfights between police and strikers and "a rock, twice the size of a baseball, whizzing by a policeman's head" struck a bus carrying scabs into the lot.[37] There was a wild street fight between strikebreakers and strikers at Paramount. On a narrow street near MGM's Culver City lot, a melee involving 200 people ensued when pickets tried to overturn cars crossing their line. Such was the climate when Judge Emmet Wilson ordered the stoppage of mass picketing at the Samuel Goldwyn Studio. That's when the strikers, in no mood to take orders, held their meeting at the Hollywood Legion Stadium and decided to throw a picket line around the Warner Bros.' studio.

During the battle of Warner Bros., Sorrell was arrested for breaking a strikebreaker's jaw. Asked whether he was defying the court injunction banning picketing, Sorrell described the protest as a "spontaneous" rank-and-file act. In the days following the Warners' donnybrook, there would be pitched battles at Paramount, RKO, and Columbia. "Give them even more at Columbia Pictures today than they got at Warner Brothers," Sorrell told a union gathering. "If they want it bloody, let's make it bloody. The words for tomorrow are, 'They shall not pass.'"[38] Warners, he stressed, were "not the only bad boys ... Some of these days we'll go to MGM. I flipped a coin to see whether it would be Columbia or Paramount today."[39]

The nationwide publicity generated by the assault on the picket line at Warner Bros. increased support for the strikers and pressure on the studios to settle. Bette Davis and John Garfield spoke out in support of the strikers at another rally at Hollywood Legion Stadium. Pete Seeger sang for the striking CSU workers. Twelve hundred UCLA students joined a picket line at Warner Bros.' Burbank lot. The National Maritime Union sent a telegram to L.A. mayor Fletcher Bowron, stating: "The brutality of the police who increasingly are assuming the role of storm troopers at the beck and call of the big studios, merits our bitter condemnation."[40]

Meanwhile, the National Labor Relations Board agreed that the CSU was the bargaining agent for studio set decorators. The strike was settled on October 24, 1945; the CSU won jurisdiction and a wage increase, but their outstanding disputes with IATSE were to be resolved by an AFL committee. On that final day, 400 pickets and their supporters were arrested at Paramount and RKO. A few days after the settlement, gunshots from a passing vehicle were fired at Sorrell as he backed his car out of his driveway in Glendale.

The studios did not accept defeat easily. In September 1946, more than 1,100 CSU workers were fired after they had refused to work on sets constructed by IATSE members, and soon after, hundreds more would be dismissed. The coordinated firings, now occurring at all the major studios, had been planned for the next time the CSU raised jurisdictional issues—what Sorrell called a "systematic lockout."[41] In defiance of court orders, the CSU threw picket lines around the studios. There were 679 arrests at Columbia on October 15. Disney, finally exacting his revenge for the animators' strike of 1941, fired 459 of his 1,073 employees.

Sorrell and thirteen other members of the CSU were indicted on conspiracy charges ranging from rioting to disregarding court orders. "A little thing like this is not going to stop our strike," Sorrell said.[42] The charges collapsed before reaching trial. In March 1947, Sorrell was abducted by three men—one wearing a police uniform—on a San Fernando Valley street, then beaten and dumped off a highway 140 miles north of L.A. "I'm certain I know who pulled this job," he said. "At least, I know who paid them off."[43]

Despite considerable support within the industry for the CSU (it even received a message from Mexico's Cinematographic Production Union saying that, in solidarity, it was outlawing technical work on American films), the lockout and attacks on CSU organizers were taking their toll. With 3,000 CSU members out, the mass trials continuing, and producers ignoring CSU calls to parley, one by one CSU affiliates—story analysts, janitors, painters, and set designers—returned to work. It would be the end for the embattled CSU. Some unions disaffiliated from them, while others were pushed out; IATSE and the studios formed a new machinists' local.

Norma Barzman was on CSU picket lines, along with Ben and her cousin Henry. This studio war was against screenwriters too. The talkies had given writers the power, one studio executive noted, "to do pretty much as (they) liked ... The result was a type of picture which should never have reached the screen."[44]

*Jimmy Stewart mops up a kind of fascism in* Destry Rides Again. © *Universal Pictures / Photofest.*

At first glance, Henry Myers' *Destry Rides Again* (1939) looks like a Buck Jones western, with every expected convention: the bouncy stage into town; the saloon distilling sex, drinks, and gambling; the corrupt town baron; the beautiful good girl and the sensual bad gal; and the hero (Jimmy Stewart) arriving to clean up the town. But all is turned on its head as Jimmy Stewart's character avoids every cliché that tamed the West, his decency drawing out the best in others along the way, until he reluctantly has to pick up the gun to defeat a kind of fascism. The violence is less than might be expected because the baron and his thugs are so quickly overcome by the sheer mass of the popular uprising—led by the womenfolk, no less.

While the picket-line combat would rage on for a time, ultimately the CSU was purged from Hollywood. Its replacement union, IATSE, had switched its allegiance from Bioff-era mobsters to right-wing politicians. L.A. IATSE leader Roy Brewer sent a telegram to L.A. mayor Bowron commending him for the "splendid work" of the police during the CSU strike, then he got to the heart of the matter: "The Conference of Studio Unions is a Communistic-designed and Communistic-dominated organization which has for its purpose the control of the unions in the motion picture industry—that the great propaganda value of the industry might be used to promote the cause of world Communism."[45] Brewer's telegram would be more prophetic than anyone might imagine because, as 1946 drew to a close, the studios, having defeated Hollywood's union, would turn on its defenders. The fury of the blacklist was under way.

## CHAPTER TWO

# The Cossacks Are Coming

"INDEPENDENT" HAS COME TO mean a kind of filmmaker, but when the studios were new, independent meant the producer. And as studios began to consolidate their vertical empire, the first obituaries for independent film appeared. "The day of the independent producer has passed," author Will Irwin proclaimed in 1928. "The industry, after all its kaleidoscopic shiftings, has settled down into seven or eight corporations or groups."[1]

While Zukor, the Warners, Laemmle, and the rest were busy constructing a studio system, not everyone was marching along in lockstep. Besides the studios' testy class war with a feisty Hollywood left, they were embattled on other fronts, mostly involving impertinent protectionist policies and uncooperative independent producers.

In 1919, a collection of major stars—Charlie Chaplin, Mary Pickford, Douglas Fairbanks, and D.W. Griffith—announced the formation of United Artists. Less of a production company than a distribution arm for independently produced films, its first press release was an opening salvo against the studios' block-booking system: "This step is positively and absolutely necessary to protect the great motion picture public from threatening combinations and trusts that would force upon them mediocre productions and machine-made entertainment."[2] In 1941, a group of high-profile independents—including Chaplin, Pickford, Samuel Goldwyn, and Orson Welles—intent on gaining access to screens by eliminating block booking joined forces to create the Society of Independent Motion Picture Producers.

In the first two decades of talking pictures, Hollywood was new enough and the times chaotic enough for the studios to hire screenwriters and directors clever enough to turn all of the Production Code nonsense on its head, coming up with sufficient round-about innuendo and subversion to later rile an army of blacklisters. Having started out as independents themselves, the moguls had a grudging admiration for the sort of filmmakers who nowadays would have to make their films outside the system. Orson Welles, for example, would recall: "I was a maverick, but the studios understood what that meant, and if there was a fight, we both enjoyed it."[3] While the studio heads opposed Hollywood unionization, for a time they didn't much care about the ideology of their employees, providing their work resulted in profits.

Within the screen unions, leftist activists were influential, particularly the CSU affiliates, including the Screen Cartoonists Guild and the Screen Publicists Guild. The autonomous Screen Writers Guild was also filled with active progressives, including Ring Lardner, Jr., Herbert Biberman, John Howard Lawson, Sidney Buchman, Donald Ogden Stewart, Abe Polonsky, Lester Cole, and Dalton Trumbo. And while SAG had its own internal left-right war, many major stars were staunch progressives, including Bette Davis, Katharine Hepburn (whose activist mother was friends with famed anarchist Emma Goldman), and others who supported the CSU strikers. Writer Ella Winter noted in the mid-1940s: "In the past few years there have been great changes in Hollywood. The town has become union conscious and world conscious."[4] But the new mood that Winter felt so good about wasn't as pleasing to the studios, which knew that the lefties they had hired to make their movies had also helped to make the movie unions. In the wake of the CSU-management confrontation, the studios were no longer so willing to turn a blind eye to their employees' politics.

‡

Norma's writing class was just up the street from Ben's apartment. Shortly after they met, she arrived at class to find a note on the door— "Gordon Kahn has flu. He'll be back next week"— canceling the class, so she walked over to Ben's apartment. "I rang, but he didn't answer. I saw lights up there. He came running down and told me. 'You can't come in. Just disappear for an hour.' And I figured he had another girl there. I said, 'I'll disappear altogether.' I went home and I cried all night, and in the morning I received flowers and a note saying, 'Meet me at the Brown Derby.' When I met Ben there, he said, 'Kid, it wasn't a girl. It was a meeting of the Communist Party. I couldn't let you up.'"

The Communist Party of the time was a mass movement in America, and like many others, Ben, and soon Norma, joined because they saw it as the organization that was rallying against racism, building unions, sending volunteers to Spain, and taking to the streets against the rising fascism at home. Their aspirations were closer to earlier utopian socialist ideas of writers such as William Morris ("when mastery has changed into fellowship") than they were to the authoritarian regimes that would abuse the "socialist" label and those ex-Party members who, under threat to their livelihoods, later stool-pigeoned against the

Hollywood Communists—claiming they had totalitarian designs—were disingenuous, self-serving hypocrites at best. Ben, Norma, and their friends did not join the CP to create a dictatorship in America. They joined because they were young idealists who saw the organization as a way to build a new, fairer world. "It was everything I believed in and cared about," said Norma. "They were active and they seemed to me to be well-organized to do the two things I wanted to do—fight fascism and make a better world. They seemed to be doing everything." The Hollywood left of the day was a remarkably creative bunch. "It was everyone I liked and loved and wanted to be like. It was an inspiration. No matter what we were working on, we all helped each other without any feeling of wanting credit."

By the time Norma and Ben were married by a defrocked rabbi in January 1943, she had become that "girl reporter" she had seen on screen at age nine, working at the *Los Angeles Examiner*, and developing movie story ideas on the side. Meanwhile, Ben's first screenplays, *You're a Lucky Fellow, Mr. Smith* and *True to Life*, were shot later that year. His renown grew in Hollywood, when he wrote, among other screenplays, *Back to Bataan* (1945) and *The Boy with Green Hair* (1948).

Before she was blacklisted for her politics, Norma was blacklisted for her gender. She left the newspaper and focused on movie writing, starting with *The Locket* (1946), which she wrote with Ben. "I wanted to marry Freud and Marx, and that's what *The Locket* is," says Barzman. "I wanted to show a woman whose neuroses, because of class society, grow worse." RKO would purchase the script and produce the film without giving her a screenwriting credit. Things were easier for a male screenwriter, as Barzman learned when she came up with the story idea for *Never Say Goodbye* (1946). "It was very pro-feminist," she says. "I gave it to Ben's agent George Wilner, who was a Communist; and you would've thought he'd fight for me, but you know what was rife in the party: looking down on women." While Ben and other men in their circle were good on issues of racism or unions, gender inequality was barely on the radar in the left of the 1940s. Warner Bros. liked Norma's story—about a wife who dumps her man-about-townish husband and lives alone with her daughter, who connives to bring them back together—enough to offer $30,000, but said they didn't want Norma co-writing with Ben.

Then Norma and her friend, novelist Janet Stevenson, wrote a story featuring "a woman who's got an awful husband," set among farmers in Northern California. Harry Warner's son-in-law, producer Milton

Sperling, read the script. "He said, 'I just love your story, I loved every-thing about it, but can we put this in the snow? We could put it on a mountain top and the guy could be a ski teacher.' And Janet began to go noodly. I can't remember what she said or what she did, but two minutes later I found myself in the parking lot with her. He had just thrown us out."

Norma and Ben were now immersed in the Hollywood progressive community Henry Myers had introduced her to on her first night in town. "The Sleepy Lagoon kids, do you know about them? They were a group of Mexican teenagers who were accused of a murder in Los Ange-les. They couldn't have done it, but they were going to get railroaded. One of our big activities was to save those kids—and we did." She also recounts campaigns to improve working conditions for Filipino lettuce workers in the Salinas Valley, the Screen Writers Guild's successful fight for pensions, and "the big strike out at Warner Brothers. I always liked picket lines because you'd see all your friends."

There had been earlier, failed attempts to whip up anti-Communist hysteria about Hollywood, so in the spring of 1947, when the House Un-American Activities Committee (HUAC) announced it would hold hearings into subversion in Hollywood, it wasn't only the left that ob-jected. "Hollywood is weary of being the national whipping boy for congressional committees," announced the Association of Motion Pic-ture Producers. "If we have committed a crime we want to know it. If not, we should not be badgered by congressional committees."[5] At first, there was a parade of "friendly" witnesses before HUAC, such as Ginger Rogers' conservative mother Lela complaining that her daughter was required to say the line "Share and share alike, that's democracy" in the movie *Tender Comrade* (1943). The "unfriendly" witnesses, such as Norma and Ben's friend Adrian Scott, announced they would not co-operate with the committee. Once before HUAC, they defiantly refused to answer questions. They were backed by the Committee for the First Amendment, a planeload of movie stars who came to Washington, in-cluding Humphrey Bogart, Lauren Bacall, and Frank Sinatra.

‡

Before World War II, anti-Hollywood voices had largely been absorbed (the puritans by the Production Code) or ignored (the Dies Commit-tee by pretty much everyone). As war approached, politicians such as Senator Gerald Nye took aim at the anti-fascist movies coming out of

Hollywood, many featuring future blacklisted writers, directors, and actors, such as Universal's anti-Franco *Blockade* (1938) and Warner Bros.' anti-Nazi *Confessions of a Nazi Spy* (1939). With fascists marching across Europe, it was difficult for Nye to find much support. *New York Post* columnist Dorothy Thompson wrote: "Senator Nye and associates intend to awaken an anti-Semitic movement in the United States, stop all attacks on Hitler and Hitlerism on the ground that criticism of the Nazi regime is war-mongering ... and pave the way for a collaborationist regime in America ... It is the greatest Nazi propaganda stunt ever pulled off in the United States."[6] The hardscrabble Warner studio, with its acting ensemble of tough city guys and gals (including Humphrey Bogart, Edward G. Robinson, Barbara Stanwyck, Jimmy Cagney, John Garfield, and Lauren Bacall), was the most New Deal-ish. Harry and Jack Warner endorsed Franklin Roosevelt and the studio released social critiques (*I Am a Fugitive From a Chain Gang* [1932]) and anti-fascist missives (*Black Fury* [1935]). Upon taking power, the Nazis demanded that the studios fire their Jewish employees in Germany. Several agreed, but not Warner Bros., who instead shut down their German operations. While some moguls, notably Louis B. Mayer, were easily cowed by politicians, Harry Warner stood defiant: "I am ready to give myself and all my personal resources to aid in the defeat of the Nazi menace to the American people ... I deny that the pictures produced by my company are 'propaganda', as has been alleged ... *Sergeant York* (1941) is a factual portrait of one of the great heroes of the last war. If that is propaganda, we plead guilty. *Confessions of a Nazi Spy* is a factual portrayal of a Nazi spy ring that actually operated in New York City. If that is propaganda, we plead guilty."[7] The Dies Committee's attack on Hollywood virtually disappeared when Pearl Harbor was attacked in December 1941. During the war, the Hollywood left's anti-fascist politics were suddenly mainstream. In 1943, Warner Bros.' *Casablanca* won the best-picture Oscar and its openly pro-Soviet *Mission to Moscow* was released.

After the war, however, the studios went to battle with the CSU and soon fell in line with the new national pastime: red-baiting. An anti-Communist hysteria accompanied the strike, as these typical headlines attest: "Link Film Riots With Disruptive Communist Plot (*Hollywood Citizen-News,* October 4, 1946); "Reds' Part in Studio Strike Investigated (*Los Angeles Times,* October 5, 1946); and "Reds Accused of Film Control Plot in Strike" (*Los Angeles Examiner,* October 20, 1945). In the *Examiner* story, IATSE head Roy Brewer charged that the CSU strike was part of a "gigantic Communist conspiracy" to dominate the film industry and destroy the AFL.

Although the Cold War was purportedly against the Soviet Bloc, it was an attack aimed more at eliminating the domestic left, and in particular trade unionists. In Hollywood, the moguls now embraced the blacklist, in no small measure because it came on the heels of the big strike, and they saw it as a means to dispose of the CSU, the Screen Writers Guild, and other union militants. Even the Warner brothers now said that they were victims of a "Communist conspiracy" and vowed never to make another "liberal" film.[8] Apparently, a "Hollywood liberal" was a Roosevelt supporter who, upon having his movie studio surrounded by pickets, announced that, in future, he would vote Republican (which Jack Warner did).[9] The studios were also fretting about the box-office repercussions of Hollywood personalities being targeted by increasingly loud anti-Communist politicians and their committee, along with non-governmental organizations such as the American Legion and the Motion Picture Alliance for the Preservation of American Ideals. The moguls had another reason for going along with the blacklist. HUAC's witch-hunters were bothered that so much studio talent was so New York, so intellectual, so smart-alecky, so left-wing ... so Jewish—un-American. HUAC spokesman John Rankin, a congressman from Mississippi, wasn't reserved when it came to his prejudices about Hollywood's "alien-minded Communistic enemies of Christianity."[10] So the frightened, essentially conservative studio heads, who were almost entirely Jewish, were at pains to distance themselves from their left-wing Jewish employees, and to prove they were first and foremost American, they enforced the blacklist. Having used red-baiting to successfully defeat the CSU in favor of IATSE, the studios were now prepared to use it on their directors, writers, and actors.

The studios also wanted to keep Washington's foreign film policies on-side. Preparing for the post-war movie world, the MPPA's Hays had sent Secretary of State Cordell Hull a reminder that forty percent of the industry's profit was made in foreign countries. "That so large a portion of industry earning must accrue abroad renders the industry peculiarly susceptible to foreign governmental discrimination," he wrote. "Just as we have dealt, and can deal, with foreign industry, we ask that our government deal with foreign governments ... The imposition of discriminatory taxes, restrictive orders, quotas and regulations in limitation of United States distribution, are matters clearly beyond our industry's effective province."[11] For its overseas efforts on behalf of the studio system, the state department wanted a Hollywood it could rely on.

Eric Johnston, former president of the US Chamber of Commerce, replaced Hays as MPPDA head in 1945. He was soon boasting that the new Hollywood had turned the corner on the blacklisted and their politics. "We'll have no more *Grapes of Wrath*s, we'll have no more *Tobacco Roads*," he said in 1947. "We'll have no more films that show the seamy side of American life. We'll have no pictures that deal with labor strikes. We'll have no more pictures that show the banker as a villain."[12]

‡

Meanwhile, Ben Barzman was having headaches with new RKO boss Howard Hughes. In those pre-auteur days, studio directors often worked by the numbers, and much of the creativity was driven by the writers. "I think people forget that it wasn't just the studios hiring a guy to write a screenplay for one of their properties; maybe it was a progressive guy so it was a humanist movie—maybe not left-wing, but at least more real," says Norma. "I think more of those films were based on a book or a play suggested by progressive writers. You would talk to a director or a producer or an actor and suddenly they would be interested and they would do it. That is how content was influenced."

*The Boy with Green Hair* evolved from a friendship between a progressive writer and producer. A couple close to the Barzmans, producer/ writer Adrian Scott and actress Anne Shirley, had returned from England after adopting a war orphan they brought back to L.A. "One day when we were vacationing with Adrian and Annie, Adrian sat with us at breakfast and said, 'Suppose there was an orphan from the war who really had within himself the anti-war spirit, who was like a living spirit against war. After all, he had lost his parents to the war.' Adrian said, 'That's all there is. I'd like to do a movie like that.' Ben said, 'Isn't there any more?' And Adrian said, 'No, that's for you to think up.'" Scott said he could get Ben a job writing the screenplay at RKO. "It became *The Boy with Green Hair*. This is how things got talked about and became a property. Adrian was a producer at RKO and he could do anything he wanted because he had just had two big hits."

The movie was Joseph Losey's directorial debut and starred an adolescent Dean Stockwell. "Howard Hughes wanted Joe Losey and Ben to change what the boy says, and they wouldn't change it. And that lovely actor [Stockwell] wouldn't do it either. The boy speaks out against war, but Hughes wanted him to say something like, 'There won't be war if

*Members of the Hollywood Ten surrounded by supporters. Photofest.*

we have the biggest army and navy in the world'—some stupid thing like that, which the boy himself wouldn't say. Hughes was so angry at Ben for *The Boy with Green Hair* that he took our names off the credits for *The Locket*."

On November 24, 1947, ten Hollywood writers and directors, including Adrian Scott, were cited for contempt of Congress for refusing to testify before HUAC. That same day, forty-eight film executives met at the Waldorf-Astoria Hotel in Manhattan to formalize the blacklist. There were divisions among independent producers in their response to it. The Society of Independent Motion Picture Producers (SIMPP) was one of the main producer associations—along with the Motion Picture Association of America (the new name for the MPPDA)—at the Waldorf conference, which resolved that the indicted Hollywood Ten would be fired. Producers at the Waldorf also pledged not to hire Communists, even though at least one prominent member of SIMPP—*Mr. Smith Goes to Washington* (1939) screenwriter Sidney Buchman—had been a CP member (and was eventually blacklisted himself). Although three SIMPP members—Sam Goldwyn, Walter Wanger, and Dore Schary— argued against the blacklist at the Waldorf meeting, they, along with everyone else there, ultimately signed the resulting blacklist agreement.

The Hollywood Ten—Adrian Scott, Alvah Bessie, Herbert Biberman, Lester Cole, Edward Dmytryk, Ring Lardner Jr., John Howard Lawson, Albert Maltz, Samuel Ornitz, and Dalton Trumbo—responded with a $65 million damage suit that listed SIMPP as one of the defendants. The Screen Writers Guild attacked the blacklist as a conspiracy between SIMPP and the two major studio producers' associations. SIMPP did try to separate itself from the Waldorf meeting, stating: "SIMPP has at no time entered into any of the alleged conspiracies set forth, nor is this organization adhering to any such conspiracy."[13] The Hollywood Ten removed SIMPP from their lawsuit.

The differences between SIMPP and the blacklisted directors and writers underscored the problem in defining a film's independence by its producers rather than its filmmakers. SIMPP members had wildly different politics, from leftists such as Welles and Chaplin to the red-baiting Hughes and Disney. While most SIMPP members were producers first, most progressives in the organization were first and foremost filmmakers who became producers as well, chiefly to retain control over their own work. Welles saw film as a directors' art form and maintained a healthy skepticism when it came to producers. "Call directing a job if you're tired of the word 'art,'" Welles wrote in 1941.

> It's the biggest job in Hollywood. (It should be anyway, and it would be, except for something called a producer.) ... Only a little less superfluous than the agent and almost as successful, unlike certain others among Hollywood's middlemen (the publicity man and the columnist, for instance), the producer is not a necessary evil. He's unnecessary, and he's an evil ... In England, a producer is a man who stages a play; on Broadway, he is the man who finances a play; in Hollywood, he is the man who interferes with a movie ... A producer has no equivalent in any other craft or profession, which is one of the good things about any other craft or profession.[14]

Welles, more than any other Hollywood-based filmmaker of the 1940s, helped to formulate the independent sensibility that would emerge in later decades. His first two films, *Citizen Kane* (1941) and *The Magnificent Ambersons* (1942), were stunningly innovative and audacious pieces of personal filmmaking. "I owe it to my ignorance. If that word seems inadequate to you, replace it with innocence," Welles would say of the unconventional stylings of *Citizen Kane*. "I said to

*Orson Welles and Dolores del Rio attend the 1941 premiere of* Citizen Kane *at Hollywood's El Capitan Theatre. Photofest.*

myself, 'This is what the camera should be really capable of doing, in a normal fashion.' When we were on the point of shooting the first sequence, I said, 'Let's do that!' [Cinematographer] Gregg Toland answered that it was impossible. I came back with, 'We can always try; we'll soon see. Why not?'"[15] Based on the life of newspaper magnate William Randolph Hearst, *Citizen Kane* was attacked by the Hearst chain, which banned advertising for it. *The Magnificent Ambersons* was chopped beyond recognition by RKO editors.

Welles arrived at RKO with supposed artistic control, on the basis of the acclaim for his work in theater and radio, and he wouldn't accept the tampering without a fight, so he and his entire crew were tossed off the studio's lot in 1942. His remaining decades in Hollywood and Europe, despite occasional acts of brilliance as an actor or director (*The Stranger*, 1946; *The Lady From Shanghai*, 1947), were mostly an ongoing struggle to get funding, complete projects, and maintain his soul. Director Henry Jaglom, who was close to Welles in his later years, noted: "You know, Orson Welles never publicly said this, but it wasn't the economics that sent him to Europe, as was said originally ... They were going to get after him because of his history, his progressive history."

So the blacklist even claimed people who weren't on it. Welles' dream project, *Don Quixote*, was never finished, but he never abandoned his love and hope for cinema. "The invention of the moving picture was a moment of historic importance equivalent to the invention of movable type," he wrote.[16] While most directors of the 1930s and '40s were hired guns, a handful besides Welles were able to find producer-director niches inside the studios, including Preston Sturges, Howard Hawks, Ernst Lubitsch, and Frank Capra. Following the success of Capra's *It Happened One Night* (1934), for example, his producer-director deal with Columbia gave him creative freedom and twenty-five percent of net profits. But Capra and the others were the exception. While the studios made some great movies that would not see a green light today, most of their productions were forgettable, made by a stable of confined directors, starring actors under stifling long-term contracts.

‡

The summer after Walter Bernstein graduated from Dartmouth in 1940, he made his way to the West Coast, finding it something to behold for a kid from Brooklyn obsessed with movies. "I'd drive around and look at the outside of MGM and Warner Brothers and the different studios. I thought it was paradise ... I bought a 1929 Model A Ford convertible and drove it up to San Francisco." In the army, he wrote for the military magazine *Yank*, spending most of the war wandering near the front ("I was young and stupid and fearless and I trooped all over Europe"), interviewing everyone from Yugoslav resistance leader Josip Tito to First Lady Eleanor Roosevelt.

Discharged in 1945, Bernstein spent a year at the *New Yorker*. A collection of magazine pieces he had written on the war were published as a book called *Keep Your Head Down*. It was a dream for a young writer to have a job at the *New Yorker* and a new book, but since his brief stay on the West Coast, he had been intent on something else. "I'd always been crazy about movies. Movies were very, very important to me, and I would go to them as much as possible. The idea of being part of that was irresistible. I had been thinking of writing for movies, and on the basis of the book I got an agent, and he got me a contract." With a ten-week Columbia Pictures contract in hand, Bernstein returned to L.A. There, he went to work for Bob Rossen, who was developing *All the King's Men* (1949), a fictionalized account of the life of Louisiana demagogue Huey P. Long.

Hollywood was in transition when Bernstein arrived, at the tail end of the first couple of decades of the talkies, during that fleeting period between the CSU strike and the full force of the blacklist. "I got there in '47, which was when the subpoenas were first being handed out, and while we took it seriously, in the left, or the left I knew, nobody thought it was *that* serious. It accelerated very quickly. But when I was there, I remember Rossen was served and he talked about how militant he was going to be, and he was upset that he wasn't named as one of the ten."

The indictments made this blacklist different than Dies' clampdown and were enough to send much of Hollywood scurrying for cover. Bogart and the rest of the Committee for the First Amendment never launched their promised campaign in support of the Hollywood Ten.

By the time Bernstein's contract was up, his agent, Harold Hecht, had formed a production company with Burt Lancaster, and they hired him to work on the adaptation of the thriller novel *Kiss the Blood off My Hands*. "I liked working for Rossen and would have stayed, but they offered me twice the amount of money. I was getting $250 a week from Rossen and they offered me $500. When that was finished, I went back home to New York. But, you know, I had a very, very good time in L.A.—and the political stuff didn't end there."

‡

While much of Hollywood was preoccupied with the blacklist, the studios were also engaged on another front—their long legal battle with independent producers was working its way through the courts. In the late 1930s, acting on behalf of independent producers and small-town theater owners upset with their lack of access to major releases, the FDR administration launched anti-trust action against the Big Eight (Paramount, 20th Century Fox, Warner Bros., MGM, RKO, Columbia, Universal, and United Artists), accusing them of illegally monopolizing production, distribution, and exhibition. The studios and the government settled out of court, a consent decree allowing the studios to keep their theater chains intact in exchange for limiting their monopolistic practices, in particular block booking (restricting packages to no more than five films) and blind bidding (now movies would have trade screenings for theater owners).

Regardless of internal differences, SIMPP's founders felt an alliance of independents was necessary to stand up to studio power, and they were united on the issue of block booking, opposing even the modified form. In the post-war era, independent companies would come and go; their achievements included Samuel Goldwyn's *The Best Years of Our Lives* (1946), Enterprise Productions' *Body and Soul* (1947), Liberty Films' *It's a Wonderful Life* (1946), California Pictures' *The Sin of Harold Diddlebock* (1947), and Stanley Kramer Productions' *High Noon* (1952). Actress Constance Bennett was one of the first women to form a production company, and she produced *Smart Woman* (1948), written by future Hollywood Ten member Alvah Bessie.

After years of legal skirmishes between the studios and SIMPP, the justice department, believing the majors hadn't adhered to the consent decree, reached the Supreme Court with its anti-trust case in late 1947. Former Supreme Court Justice James Byrnes, now the studios' lawyer, said the government was out to destroy the film industry, which had "its back to the wall and is fighting for its life."[17] In May 1948, the Supreme Court ruled that the studios were in violation of anti-trust laws. Block booking was outlawed, and the studios were ordered to divest themselves of their theater chains. Some were quick to cheer the death of studios. "The backbone of the motion picture trust shall be broken," said Abram Myers of the Allied States Exhibitors.[18] Others predicted the ruling would make independent producers out of the studios—instead of a handful of monopolies, there would be hundreds of smaller companies.

‡

The witch-hunt didn't stop at Hollywood's city limits. In 1949, in the town of Peekskill, about an hour north of New York City, Walter Bernstein had gotten a taste of the new American mood at a benefit concert for the Civil Rights Congress featuring Paul Robeson—opera singer, Shakespearean actor, author, movie star, social critic, folk singer, all-American football player, and lawyer. Robeson was also a leftist, which, for the blacklisters, trumped all. "There had been threats against Robeson, and so we organized a cordon around this a field where he was going to perform," says Bernstein. "Outside on the road, the American Legion picketers called us reds and all that kind of stuff. It was just one rather narrow road leading out to the main road. When the concert was over, we were all funneled out that road, and the cars couldn't go more than two, three miles an hour. These people who had been picketing began throwing rocks at us, beating on the cars, hitting people. The cops were on the road, but they didn't do anything. It wouldn't have happened without the cops protecting them; it was essentially a police riot. Of course, the Communists were blamed."

Bernstein had gotten involved with the Young Communist League while at Dartmouth and joined the Communist Party after returning from the war. "The things that we wanted or tried to organize around were things like housing and racism. We organized a big housing-for-veterans rally in New York. That was the kind of stuff that we did." In 1950 Bernstein was writing for *Danger*, a half-hour weekly melodrama produced by Martin Ritt, directed by Yul Brynner, and assistant-directed by Sidney Lumet. Brynner left to do *The King and I* on Broadway, and then Ritt left too, leaving Lumet as the show's director and Charles Russell its producer.

> Russell said, 'I can't use you any more.' By that time, I had
> a sense of what was going on, and he confirmed it. He said,
> 'You're on some kind of list, and I'm not to tell you that
> that's the reason. I'm just supposed to tell you we're going
> in a different direction.' He said, 'Use another name. Keep
> writing, but use another name.' He was a wonderful guy.
> He was totally nonpolitical. He had been an actor, and he
> just thought it was bad. Had they known that he was using
> me, he would have lost his job. But I continued working
> under another name for awhile. And then he came and said,
> 'They're catching on that blacklisted writers are using differ-
> ent names, so you're going to have to produce a real person
> to be you.'

So began the practice of getting fronts—people willing to have their names used on blacklisted writers' scripts and articulate enough to fake it at meetings with producers. "This is what I did for the next eight years," Bernstein says.

*Dead End* (1937) was realism before the neo. It's a wrenching recreation of Depression-era New York, and it's as homegrown as Hollywood could be in 1937: its screenplay was written by the soon-to-be blacklisted Lillian Hellman, who attended New York public schools; it was directed by William Wyler, a European immigrant to New York; it was adapted from a play by New York's Sidney Kingsley, formerly of the Group Theatre;

it introduced Billy Halop, Leo Gorcey, and their Bowery Boys, the quintessential New York street urchins; and it starred the Upper West Side's Humphrey Bogart and the Bronx's Sylvia Sidney. This dead end is where a slum street and tenement rooftops meet a ritzy new apartment with an East River view. Sidney was a real-life lefty who made a career out of soulful portrayals of working-class women. In this film, she's luminous as Drina, coping as best she can amidst poverty while doing her bit on the picket line. When a cop questions Drina about her brother's whereabouts, she says, "See this," pulling her hat back to show a lump on her forehead. "We were picketing the store today and one of you dirty cops hit me."

The cop: "Well, you were picketing, weren't you?"

Drina: "Sure, we got a right to picket. They hit us right and left. Three of the girls were hurt bad. Yeah, I'll tell you anything." Sidney turns her back and walks off.

"It happened suddenly," says Barzman. "We were shocked. We were frightened. We didn't think that we would lose the fight. We thought that we would show them up." The Hollywood Ten were sent to prison and there were new batches of hearings. Anyone accused of having been a Communist or who refused to sign a studio loyalty oath was blacklisted from working in Hollywood. There was one way out, according to this ritual—name names. To keep off the blacklist, you had to give names of "subversives" to the witch-hunters. Those named lost their livelihoods. Most called before HUAC, like Lillian Hellman and Adrian Scott, stood strong; some, like Clifford Odets and Robert Rossen, did break, giving names that, in most cases, the committee already had.

"It is very important to know that all through the war the witch-hunters were quiet," Norma says. "But by '47, as soon as the war was over, the right stopped lying in wait, really because of the labor situation, because we were important in the guilds and the unions in those years and doing wonderful things. Our closest, dearest friend was Adrian Scott. Adrian had lived with us. I've never known such a good man. He went to jail. He was one of the Ten. We knew them all pretty damn well."

The fear set in, and one by one, the Hollywood left was picked off. Director Edward Dmytryk, banned from entering any studio, sneaked into MGM and dropped a book, Pietro di Donato's *Christ in Concrete*, on

*Sylvia Sidney is a street-smart, working-class New Yorker in Dead End. © United Artists / Photofest.*

Ben Barzman's desk. Norma, who was about to have lunch with Ben at the studio commissary, took one look at her favorite novel and got excited about the prospect of turning it into a film. Dmytryk said he had a deal with Rank Productions to make the movie in England if Ben wrote the script. So Norma, Ben, and their two young children took the RMS *Queen Mary* across the Atlantic in early 1949. Norma says they didn't have a choice—their future in Hollywood was so dicey: "Remember the times. You had to do it."

Before they left, they took Ben's mother for ice cream at the Pig N' Whistle café on Hollywood Boulevard. "Ben said, 'Momma, we are going to go to England to make this film, but I don't know how long we will be gone. You know as well as I that we could be named and then we wouldn't be able to work [in the US], and then we couldn't come back.' She said, 'I understand. The Cossacks are coming after you.' Ben said, 'No, Momma. They're US congressmen, not Cossacks.' And she said, 'I know. Cossacks dress in different ways. If you are going somewhere, go somewhere where there are no Cossacks.'"

CHAPTER THREE

## *Hollywood Exiles*

NORMA AND BEN WALKED across the room to meet Pablo Picasso, who had not returned to his Spain since Franco's victory. The Barzmans, not long in Paris, were introduced to him as Hollywood screenwriters. "Picasso threw his arms around me, hugged me tight, and said, 'We are the same, we are the same. Exile, exile.' Ben said, 'We have been away from the States for only two-and-a-half months.' Picasso said, 'Exiles—who don't know yet they are exiles.' He took us by the hand and introduced us to everyone in the room, as 'Hollywood exiles who don't know yet they are exiles.'"

Norma and Ben and their growing family had stayed a couple of months in England for *Give Us This Day* (1949), the adaptation of *Christ in Concrete*, then settled in France. "In April '49, when we went to Paris, it was already clear that neither of us would work again in Hollywood. Our friends were already not getting jobs. The blacklist was growing. You could have trouble getting a job even if you hadn't been named in the congressional hearings yet."

The first American exile colony in Europe—the blacklisted—was forming. Although the US government now prohibited "subversives" from leaving the country, the Barzmans would have a stream of visitors, some of whom they helped escape from the US, such as Joseph Losey. Norma, Ben, and others formed a production company that was about to make a picture based on Ben's *Stranger on the Prowl* (1953). "I said, 'Joe Losey should direct it. If we get him out [of the US] now, we don't wait.' He had a hard time getting out, but he got out." In England, Ben also worked on *Time Without Pity* (1957) with Losey, who would go on to great acclaim directing *The Servant* (1963) and *Accident* (1967).

While in exile, Norma and Ben learned they had been named. "Eddie Dymytrk, I was told, had named us at the hearings. But we got named over and over, and we might have been named before Eddie did. We got letters from friends saying 'So-and-so is going to name you.'" Ben used the alias Andrea Forzano in the *Stranger on the Prowl* credits, S.B. Levenson when he wrote *It Happened in Paris* (both 1952), and was uncredited for *El Cid* (1961). Norma, with Italian writer Ennio Flaiano as her front, had written a screenplay about a teenage girl who gets pregnant. Her parents want her to go away to have the baby, but she wants an abortion. "United Artists distributed it with Ennio Flaiano's name on it, not mine, and instead of the [blacklisted] director Bernard Vorhaus, they used the Italian assistant-director's name. Instead of calling it *Finishing School*, it was called *Luxury Girl*. United Artists put it into an all-night theater on 42nd Street, with nudie photographs outside that had nothing to do with the story. That has always hurt me. It was a lovely picture, and it did well all over Europe [released as *Fanciulle di lusso*, 1953]."

The growing Barzman family—there would be seven children—lived in Paris for a few years, then settled in an old country house near Cannes. In the 1950s, Norma wrote television for Hannah Weinstein, a lefty US producer who set up shop in London to hire exiled Americans, making TV series about fighting the good fight, such as *The Adventures of Robin Hood*. "When the blacklist hit, [Weinstein] gathered together a lot of money from progressive people all over the States. She told them that she would buy a studio in England, make television, and employ the blacklisted writers. And she did it, by god, she did it."

Not everyone was as brave as Weinstein. Any association with the blacklisted could hurt a career. US filmmaker Jules Dassin, in exile in France, recalled movie stars at the Cannes festival holding up champagne glasses to cover their faces from him as he passed by. Gene Kelly was a courageous exception. When Dassin was at Cannes in 1955 with his outstanding heist film *Rififi* (1955)—co-written by Ben Barzman—he saw Kelly as he entered the Palais theater. "I kind of ducked away so that he wouldn't be embarrassed by fleeing from me. He saw this. And I shall always appreciate him coming after me and saying, 'What the hell are you doing? Are you avoiding me?' He took me by the arm and led me up the steps of the Palais. He was the only one I knew willing at that time to be photographed with me."[1]

‡

Norma and Ben weren't the only ones in Hollywood drawn to France and England. The studios had designs on both countries.

Former French prime minister Léon Blum, representing his country during post-war economic negotiations in Washington, proposed that French theaters screen domestic films twenty-eight weeks a year. He settled for sixteen, and no ceiling on US imports. Blum also negotiated a line of credit and cancellation of French debts. "I admit that if it had been necessary in the higher interests of France as a whole to sacrifice the French film industry, I would not have hesitated," he

*Actress Betsy Blair and her husband Gene Kelly were active in Hollywood's progessive community. Photofest.*

said.[2] France's film community reacted angrily to the concessions. Soon, with French production down, protestors, including actors Simone Signoret and Jacques Becker, took to the streets demanding the nationalization of film, while politicians called for a tougher quota. "This political situation has been created by Communist propaganda against American films," said US ambassador Jefferson Caffery, "which has gained support from non-Communists who consider that American films are threatening French films as an art form and expression of French genius."[3] US Secretary of State George Marshall cautioned his government that pushing too hard on film issues might ignite opposition to other American policies in Europe. The French–US agreement was changed to twenty weeks and a limit of 121 US films a year, leaving SIMPP angry that 110 of those slots were reserved for studio products.

At one point in negotiations, the state department suggested an end to the Marshall Plan—post-war US aid to reconstruct Europe—in France and England as retaliation against restrictions on US movies. British movies, with help from the quota, had come of age, and there was confidence they could fill domestic screens in 1947 when the new Labour government slapped a tax on foreign films: for every pound the studios took out of the UK, they would pay three pounds. The studio response was immediate. The following day, they announced a boycott of UK theaters. MPAA president Eric Johnston lambasted Labour intentions "to socialize the film industry."[4]

The Labour government seemed unmoved at first. "I am sure that I can say to Hollywood that if they believe they can squeeze us into modifying our attitude on the duty by continuing the embargo, they are backing a loser," Prime Minister Harold Wilson said.[5] But British exhibitors, uncertain about UK production and disdainful of subtitled movies, worried that they'd soon run through their backlog of Hollywood movies and be left with empty screens. The British government feared that the MPAA would use its influence in Washington to scuttle Marshall Plan funding. Negotiations ensued between the UK and the MPAA. In the end, Wilson and his government capitulated, producing a new formula that allowed Hollywood studios to take more of their earnings out of the country and avoid taxes through film-related spending in the UK. The studios were not as pleased by Wilson's decision to increase the British quota to forty-five percent of screen time. Under considerable heat, Wilson reduced that to forty percent in 1949—still not enough for Johnston, who said: "Because the quota is so clearly unreasonable and excessive and runs directly counter to the spirit and purposes of trade agreements between Britain and the United States, we feel that the State Department should immediately and vigorously take up the matter again with the British government to relieve this intolerable condition."[6] It was reduced again to thirty percent in 1950 and would continue to be trimmed until being eliminated altogether in 1983.

‡

Walking in midtown Manhattan, Walter Bernstein and his equally blacklisted friend, comic actor Zero Mostel, saw another actor, Lee J. Cobb, who had named names, coming toward them. "I think he had named Zero, and so when Zero saw him coming, all his rage—which was a lot—started to percolate, and I really thought that he was going to kill Cobb," says Bernstein. "Cobb thought that also because his face changed when he saw Zero. But nothing happened. I mean, we just walked past him."

In New York, Bernstein and fellow blacklisted screenwriters Abe Polonsky and Arnold Manhoff met regularly at Steinberg's deli sharing ideas and work that would come their way, often utilizing fronts. Bernstein found work on Sidney Lumet's TV series *You Are There*, which recreated historic events, and TV theater such as *Philco Playhouse* and *Westinghouse Theater*.

In 1950, Bernstein's name was among the 151 published in *Red Channels*, the best-known blacklist. A publication of American Business Consultants, Inc., *Red Channels*' randomly compiled "subversives" ranged from movie stars Judy Holliday, Jose Ferrer, and Edward G. Robinson to musicians such as Artie Shaw, Pete Seeger, and Leonard Bernstein. "I was lucky in that there was a very strong support system in New York of other blacklisted people, left-wing people, some of whom had come from Hollywood and were living there, like Polonsky or Waldo Salt and Ring Lardner, and they were enormously supportive," said Bernstein.

> Everybody helped everybody else. If I had a job and heard about another job that I couldn't take, I would try to get it for another blacklisted writer, and they would do the same for me. I was very lucky to have a relationship with Sidney Lumet. *You Are There* and *Danger* ran for several years, and by the time those shows finished, I had enough of a name, even though it was an underground name, so that I was able to pick up work. So I made a living, not a good living, but it was a living. I survived. I wasn't blacklisted by accident, and I knew what my position was going to be. I mean, it was ten years out of my life, but I knew what I was doing and believed in what I was doing.

While writers, unlike performers, could sometimes find ways to continue working anonymously, there was the emotional toll that comes with being told you are no longer allowed to do what you do well. The blacklisted would get the occasional offers to lecture on writing or acting or the movies to receptive Catskills audiences. "One of the resorts in the Catskills was kind of a left-wing resort," Bernstein said, "and the very nice woman who ran it would offer a free weekend if you'd come up and give a talk or perform." Bernstein drove Mostel, a nightclub headliner before the blacklist, to a Catskills hotel where the audience's bittersweet roar of approval reminded him of what he had lost.

‡

After the 1948 Supreme Court anti-trust ruling against the studios, producer David Selznick predicted: "Hollywood's like Egypt, full of pyramids. It'll never come back. It'll just keep on crumbling until finally the wind blows the last studio props across the sand."[7] The studios proved more resilient than many anticipated, soon discovering that the only indispensable element of their old three-part system was distribution. Control distribution, and you've got the world's screens. Instead of disappearing as a result of the court ruling, the studios thrived by transforming into primarily financiers and distributors.

The Society of Independent Motion Picture Producers didn't suddenly disappear either. "Indies War on Majors," declared *Variety*'s front page a couple months after the ruling, when SIMPP announced it would continue to sue theater chains, starting in Detroit, where ninety percent of screens were under Paramount control.[8] Some in SIMPP were concerned that theaters, while under new ownership—the studios were forced to divest their theater holdings—would still be coerced by studios. SIMPP President Ellis G. Arnall likened it to an anti-trust case that had divided the Pullman railroad company, in which: "One-half [of the company] set up business on the other side of the street under a new name."[9] While the Detroit case dragged on, Paramount refocused on television, merging with the ABC network and urging independent producers to provide product. Walt Disney, in particular, formed a close working relationship with Paramount-ABC, producing a series, *Disneyland*, for the network, which in turn invested in the planned theme park. SIMPP's Disney now rushed to settle the Detroit suit before Disneyland's grand opening in 1955, dispatching his vice-president Gunther Lessing to Detroit, where an out-of-court settlement was reached and the case dismissed.

The MPAA, under the presidency of Eric Johnston, set out its own foreign agenda, rooted in free-trade arguments, including the freedom of studios to use the vertical integration model in foreign countries because the 1948 anti-trust decision ruling was confined to the US. With independent producers soon in tow following the Supreme Court decision and with the Hollywood left in exile, the studios could concentrate on their global mission. Johnston had emerged as the studios' foreign ambassador/salesman—the "MPAA Prez Who Sold Hollywood Around," *Variety* called him.[10] From the first, Johnston enlisted the departments of state (because the studios sold the American way) and commerce (because they sold American goods) to assist his policy. Hollywood was eager to enter into co-productions with foreign investors, in part to avoid the US-based film unions, but also to spread the word. "Dr. Rudolf Vogel has been in the United States," noted secretary of state Dean Acheson in 1951, "interviewing motion picture producers concerning plans for co-production by German and US firms of anti-communist films."[11]

‡

Stewart Stern did his bit as a struggling actor in New York, then drove to the West Coast. The Actors Lab—the closest thing to an L.A. version of New York's Actors Studio until an actual Actors Studio West opened in 1965—seemed a natural home for Stern. "Morris Carnovsky and Phoebe Brand, his wife, were there ... [along with] Roman Bohnen, who had been in the Group Theatre. It was great training."

Many men and women, regardless of their politics, protested with daily acts of quiet resistance to the witch-hunt. Stern was directly warned by Adolph Zukor about his association with the Actors Lab. "My uncle called me and said, 'You've got to get out of that school. It's a red front.' And I said, 'I'm going to it on the G.I. Bill of Rights. As long as they're paying and I'm going as a veteran of the war, I'm going to stay.' He was very upset with me. He said, 'Also, I think you should change your name. It's too Jewish.'"

Making the transition from acting to writing was a natural for Stern, and he found work as dialogue director on noir films at the small Eagle-Lion studio where he worked with these "great people [such as] John Alton who just revolutionized the camera, and Anthony Mann." However, recalls Stern, "The scripts were mostly so awful. In the morning, I'd sit with Virginia Mayo or Carol Landis or Ann Dvorak or Wally Ford and just see whether they knew their lines, which was my job. To see them try to make something real out of this dialogue had me rewriting their lines in the dressing trailer."

The film noir era was launched largely by European filmmakers sent into Hollywood exile by the rise of Nazism. The unlikely mix of dark European criminality with warm evenings on the hills and beaches of L.A. resulted in alluring films about private eyes and femme fatales and other engaging outsiders maneuvering through California nights. Fritz Lang brought the sensibility of his expressionist thriller *M* (1931) to Hollywood with movies such as *The Big Heat* (1953) and *You Only Live Once* (1937). Other Europeans, such as Otto Preminger (*Laura*, 1944), Billy Wilder (*Sunset Boulevard*, 1950), and Robert Siodmak (*The Killers*, 1946) were also mainstays of Hollywood noir. The noir films were often made by independent producers and distributed by the studios, and while they were the most entertaining Hollywood productions of the blacklist period, true to their times they usually steered clear of social critique. Still, some early noir filmmakers—including Orson Welles and Jules Dassin before they departed Hollywood, and the Robert Aldrich–A.I. Bezzerides team behind *Kiss Me Deadly* (1955)—utilized the dark stylings of noir to portray an underside of American society, counter to the wholesome distortions that dominated screens in the 1950s. The noir genre caught exiles coming (from Europe before the war) and going (to Europe after the blacklist). For some, such as the great German socialist writer Bertolt Brecht, it was difficult to know whether they were coming or going, having been driven out of Europe to Hollywood by the Nazis, only to be later driven out of Hollywood to Europe by HUAC.

One evening, Stewart Stern's other uncle, Arthur Loew, screened his new film *The Search* (1948) for him and his cousin, Arthur Jr. Starring Montgomery Clift and directed by Fred Zinnemann, it was American neorealism about a young Auschwitz survivor and his mother searching for each other in post-war Europe. "And I was blown away," recalls Stern, "by the relationships and the caring. This was about a small relationship and people exposing emotion in a way that I believed and never had seen. I said, I have got to meet Fred Zinnemann. But Zinnemann said, 'I don't like to meet people who tell me I'm good because I never know what to say.' But Arthur took some of my short stories out of my desk and, without telling me, gave them to Zinnemann, whose secretary called me and said that he wanted me to come in."

Their first project together, involving Clift and Leonard Bernstein, fell through, as film plans are wont to do. But Stern did do a film with Zinnemann, *Teresa* (1951), about a young Italian woman who marries an American soldier and moves to the US. Besides writing the Oscar-nominated screenplay, Stern did some scouting for the production in Italy and discovered its star: "Anna Maria [Pierangeli] walked in, and it was Teresa.'" Stern told the young actress she should return to live in Italy after shooting the movie. "I told her, 'Stay here and you will stay sane.'" The talented Pierangeli, using the name Pier Angeli, would be offered Hollywood stardom after *Teresa*.

‡

SIMPP disappeared in 1958. When it came to studio adversaries, SIMPP was far easier to settle with than the Hollywood left, and its big intentions, including a foreign office in Paris, were abandoned as the organization began to crumble. Although they often resented the studios' power, the handful of high-profile independent producers working outside the system prior to the 1948 ruling usually had distribution arrangements with one. After winning its big issues—block booking and theater divestiture—there was little reason for SIMPP to continue. Independent producers were so much a part of the new emerging studio system that they were simply absorbed, and instead of maintaining their own movie factories, it was less expensive for studios to contract independent producers to make the movies they distributed. "Independent production" now meant packaging a script, director, and cast for a major studio/distributor. By 1957, seventy-one percent of the major studios' movies were partnered with independent producers. While studios still produced their own films on occasion, "studio heads now are accountants," John Huston decided, "tax experts, a sprinkling of financial wizards, and ex-agents. They are hardly a creative breed ... [and are] illiterate when it comes to making pictures."[12] While a few SIMPP members were determined independents, others would have liked nothing more than to transition to a major studio, but didn't have the smarts or the luck to pull it off. One did—Walt Disney, like Zukor and the Warners before him, was an independent producer-turned-studio boss.

This new studio system made fewer movies (the Big Eight, which had together produced 500 films in 1940, now made just fifteen to twenty a year each). The end of block booking resulted in a shortage of films for small neighborhood theaters, already under siege from television, but it didn't mean the studios lost control of exhibition. They would continue to block book by a different name, releasing their movie packages one-by-one with the understanding that an exhibitor who didn't take it all might not get any, especially the most profitable releases. As the 1950s wore on, there wasn't enough studio production to maintain long-term contracts with talent, so actors and directors formed their own production companies linked to the majors. The producer-driven "independent" movement, as studio adversary, was non-existent by the end of the decade. Even Jack Warner, who left Warner Bros., was piecing together his own projects for studio release. Independence, for producers, had meant working outside the studios, but now the Hollywood mainstream was made up of producers not permanently employed by the studios.

‡

When the Hollywood Ten's Dalton Trumbo was given a screen credit by Kirk Douglas for writing *Spartacus* (1960) and by Otto Preminger for *Exodus* (1960), the blacklist showed its cracks for all to see. Frank Sinatra was the first to publicly try to break the blacklist when he earlier announced that he had hired Hollywood Ten member Albert Maltz to write *The Execution of Private Slovik* (never produced). John F. Kennedy, who Sinatra was supporting for president, eventually prevailed upon him to back down. But by the early 1960s, the worst of the McCarthy era had passed. Some of the blacklisted, without having named names, were back at work. Yet there wasn't a defining moment when the blacklist stopped all at once for everyone. "For me, it was when Sidney Lumet hired me to do a Sophia Loren movie," says Walter Bernstein, "and I squeaked through then because the producers, who were her husband and his partner, didn't know who I was. They just took Sidney's word for it and then Paramount went ahead, until I got the subpoena. By then I knew [the blacklist] was cracking."

None of this made much sense to Loren, as Italian cinema was full of socialists, and the Communist Party had the second largest bloc of seats in Italy's chamber of deputies. The subpoena for Bernstein to testify came toward the end of the hearings while he was writing *That Kind of Woman* (1959) for Loren and Lumet. "I was not served, but I heard from my agent, who heard from Paramount that they were not going through with the contract because of the subpoena. I just packed a bag and went on the lam until they finished with their hearings and then I surfaced again. I was never served." Bernstein returned to Hollywood. "I finished the job, and they shot the movie. And then I got a passport. That was a big thing. I went to Europe."

‡

Norma Barzman received a note from the US embassy in Paris saying there was a minor detail in her passport which needed correcting. She wondered if it was some government ploy she should ignore, and she talked it over with friends. No one was sure what it meant. So Norma agreed to go to the embassy.

> I showed the letter to the girl behind the counter, and she said, 'Show me your passport.' She pinched it out of my hand and ran away with it. I waited for about an hour before the consul-general general came out. Her name was Agnes Schneider. We later called her Aggie Schneider the Spider. She had purple hair. She said, 'You will leave France on a ship for America. When you get to America, your passport will be taken from you. You cannot travel any more.' I protested and protested but she said, 'Not only that, but you better tell your husband that if he doesn't come in and give up his passport, we will eventually get it from one of the borders when he is trying to cross.'

Norma was stranded in France without a passport from 1951 to 1958. Born-in-Toronto Ben was stripped of his US citizenship but could get a stateless person's visa in Paris. "He could go everywhere and I could go nowhere. I learnt to live without it for several years."

In 1958, Norma's lawyer Leonard Boudin cabled from New York: "Go into the American consulate in Nice and just say, 'I want my passport.'" With trepidation she walked into the consulate. "I waited for the consul-general and there she was, a beautiful young black woman, and before she did anything she kissed me and said, 'I'm so happy I can give you back your passport. Do you know what I did all those years when this was American policy? I had myself stationed in Asia for seven years. I couldn't bear it.' She congratulated me, hugged me some more, gave me my passport, and said, 'Enjoy.' I cried."

Norma's first stop was London, then in November 1960, she traveled to Spain where Ben was writing *El Cid*. Sophia Loren had seen *Give Us This Day* and wanted Ben to rewrite an un-shootable script about the eponymous heroic Spaniard (played by Charlton Heston) and his great love, Jimena (Loren). Ben arrived in Spain on a Friday to rework the script for a shoot that began on Monday. "He said, 'I can't save anything. I have to start from scratch.' And Sophia said, 'My life is in your hands.'"

*El Cid* producer Sam Bronston's original family name was Bronstein. He was the nephew of Leon Bronstein, who later changed his name to Trotsky. Ben was not part of the stable of blacklisted talent Bronston maintained in Spain, where he shot a series of relatively low-budget epics, including *John Paul Jones* (1959) and *King of Kings* (1961). Now Ben was in Madrid writing furiously. Loren invited Ben and Norma to come to dinner at the penthouse where the actress and her husband Carlo Ponti were staying. "She had her hair wrapped in a towel and wore one of Carlo's long shirts. That was my introduction." It was the beginning of a lifelong friendship. "I love her very much, and she is a really good person," Norma tells me.

Ben Barzman, the Communist who contemplated volunteering for the Spanish Civil War, was finally in Spain—Franco's Spain—writing, under the fascists' noses, dialogue about resistance and exile. In the script, Loren's Jimena, having enjoyed an evening of good food, wine, and love in a remote farmhouse with Heston's El Cid, tells him: "We will find some hidden place where you're not known ... and we will make our lives there." Says El Cid: "If all men knew that banishment could be like this, we'd have a world of exiles."

*Ben Barzman. Photo courtesy of Norma Barzman.*

Back in Hollywood, the Academy revoked a bylaw making anyone who hadn't cooperated with HUAC ineligible for an Oscar. Robert Rich, a no-show when he won the 1956 best-story Oscar for *The Brave One*, turned out to be Dalton Trumbo. The following year, Pierre Boulle, author of the novel *Bridge on the River Kwai*, won an Oscar for its screenplay, although it was really written by Carl Foreman and Michael Wilson. The year after that, Nathan E. Douglas (actually blacklisted writer and actor Nedrick Young) won for *The Defiant Ones*.

After the blacklist dust had settled, the ones who hadn't collaborated with the witch-hunters were bloodied but unbowed. The ones who buckled, appearing before Congress to inform on friends, hadn't simply tarnished their images, they had destroyed lives. Actor Phil Loeb, of TV's *The Goldbergs* (1949), named by Lee J. Cobb and director Elia Kazan, committed suicide: "Died of a sickness commonly called the blacklist," said a letter to the *New York Times*.[13] Actress Mady Christians (*All My Sons*, 1949), unable to find work for three years after being named, died of a cerebral hemorrhage in 1951. Hollywood roles ended abruptly for Phoebe Brand and Morrie Carnovsky after they were named by Kazan and actor Sterling Hayden. Called before HUAC to name names and save his career, Carnovsky refused to cooperate. Norma and Ben saw their friend Adrian Scott for the last time when, un-hirable in

Hollywood, he visited them in France. "He was utterly despondent," Norma says. John Garfield, who grew up Jacob Julius Garfinkle in gangs on the streets of New York, was among HUAC's most prized prey, having just starred in *The Postman Always Rings Twice* (1946) and *Body and Soul* (1947) when he was swept up in the clampdown. The witch-hunt drove Garfield from Hollywood, back to New York where he would die of a heart attack at age thirty-nine the day before he was scheduled to appear before HUAC. "He was caught in that blacklist period between wanting to be a movie star, which he liked being very much, and being this kid from the streets, Julie Garfinkle, who never ratted," Bernstein says. "The biggest crime was being a rat. He was torn, and they were merciless in hounding him. He solved it by dying."

The blacklist would leave a broken Hollywood. Those sent into exile had helped to create much of the best of the first twenty years of talkies, and the studio movies, qualitatively, would never recover from their loss. "Certainly during the '50s, it put a stop to a lot of content," Bernstein says.

> You can't divorce [film] from the society, which in that
> Eisenhower period had a kind of blandness. There was no real
> tough content being done. The studios would do anything in
> order to make money. They would go along with whatever.
> They were friends of the Soviet Union during the war because
> the government told them to be, and after the war, when
> the blacklist started, they became enemies. It was a bad, bad
> period. The blacklist was part of the Cold War; it didn't stand
> by itself. The Committee loved Hollywood because they got
> their name in the papers when they had hearings with celeb-
> rities. The purpose of the blacklist was to break the left wing
> of the labor movement—which they did. They went after
> teachers, they went after doctors, they went after lawyers. We
> were just a small part of it.

As Norma and I prepare, finally, to leave Nate 'n Al's, she tells me: "I want to say something that the blacklist did. It silenced America. I think so much fear was sown then that people are still afraid. It's almost engrained."

*Kiss Me Deadly* is a road movie set inside the road city. Without ever leaving L.A., private detective Mike Hammer (Ralph Meeker) drives from flop house to mansion to beach house, meeting a parade of eccentrics. In some noir pictures these characters might seem ridiculous or even cool, but here they're sad—as empty as these L.A. streets after dark, filled with fears and hoping to find "the great whatsit" that everybody's seeking. In screenwriter A.I. Bezzeride's hands, this is more of a reconfiguration than an adaptation of Mickey Spillane's novel. Released near the end of the noir era in 1955 (many of Bezzeride's and director Robert Aldrich's friends were caught in the blacklist), our hero has none of the niceties of Spade and Archer. This private dick is as brutal as any of the movie's bad guys, except its ultimate bad guy: a nuclear future.

It wasn't only the blacklist that drove talent from Hollywood in the 1950s. For Stern, it was the contraction of the studio system. "I got fired after *Teresa* even though I was nominated [for an Oscar]," Stern says. "MGM decided to cut out a lot of people, and I was a junior writer." Stern returned to New York, where he wrote for television and worked with the New Dramatists Committee, which arranged readings of new plays. "Equity had agreed to supply the actors. Any actor who wasn't working could come and be in these readings. I was directing really incredible casts, and everybody kept suggesting James Dean. I didn't know who he was. But I called, and the answering service said he was out of town. It wasn't till Arthur, my cousin, invited me to go to California for two weeks at Christmas that I met Jimmy, because he was a friend of Arthur's and he was in love with Pier Angeli."

## CHAPTER 4

## The Actor Rebellion

JAMES DEAN SAT ACROSS from Stewart Stern as they both spun around in their chairs.

"We didn't know what to say," Stern says. "Here was this kid at Arthur's place. I knew that he was an actor and that's really all I knew. I was scared of him because of his reputation—I'd heard that he was crazy, disrespectful, dangerous. Then we saw our reflections in the glass door that led to the garden, and—we were spinning—he mooed at me. I knew I could outdo him, so I gave him my moo. Then I did my flock of sheep, and then I did· my three pigs eating at the same time. We laughed and laughed, and I don't remember any more to the conversation. You couldn't help liking him. I thought, *This isn't the guy they're talking about.*" Later that week, Stern went to a party at Gene Kelly's house. "Nick Ray came over and said that he had seen *Teresa* and liked it a lot. He was making a movie at Warners and he said, 'Come and see me.' That turned out to be the assignment for *Rebel Without a Cause.*"

*Rebel* would touch audiences around the world, but it began as a local story. The director Nicholas Ray kept seeing articles in the L.A. papers about a new kind of middle-class teenage crime. "Kids were tearing up places, having these 'chickie runs' and knife fights," says Stern. "Ray thought, There's got to be a reason for this whole thing that's happening in L.A., and then he realized it was happening in other cities too. So he said, 'There's got to be a story in this. Let's find out what's making this happen.'"

Ray spoke with Warner Bros. producers, who asked him to put it on paper. He wrote seven pages detailing a proposed film he called *The Blind Run*. "The blind run was something that was going on, on Mulholland Drive where there was a tunnel, and people from different school gangs would challenge each other," Stern says. "They'd steal a jalopy and race toward each other through this tunnel, and the first one to veer was chicken."

Novelists Leon Uris and Irving Schulman were hired to come up with the screenplay for Ray's idea, which was now called *Rebel Without a Cause*. The title was taken from a book by psychiatrist Robert Lindner about a youth in prison being interviewed by a psychiatrist. "I looked at the script, because I figured Schulman was off the picture. I told Nick that I would have to start from scratch. I would have to meet these kids, pose as a social worker from Wisconsin, and sit with the cops and be there when the parents came for them."

‡

Although Stern kept the occasional image from Schulman's script, such as setting a scene at the Griffith Park Conservatory, he was essentially starting over, with different characters and relationships. It was method screenwriting. Stern drew on his own family history, friendships he'd had at school and the army, and his identification with *Peter Pan*'s forever-young, parentless protagonist and adventurous lost children. The result was James Dean's Jimmy Stark, the teen outsider who moved to suburban L.A. with his detached mother and timid father; Sal Mineo's Plato, a motherless wild child looking for affection and guidance; and Natalie Wood's Judy, the rebel girl looking to escape unrelenting pressures from her peers and parents.

"The sequence where they come to the mansion—that's Peter, wrapped up in Plato, taking all the Lost Boys in. That was quite conscious; that character was very, very close to Peter and to my own experience. Dean's background with his parents was very like mine because he was an orphan for all intents and purposes."

After Jim Dean's mother died when he was a child, his father shipped him off to be raised on an Indiana farm by an aunt and uncle, leaving him with a sense of abandonment and vulnerability that would later jump off the screen. Meanwhile, Stern learned from his mother that she didn't want him after finding out she was pregnant. "She just couldn't bear it because it meant that she would not be allowed to be an actress, which she had always dreamt of. She tried every way to get rid of me." His response was to give her a Mother's Day card that read: "I have never felt welcome." Stern put his own parents in *Rebel*. "I knew this had to be a story about a kid who was motherless and fatherless, whose mother used him as an excuse to keep moving because she couldn't bear herself, and a father who couldn't stand up, as mine couldn't. So he's looking for a father and, at the same time, without realizing it, becoming what he's looking for with this other kid, Plato."

Stern's rebel research didn't stop at his personal history. When he read about a man who couldn't bear to see his adolescent daughter in lipstick, the idea of a father uncomfortable with his daughter's pubescent sexuality became key to the Judy character. Plato was also drawn

*Stewart Stern. Photographed by Paul Newman, courtesy of Stewart Stern.*

from an incident in which a teen had shot his neighbor's ducklings.

> But it became puppies. Plato would have killed the puppies
> because they had a mother, and he didn't want to see a lot of
> noisy suckling little puppies on their mother's breast when
> he had no mother except somebody who was always away.
> So I began to build the characters. I thought, this has to have
> Aristotle's unities—one major action behind one major hero.
> The action is to find a father, and the prize is that he [the
> hero] becomes a father. It's the most unexpected prize of all.
> What he wants to be is good, and what he wants to find is a

society where he can belong, that will accept him, and kids that will accept him. I wanted Jimmy to be shot while he's trying to protect Plato. The father comes up to him and says, 'We got to talk, we got to talk,' and Jimmy says, 'I'm busy, I can't talk. I'm busy dying.'

‡

Like sound before and digital afterward, television in the 1950s would change the movies. As movie attendance dropped, the studios debated television. While some saw it as an audience-stealing enemy to be vanquished (as in 20th Century Fox's *The Man in the Gray Flannel Suit* [1956]), others (Walt Disney, David Selznick) saw it as their future. TV soon shifted from its live-in-New York base to in-studio Hollywood productions, often shooting at studio lots. When what had passed for independent filmmaking was incorporated into the studio system, the old categories of production, divided by A and B pictures, were shelved. The new TV networks' series were the descendants of the B pictures. Producers received financing and distribution through one-off deals with studios that made the new A movies—"big pictures" with broad appeal (*The Greatest Show on Earth* [1952], *The Egyptian* [1954], *Vera Cruz* [1954]) or "small pictures" with niche audiences (*Marty* [1955], *The Defiant Ones* [1958], *Rebel Without a Cause*).

Directors such as John Ford and actors like Burt Lancaster rushed to fill the studios' sudden need for external production companies. HHL (Harold Hecht, James Hill, and Lancaster) was a new production company, combining big (like *Trapeze* [1956]) and small. It produced a feature film based on a teleplay, *Marty* (which had been originally broadcast live from New York in 1953) for $350,000; this working-class Bronx romance would win Cannes' Palme d'Or award and the best picture Oscar while earning $6 million at the box office. But for every *Marty* that drew audiences, there was a slew of ambitious "small pictures" with dismal box-office returns such as HHL's *Sweet Smell of Success* (1957). TV wasn't the movies' only problem, however. From the early 1950s until the late '60s, which saw the rise of a "New Hollywood," American film, with a handful of exceptions (a good low-budget noir or a *Sweet Smell of Success*), was rarely worth watching. Along with the quality independent productions of an HHL, there were the cheapo drive-in movies of American International Pictures or Roger Corman's Filmgroup. In the 1950s, they churned out shows like *Hot Rod Girl* (1956) to fill double bills. Some had believed the end of block booking would mean fewer but better studio films, but it resulted in fewer bad movies *and* fewer good movies.

There was, however, the beginnings of an acting breakthrough that would change the face of film. It's no coincidence that terms applied to the "method" insurgency—real, tough, honest—would later be used to describe independent film. The American method actors, combined with the naturalistic acting in Italian neorealism and the French New Wave, made possible the realistic storytelling that would largely define independent cinema. It is a character-driven filmmaking, so it's no surprise that many of its best directors started out as actors. Nor should it be a surprise that a writer, Stewart Stern, so suited to the new style, would have started out as an actor.

‡

By the late 1940s, the Group Theatre had disbanded and the method style of acting was being taken to new heights by its successors, the Actors Studio and the Stella Adler Studio of Acting. "When the Group Theatre alumni began teaching in New York—Elia Kazan, Lee Strasberg, Sandy Meisner, Stella Adler—they taught what they had been doing for ten of the most successful years on Broadway with Clifford Odets, who had four plays on Broadway at the same time. And they were without peer, these people," says Stern.

Their teachings fomented an actors' rebellion, which made its grand entrance when Marlon Brando astonished audiences with his raw naturalism in *A Streetcar Named Desire* on Broadway in 1947, then on screen in 1951. It was like witnessing, Stern says, a moment of "absolute authenticity." He saw Brando in the play at the Ethel Barrymore Theater. "When Marlon made his entrance in *Streetcar* it was like a mistake. It was like somebody walked on not realizing the curtain was up. It was uncomfortable to watch because it was the kind of acting that no one had ever done before. Everybody in the audience was looking at everybody else. And then, when he sat down and started to play cards, you went, 'Who is this?' You looked at your program. This is Stanley Kowalski. It was a revelation."

Brando was just the beginning. The Actors Studio, with Strasberg as artistic director, and slightly later, the Stella Adler Studio of Acting, unleashed a method onslaught on Hollywood. "They were nail biters and they ate with their hands and they scratched their asses and they turned their backs to the camera and they talked to the director—and it just blew everything sky high," says Stern. "Robert Wagner said his experience with Paul Newman in *Winning* [1969] changed his life. He had never been with a star like Paul, who would never let him do a close-up without being behind the camera for him to talk to, and to have that contact with. It was a shock."

Students of the method schools include: Carroll Baker, Anne Bancroft, Warren Beatty, Ellen Burstyn, Montgomery Clift, James Dean, Robert De Niro, Sally Field, Jane Fonda, Ben Gazzara, Dustin Hoffman, Harvey Keitel, Martin Landau, Steve McQueen, Marilyn Monroe, Jack Nicholson, Paul Newman, Al Pacino, Geraldine Page, Sidney Poitier, Mickey Rourke, Eva Marie Saint, Martin Sheen, Rod Steiger, Susan Strasberg, Rip Torn, Eli Wallach, Shelley Winters, and Joanne Woodward.

‡

While the method movies of the 1950s portended the cultural revolution on the horizon, they were made in the shadow of the blacklist. "Kazan gave the names of everybody at the Group Theatre. And so did Odets," Stern says. "I knew some of those people. I didn't know their histories until later. Marty Ritt never did a movie that didn't have social foundations, so I think he was one of the best to come out of it. I don't think Trumbo ever really did what he could have done after [the blacklist]. He might have just been too mutilated."

*On the Waterfront* (1954) was a great platform for the new naturalistic acting, with an outstanding cast of method actors and non-professionals. Brando is as good as acting gets on screen, again displaying his singular mix of power, vulnerability, and intelligence. And Eva Marie Saint and Lee J. Cobb were also remarkable. *On the Waterfront*—about a tough New York dockworker who testifies against corruption—was also director Kazan and writer Bud Schulberg's self-serving way of absolving themselves after naming names, and despite its greatness, the film was later disavowed by Brando.

‡

A young French acting student at Le Studio Jack Garfein stops by our table in a Paris café to say a warm hello to Jack Garfein. "She works here and gives me free coffee whenever I come," he smiles.

Jack Garfein directed two of the great unheralded method-driven movies, *The Strange One* (1957) and *Something Wild* (1961). He applied at the Actors Studio after witnessing *A Streetcar Named Desire* on Broadway. By his early twenties, Garfein dropped his acting aspirations and was directing and teaching at the Actors Studio. At twenty-three, he directed *End as a Man*, starring Ben Gazzara as a scheming southern cadet at a military academy, the first play to move from off-Broadway to Broadway. He wasn't expecting a lot when a young actress, who was hoping to study at the Actors Studio, asked to perform a scene. "I was amazed; she did something that was quite remarkable, so I said to her, 'I think you should take a class with Strasberg. I could recommend you.' She called me, wanting to have lunch to talk, and I was attracted to her, you know. She told me she was married to a man who was in his sixties—she was twenty—but she was getting a divorce."

Carroll Baker called Garfein back a week later. "She said, 'I have my own place now, and I'm divorced.' I said, 'I'll tell you what, let's celebrate your divorce.' And our relationship started. Then, one day, I'm walking down the street and these guys follow me and start to beat me up. I ran into a restaurant and called the police. When I got home to my apartment, it was wrecked." Garfein was in love with Baker, however, and after what he had experienced during the war, it took more to scare him than her ex, a furrier with gangland ties.

Born in Czechoslovakia, Garfein had survived Auschwitz as a child. His parents and sister had died in concentration camps. When he was fifteen, he arrived in New York to stay with an uncle. Although he spoke no English at first, he was a fast study and soon decided to be an actor. At seventeen, he won a scholarship to the New School's dramatic workshop. He quickly learned he liked directing even more than acting, so he both studied at the Actors Studio, then taught there.

A year after Garfein and Baker met, they married. She first took small roles on Broadway and in movies, but possessed the talent to be the female answer to Brando or Montgomery Clift, and it didn't take long for her to land the film role that proved it, winning the lead in *Baby Doll* (1956) by reading for its author, Tennessee Williams, in his New York apartment. Baker radiates a riveting, frustrated cool as the sensuous Mississippian Baby Doll Meighan, married to a distracted middle-aged cotton-gin proprietor (Karl Malden), but drawn to an outsider (Eli Wallach) from the north. The result is pure steaminess in the Deep South. Directed by Elia Kazan, the movie would be banned in much of the US and several other countries.

Meanwhile, Garfein was hired by *On the Waterfront* producer Sam

Spiegel to direct the movie version of *End as a Man*, and with a cast selected from the Actors Studio, he relocated to Florida for the shoot. With *The African Queen* in 1951, Spiegel pioneered the now standard financing method of pre-selling foreign distribution rights. He was also among the first to advance co-productions, setting up a London office for his Horizon Pictures and producing *The Bridge on the River Kwai* (1957). Spiegel was living proof that Hollywood's new bosses, "independent" producers partnered with the studios, weren't much different from the old ones. Along with being a legendary producer, Spiegel was an intrusive one who would often show up on set. "He would come and try to direct us," Garfein says. Garfein asked his friend, director George Stevens, if he should suggest that the producer leave his set. "He said, 'Jack, he's been thrown off bigger sets than yours. By all means, ask him to leave the set, leave you alone.' So I did. I asked him to leave because he was undermining my authority." Spiegel wasn't happy with the outspoken young director, but he left.

Garfein had another concern—no ending to *End as a Man*, now called *The Strange One*. While researching military schools in the south, Garfein had seen a train, its aisles filled with black workers coming from cotton fields, and thought a strong ending for the film would show the redneck cadet Jocko (Gazzara) on that train: "perfect punishment." Spiegel loved the idea and Garfein made the arrangements. But the producer had second thoughts. "No blacks in a movie. It won't get any southern exhibition. So he says, 'We'll do it on a milk train.' I said, 'Sam, a milk train doesn't mean anything.' He told the assistant directors to make sure there were no blacks in the shot." But Garfein, with the help of one assistant director, who sneaked black extras onto the set, stuck to his plans. "Spiegel must have suspected something," Garfein recalls. "He showed up that night for the shoot. So [actor] Pat Hingle came up with an idea. He said, 'He hasn't got out of the limousine yet. Let's start a rumor that there are snakes around.' We started the rumor and Spiegel wouldn't move out of his car. And I shot my scene." A case study in how to deal with a difficult producer. But when Spiegel saw the movie before its release, he insisted Garfein cut the scene. "I said, 'Sam, you're asking an Auschwitz survivor to cut blacks out of a movie? Is that what you're asking, to cut them out because they're black?'" Garfein told Spiegel that he would not, under any circumstances, remove a black person from his movie. "And Spiegel told me, 'I don't care. I just want them out.' Spiegel went to Ben Gazzara and said, 'I want to re-shoot the scene with another director,' but Gazzara refused. So I became Sam's enemy, and he decided to cancel my contract with Columbia. George Stevens said to me, 'You're on the country-club blacklist; they say, stay away from Garfein.'"

Garfein and Strasberg had ongoing differences that came to a head during the Actors Studio's production of *Shadow of a Gunman,* which featured Strasberg's sublimely talented daughter Susan. With Garfein directing, Strasberg wanted to cancel the play, then agreed to proceed, but with serious reworking. Garfein resigned, returning only when Strasberg withdrew from the show. The Garfein production was roundly acclaimed, but the two didn't speak again for four years. Years later, when Strasberg was receiving applause for his portrayal of a gangster in *The Godfather* (1972), the two met at a party. Recalls Garfein, "I said, 'I must congratulate you. You were not afraid to show what a son of a bitch you are.' And he laughed."

*The Strange One* was ahead of its time, featuring blacks and gays, and the focus is on its actor-driven characters rather than a "filmic" look. Gazzara delivers one of the classic method performances, but the movie had an unhappy producer and was overlooked. After *The Strange One*'s limited release, Garfein pitched the studios Alex Karmel's novel *Mary Ann,* about a young woman who has been raped. The film adaptation, now called *Something Wild* (1961), was co-scripted by Garfein and Karmel. Caroll Baker starred as Mary Ann, Aaron Copeland wrote the music, and United Artists signed on to produce. "I wanted it to be a film that touched me deeply. It was close to my story in some way. United Artists said they would do the film as long as Carroll got minimum screen actors' pay and I got minimum directors' pay. When Carroll saw the film, she got all excited and thought she would finally get the recognition that she should have gotten with *Baby Doll*. But the guy who was head of United Artists just hated it. It opened for one week in the theaters and then they threw it away. It opened in Europe and got phenomenal reviews, but United Artists didn't put much money behind it. When Aaron Copeland had his eightieth birthday, the city of New York asked him what he wanted as a tribute. They thought he'd ask for an orchestra with a chorus. He said, 'I want a showing of *Something Wild*.' They set it up in the Metropolitan Museum of Art. Aaron said to me, 'I know you are disappointed. Just live long enough, Jack, and this film will survive.'"

‡

After United Artists dumped *Something Wild*, Hollywood showed little interest in Garfein. "Except Paul Newman, who wrote me a letter and said, 'Jack, would you find me a script like *Something Wild*? I'm ready to do it.' It was really wonderful."

When live television took hold, Stern wrote for the best—programs such as *Goodyear Television Playhouse* and *Playhouse 90*. It was on a *Goodyear* production, *Guilty Is the Stranger*, that Stern first took notice of Newman. "He played Fay Bainter's son, who had been traumatized in the war, and he gave a moan that was unlike any moan I had ever heard." Stern sent Newman his script for *The Rack* (1956), about a returning soldier who did time in a Korean prison camp, and it was the beginning of a lasting friendship.

The method insurgency included Newman, who almost single-handedly kept quality alive in the Hollywood of the late 1950s and '60s with films such as *Somebody Up There Likes Me* (1956), *The Hustler* (1961), *Hud* (1963), and *Cool Hand Luke* (1967). Somehow it's been easy to forget how popular he was, and how good. "He always said, 'I'm an emotional Republican,'" says Stern. "He had to work hard for authentic emotions, and he had to use substitutions." Newman would, for instance, re-live seeing a friend of his, a pilot during the war, walk backward into a propeller and be chopped to pieces. "Paul had to use images like that in order to bring on tears until gradually it happened for him, and he was able to just be with the character, with what came off the page ... The other thing is that he walked out on Hollywood. And Hollywood never forgave him." Newman eventually bought out his contract with Warner Bros. and he and Joanne Woodward settled in Connecticut, choosing their work deliberately.

Newman's substitutions were at the core of Strasberg's method. While method techniques varied depending upon the instructor, the shared goal was finding a character's deepest emotions, and then being the character. While there were engaging actors in the earlier studio system, from Clark Gable to Jimmy Stewart, they came out of a less naturalistic tradition, and the new realism stupefied Hollywood, challenging the very notion of a Dream Factory. "It was just different when they came along," says Stern. "Their attitude about Hollywood was, it's all fake—the movies are fake, the people are fake, the lifestyle is fake. It's all bullshit."

‡

*James Dean's improv with a toy monkey captures the essence of* Rebel Without a Cause.

When *Rebel Without a Cause* was released a month after James Dean died in a car crash on September 30, 1955, the actor became an instant and enduring legend. *Rebel* articulated deep feelings that existed in abundance among the era's teens, but which hadn't been spoken aloud before. Many who lined up for the movie when it was first released would themselves participate in the cultural combustion of succeeding years. Elvis Presley, Phil Ochs, Tom Hayden, and Dustin Hoffman are among the many who have cited the influence of *Rebel*. "It's *Rebel Without a Cause* that really altered my consciousness 'cause I was a teenager when that came out, and I had never seen a film that portrayed an adolescent in pain in quite that way," says Hoffman. "But to be feeling all that angst underneath, which is what I felt, and god knows how many millions of us felt that. It had not been portrayed."[1]

Dean's version of the method—mumbling, sensitive, crying to get out—would have an enormous imprint on acting. His *Rebel* inspired many in Hoffman's generation to become actors. Some of these would-be actors would instead become pioneering independent directors. Says American independent filmmaker Henry Jaglom: "I was in high school.

[*Rebel*] told the truth about the hurt, anger, frustration, and inarticulate rage we felt as teenagers. It was a generational thing for the first time. Emotionally I was starved, and this film spoke to that—and James Dean's performance spoke to that. My first acting pictures were taken at that period of time, and I've got a zippered jacket, a cigarette: I'm doing James Dean. I am completely under the influence of *Rebel Without a Cause*."

Says early Canadian independent Larry Kent: "*Rebel Without a Cause* is absolutely devastating, and I identified with that film completely. I just thought, *That's me*, you know. I've identified with a lot of performances and actors, but never, except for *Rebel Without a Cause*, have I had a deep feeling that you've got it, and I feel it from the bottom of my seat. The impact of *Streetcar* and *On the Waterfront* were great, but they were far removed from my life, whereas I felt that, in some documentary fashion, *Rebel* identified with my life. It had a profound effect on me."

New York independent filmmaker Nancy Savoca recalls: "My mother called me a rebel without a cause, and I didn't know why until I was about eleven when I saw the film and I went, 'Oh my god, that's me.'"

When Stern traveled to the Philippines with Brando for *The Ugly American* (1963), which he scripted, he was approached by a *Rebel* fan.

> This kid came with his family. We had tea together, and they spoke very little. All of a sudden the kid blurted out, 'You tearing me apart!' And then he started reciting lines from the script. He said, 'I saw it thirty times, and every time I asked my parents to come and see it and they wouldn't. They said, 'It's bad to see something so many times. It's all you think about.' But he said, 'I want you to come.' Eventually, though, they went to see the film, and then the father started crying. Life in that family changed completely when they got home and had dinner that night. It was the first time that the boy knew who his father and mother were, and he was able to unload everything in his heart.

Stern says Dean "was watchful. He observed everything, he recorded everything, he wanted to know everything. He wanted to be a part of all that he had met, to quote the poet, and it was fairly shallow because he was twenty-four when he died, and he never stayed still long enough with anything to really get through into the center of it."

Dean had loved Pier Angeli, who shocked him by abruptly marrying crooner Vic Damone. ("Oh well, maybe she likes his singing," Dean said.)[2] "Jimmy never could describe why he did something or articulate his creativity," says Stern, "and it sickens me that one of the most important pieces of writing that an actor ever did is behind the titles." In the opening credits, Dean does an improv with a toy monkey.

> They didn't have the sensitivity or the awareness (and neither did Nick Ray) to put the titles on the side and let that scene play itself out, because in that scene Jimmy contracts the entire film. In screenwriting, you have to tell the whole story of the film at the beginning. Even if people don't get it, they're prepared emotionally for what's going to happen. Jimmy walked over to that toy monkey and wound it up and then, when it ran down, he held it, and took the fetal position himself while he was holding that little monkey and patting it—it was the whole story of Jimmy's jacket: when Plato finally took it, then felt he had Jimmy's skin on. It was Jimmy giving Plato the jacket and finding that the father you're looking for is in you. It was all there in that unrehearsed scene that Jimmy did.

When *East of Eden* (1955) opened (prior to *Rebel*), Garfein arranged a benefit screening for the Actors Studio. Dean was feeling down when the two met the following day for lunch at the Russian Tea Room.

"Did you read the review in the *New York Times* this morning?" asked Dean.

Garfein said, "Yeah. So?'"

"Oh shit, they always say I imitate Brando. You know I don't."

"Jimmy," Garfein said, "do you pay attention to this stuff?"

Garfein couldn't get Dean out of his funk, so finally, he said, "What will help you, Jimmy?'"

"If I could talk to Strasberg," Dean said.

"Jimmy, here's his number. Go to a phone booth and call him."

Dean left and returned smiling.

"What," Garfein asked, "did the great man say to you to change all this?"

"I told him they compare me always to Brando. He said, 'Well, do you want them to compare you to John Derek?'"

Says Stern: "Dean used life in his work, like any great artist. That's why he was upset when they said he was imitating Brando; there was no imitation. All art is personal, and Dean's work was that."

The two schools of movie acting first came face-to-face, fist-to-fist, when Montgomery Clift played John Wayne's wayward "son" in the 1948 Howard Hawks' western *Red River*. Clift had been on Broadway before Brando and was a kind of transitional method star, arriving between the Group and Brando's followers. Wayne was an old-time cowboy star with little patience for the method or the left. Other than its stirring cinematography, *Red River* is hardly black and white, and its uncertainties make it one of the great westerns. Thomas Dunson (Wayne) starts out like any hero aiming to tame the west, but having taken Indian and Mexican land and subordinated every relationship to the business of cattle, his stoic heroism is spent. Unlike Dunson, Matthew Garth (Clift), wears sensitivity on his sleeve, puts people before profit, and is able to develop a relationship with the sort of strong woman (Joanne Dru) that populates Hawks' movies. The struggle between Clift and Wayne is a warning shot of what's ahead for Hollywood.

"Jimmy and I were walking to the commissary to get some coffee," Stern says, and Jack Warner came up the studio street with this money man.

'I'd like you to meet James Dean, one of our up-and-comers,' Warner said. This guy said, 'Oh, I know, I know. Very nice meeting you.' Dean looked sort of quizzical. Warner said, 'This is our money man. He's very important.' Jimmy then reached into his pocket and pulled out a handful of change and just dropped it on the pavement in front of this guy. They were both stunned. As was I. As was Jimmy. We went on sort of giggling to the commissary and sat at the counter. He said: 'Why did I do it? What makes me do things like that?'

## CHAPTER FIVE

## The Cassavetes Group

LELIA GOLDONI WAS A young dancer from L.A. who had been living in Manhattan when she heard about John Cassavetes' acting classes. "[At first,] I went to watch a class and I thought it was interesting. John asked if I'd like to come and study at the school." Although she couldn't afford tuition, Goldoni offered to teach dance to Cassavetes' students in exchange for acting classes. "And that's how it all started."

‡

Like other smart young actors in the early 1950s, John Cassavetes was drawn to the method. He started out on television, including *Kraft Television Theater*, the *Goodyear Television Playhouse*, and an episode of *You Are There*, directed by Sidney Lumet, with a small role by another aspiring actor, Paul Newman. Cassavetes' first movie lead was as a wayward teen in *Crime in the Streets* (1956), a more one-dimensional version of *Rebel*, even featuring Sal Mineo as the tormented sidekick.

Having been rejected for the Actors Studio, Cassavetes, a New York son of Greek immigrants, studied at the American Academy of Dramatic Arts; then, in 1956, he rented his own space at 225 West 46th Street and began teaching acting. In a small item in the January 20, 1957 *New York Times*, Cassavetes explained that his studio "hasn't even got a name, but our classes have grown to more than seventy pupils who work as a cooperative unit—actors, writers, and others [who] chip in to build scenery and contribute props as well as write and act. Not so long ago—about a month ago, I think—we developed a study project which we called *Shadows*—it deals with a Negro-white problem—and we intend to film it as a nonprofit, ninety-minute feature."[1]

Goldoni was never told why she was chosen to participate. "One day we were in class. John comes up to me and says, 'Can you come here on Saturday around one o'clock?' And he walked away. He went and talked to all of the other people who wound up being in *Shadows*, and we all showed up. He said, 'We're just looking to try some stuff,' and he set up certain improvisations."

Like others in *Shadows*, Goldoni only learned that Cassavetes planned to make a movie when word spread of his appearance on the late-night

New York radio show *Jean Shepherd's Night People*. Cassavetes appealed to listeners to send donations to help make the kind of real-life movie they had never seen. "You know, the minute they got fifty cents, we had to make the film," says Goldoni. Some $2,000 in small bills poured in and Cassavetes borrowed equipment and took to the streets of New York to shoot a stripped-down, hand-held, black-and-white story of America, circa 1957. This experience of being able to just do it would shape all of his subsequent work and define independent filmmaking for generations to come.

It was an exciting time for New York. "Oh, I loved it," says Goldoni. "It was time for me to be an independent person. That was part of my desire to go to New York." Goldoni's Italian immigrant parents had met in New York. Her mother Sara was a seamstress, her father Carlo an organizer with the International Ladies Garment Workers Union. He was also an actor and writer with a degree from the University of Palermo. "My father had to get the hell out of there. He was involved with the Italian anarchist movement."

Goldoni's father died not long after she was born. Until she was seven, she and her mother lived in Greenwich Village, then moved to L.A. "I was in a state of shock for about a month, looking at the greenery. I'd seen it in the movies, but they were always black-and-white films." Sara married another anarchist who also died soon after. Smitten with the movies, Lelia attended a cattle call at Columbia Studios where John Huston selected fifty children for *We Were Strangers* (1949), starring John Garfield as a Cuban revolutionary. "This was the first time I had ever been on a movie set. I wasn't interested in John Huston at all. I was so flabbergasted; can you imagine going on a film set and seeing the lights and how big it was and all that? Huston was absolutely fascinated that I wasn't interested in getting the job and all these other little girls were. I got the job playing Jennifer Jones's sister. No lines."

Goldoni attended Hollywood High, her focus mostly on dance, and by graduation in 1954, she was performing on stage and television as a member of the renowned Lester Horton Dance Theater. It was a trailblazing interracial troupe in segregated America, and Goldoni's experience with it helped set the stage for *Shadows*.

> There's a profound kind of intimacy. When you're dancing,
> you're tossing each other in the air. There was never any
> thought about what color somebody was. You needed so-and-
> so to catch you when you jumped off the box. It was as close

to having a family as you can imagine; the racial aspect of it was always what happened outside the theater. If one of the black guys drove you home after rehearsal, you might get stopped by a policeman. That happened to me three different times. Nothing about the relationships in *Shadows* was uncomfortable for me. I didn't have to overcome a lot of stuff.

Composer George Antile asked Goldoni to dance in a production he was staging in New York. Her generation was the last to come of age before rock 'n' roll, and for her the 1950s was about jazzy clubs and innovative dance, acting, comedy, and art. Before she left L.A., she studied with Jeff Corey who, upon being blacklisted, had turned to teaching acting. Her classmates included Dean Stockwell, Sally Kellerman, and Robert Blake. "In L.A., it was a very stimulating time because all the arts were co-mingling. I remember going over to somebody's house with the Horton company because this guy just got back from Africa and had this recording of music that nobody had ever heard before. We were all looking at each other's art forms. We went to galleries all the time. [Dave] Brubeck broke all kinds of rules in terms of jazz ... We would also all go and see Lenny Bruce."

There was a new youth culture starting to cut loose with its own music (rock 'n' roll), its own fashion (Brando's T-shirts and Dean's red jacket were popular), its own bedrooms (a jalopy's back seat), and its own movies—some good (*Blackboard Jungle*, 1955), some uninspired (*High School Confidential*, 1958), some Elvis. While Elvis and Dean were shaking up the broader culture, there was something smaller and oftentimes deeper taking place in the night-time downtown streets, clubs, and coffee houses. "Beat, meaning down and out but full of intense conviction," Jack Kerouac wrote.[2] The Beat movement offered up spontaneity and sexuality and, along with its own free-form *Howl*, *On the Road*, and *Naked Lunch*, inspired clichéd movie depictions like *The Beat Generation* (1959). The Beats challenged the sacred and the sanctimonious. "If you're supposed to get married, the one thing all those people didn't do is get married, and if you were supposed to be heterosexual, they experimented in being not heterosexual," Goldoni says. "It was about looking at those restrictions that society was laying on you, about how you needed to be, how you needed to behave."

Even for a jazzy, artsy young woman it was still the 1950s, and the cultural breakthroughs were slivers in an overwhelmingly stultifying atmosphere. "There was so much to fight against," she says. "But we were beginning to break it down." Immersed in the bohemia of 1950s Manhattan, Goldoni and the rest of the *Shadows* ensemble easily embraced Cassavetes' freewheeling acting class.

> It's my impression that he did not have any curriculum that he was following. He would do what he did in the moment. Once I was doing a monologue from Oscar Wilde's *Salome* and John got up on the stage and said, 'I'm John the Baptist. What do you want to do with me?' Salome actually wants to have sex with him, but you're not going to do that on stage. So we did this rough-tumble thing, all over the stage, him kissing me or not kissing me. I was pulling his hair, and he was throwing me across the stage. Everybody in the audience was terrified about what was going on. It was an amazing exercise. That's the kind of thing he did all the time in class. He would invent things like that.

‡

Meanwhile, RKO quietly became the first of the major studios to be bought out by a company outside the entertainment industry. RKO was the last of the major studios to form (1929) and the first to dissolve (1957). An offshoot of RCA radio, it had some heady days in the 1930s with *King Kong* (1933) and the Astaire-Rogers pictures. In the 1950s, though, domestic attendance was in a free-fall, and RKO production was cut back. In 1955, Howard Hughes sold the studio to the General Tire and Rubber Company, an Akron-based manufacturer. The rubber baron soon stopped production, selling its lot to the TV production company Desilu.

As the 1950s wore on, Hollywood's once cocksure moguls were replaced by unsure suits. Besides partnering off with autonomous producers, studios were now dealing with the increasing power of talent agencies. With studios no longer maintaining a stable of contract players, movie stars appeared to have more clout. Unlike Burt Lancaster's hands-on approach at HHL, however, many production companies belonged to actors in name only, being controlled instead by their talent agencies. The Music Corporation of America was the most powerful of the agencies, with studios accepting MCA's terms or finding its talent unavailable. Soon an agency was as likely as a studio to put together a talent package for a picture, assembling its writers, producers, directors, and actors, and giving the producer and studio an all-or-nothing prop-osition. With so many—agents, producers, talent—absorbed in the new production mix, old adversarial relationships vanished. How can an agent or "independent producer" confront the system when they *are* the system?

With all of this newfound agency power in movies, MCA's Lew Was-serman turned his attention to television. The MCA-owned Revue Stu-dios, formed in 1943 to produce radio programming, became a major TV production company, turning out everything from *The Jack Benny Program* to *Leave It to Beaver*. A 1952 sweetheart waiver deal between the agency and Screen Actors Guild president Ronald Reagan enabled MCA agents to represent clients while hiring them to work on Revue productions. "The waiver shocked, amazed, distressed, bowled over and annoyed large and various segments of the entertainment industry," noted an article in the *New York Post*.[3] Revue would get first dibs on MCA talent, including Reagan, and in 1954, he was hired by MCA to host Revue Studios' *General Electric Theater*. The show would make Rea-gan wealthy—and the household name that would catapult him into political office.

The MCA-SAG agreement ended in a 1962 antitrust case, but by then the agency had accumulated so much power that the decision barely caused it to pause. For instance, it refused to renew *The Jack Benny Pro-gram* with CBS unless the network also bought an MCA series it didn't want, the aptly named *Checkmate*. "I've never seen anything like this in my life," said Federal Communications Commissioner Frederick Ford. "It seems as if you can't even go to the bathroom in Hollywood without asking MCA's permission."[4] Lew Wasserman even turned down an offer to head up MGM. "I run all the studios," he noted.[5]

‡

Although the civil-rights movement was beginning its battle with seg-regation as *Shadows* was shot, the movie's groundbreaking interracial relationships weren't the ensemble's focus of discussion, but seemed a natural extension of the characters under development. "Did I think people needed a lesson?" recalled Goldoni. "I certainly did. Did I think the film was a lesson? I had no idea. I was, in a funny kind of way, too involved in the making of it." *Shadows* was set in the hipster milieu Goldoni was comfortable with, and she threw herself with abandon into making movies, Cassavetes-style.

Shadows. *Shown: Anthony Ray, Lelia Goldoni.* © *Lion International / Photofest.*

Her character, Lelia Carruthers, is a half-white, half-black New Yorker interacting with her musical brothers Ben (Ben Carruthers) and Hugh (Hugh Hurd), Hugh's manager Rupert (Rupert Crosse), the writer David (David Poktillow), and boyfriend Tony (Anthony Ray), while dealing with race and family and life in the streets and cafés. She does it with a carefree cool and sensuality that reflected bohemian Manhattan and, even more, Goldoni herself. "Some of the stuff was unconscious because it was me as well as the character. [Lelia Carruthers] was trying to figure out who she was in the world and David is trying to get her to be a writer. All she wants to do is find out who she is."

With Cassavetes, she developed much of her own dialogue and character. "It was all improvised, but there was a storyline created by John that had to be met. It wasn't so much that we knew what we were going to say. We went to shoot, and we knew what had to happen. We rehearsed it a little bit, and then we would do it with a camera running."

While Cassavetes and company didn't know it at the time, they were inventing a filmmaking-as-guerrilla-war approach that would be adapted by countless filmmakers—improvised scenes shot on the fly without permits. And just as France's New Wave was about to do with Paris,

Cassavetes made New York a star in his movie. "The cameraman was almost across the street while we were doing the scene going into Tony's apartment. We shot the bed scene in somebody's basement apartment. We shot in Central Park. The bar sequence was done in a bar that we all knew, so we did it when they were closed. That's how we got away with a lot of the stuff that we did."

‡

Seymour Cassel's movie debut was an uncredited bit in *Shadows*. The shoot was his film school. "I learned everything I didn't want to do on that film—I didn't want to be an editor, I didn't want to do lighting, I didn't want to be a cameraman."

While studying at Stella Adler's Carnegie Hall-based classes, Cassel saw an intriguing ad.

> It said, 'Free Scholarships—John Cassavetes workshop, Variety Arts Building.' I went there and said, 'I'm looking for one of the scholarships.' John talked to me for about an hour and then said, 'I've got to go. We're shooting a movie.' I said, 'Can I watch?' and he said, 'Sure.' I just started helping the cameraman. I worked all night. John took us to breakfast and said, 'What do you think?' I said, 'It's great. Can I come back?' He said, 'Sure.' And I kept coming back. Not only did it enhance my knowledge, but I found the best friend I ever had.

‡

Moment by moment, Cassavetes pushed *Shadows* forward, cobbling together the necessary $40,000, with cast and crew carried along by his enthusiasm. The original shoot lasted a couple of months in 1957. There was a buzz about it in New York's underground, which included filmmakers Shirley Clarke, who lent Cassavetes her camera, and Jonas Mekas, who watched footage during post-production. When *Shadows* first screened in 1958 at New York's Paris Theatre, some saw an instant classic, but others were underwhelmed. After the screening, Cassavetes decided to shoot a few more scenes.

*Shadows* made waves in Europe where it won the critics' prize at the 1960 Venice Film Festival and Cassavetes was embraced as a kindred auteur. "We got to bring *Shadows* to [Cinémathèque Francaise's Henri]

Langlois," Cassel says. "After screening in Paris, I said, 'See, John, I told you they'd love it.'" Goldoni didn't see *Shadows* until it screened in London. The distributor, British Lions, brought her over to do interviews with the press for the opening. "There were three weeks of unbelievable coverage. It played fifteen months at the Oxford Theatre, and there were lines around the block."

Back in America, *Shadows* was unable to find wide distribution. "It's not a commercial picture, it's an art picture," Cassavetes said. "Maybe it's rough and uneven, maybe bad in places. But it tries to do something worth doing, tries to say something. Why does the word art have to mean lousy, dull, uninteresting? Why are we all afraid of words like art? Me, I'm conscientiously trying to be an artist doing works of art—in acting, in directing, in whatever I do. I want to be an artist—who's ashamed of it?"[6]

In L.A., Goldoni did a couple episodes of *Johnny Staccato*, a short-lived NBC series starring Cassavetes as a jazz musician-turned-detective, then moved to London where she continued acting. There were few American independent filmmakers to embrace Goldoni after *Shadows*. "There were people that were making movies, but they didn't make the kind of impact John had," she says.

‡

Cassavetes was inspired by Ray Ashley and Morris Engel's *Little Fugitive* (1953) and Lionel Rogosin's *On the Bowery* (1957), both director-driven independent movies that had little in common with the so-called independent big-budget producers now in league with the studios. (*Little Fugitive*, about a Manhattan boy who runs away to Coney Island, featured young untrained actors, a script written on the run, and a scant budget.) The art house had landed on North American shores in the late 1940s, with theaters screening Italian neorealists (*Open City*, 1945; *Paisan*, 1946) following their acclaim at the Venice festival. In New York, Amos Vogel founded Cinema 16, a popular film society that screened the films of Cassavetes and more experimental independents. *Shadows* was part of an emerging American independent sensibility, mostly set in New York, that also included Jonas Mekas (*Guns of Trees*, 1961), Shirley Clarke (*Portrait of Jason*, 1967), Edward Bland (*Cry of Jazz*, 1959), and Alfred Leslie and Robert Frank (*Pull My Daisy*, 1959).

It wasn't all New York. In 1953, a group of blacklisted filmmakers made *Salt of the Earth*. Directed by Hollywood Ten member Herbert

Biberman and financed by the International Union of Mine, Mill, and Smelter Workers of America, it's a powerful, realistic enactment of the rising of Mexican mine workers against the Empire Zinc Mine in Bayard, New Mexico. Although one of the great early examples of independent filmmaking, it was barely distributed. On the West Coast, Sam Fuller moved between low-budget studio and independent work such as the Korean War story *The Steel Helmet* (1951) and *Shock Corridor* (1963), which featured Peter Breck as a journalist posing as an inmate in a mental institution, leaving viewers to wonder if anyone could maintain sanity in this disturbed world. L.A. was also home to the Sanders brothers (Denis and Terry) and their *Crime & Punishment, USA* (1959), and lest we forget, Ed Wood, whose genre work, though sometimes barely watchable, was made with a perseverance and creative fundraising that was a lesson to independents.

The New York-based New American Cinema Group was founded in 1960 to deal with the concerns of independent filmmakers, and two years later it added a distribution wing, the Film-Makers Cooperative. The group's manifesto proclaimed:

> In the course of the past three years we have been witnessing the spontaneous growth of a new generation of film makers— the Free Cinema in England, the Nouvelle Vague in France, the young movements in Poland, Italy, and Russia, and, in this country, the work of Lionel Rogosin, John Cassavetes, Alfred Leslie, Robert Frank, Edward Bland, Bert Stern and the Sanders brothers ... If the New American Cinema has until now been an unconscious and sporadic manifestation, we feel the time has come to join together. There are many of us—the movement is reaching significant proportions—and we know what needs to be destroyed and what we stand for ...

> We believe that cinema is indivisibly a personal expression. We therefore reject the interference of producers, distributors and investors until our work is ready to be projected on the screen ... The New American Cinema is abolishing the Budget Myth, proving that good, internationally marketable films can be made on a budget of $25,000 to $200,000. *Shadows, Pull My Daisy, The Little Fugitive* prove it. Our realistic budgets give us freedom from stars, studios, and producers ... The low budget is not a purely commercial consideration. It

goes with our ethical and aesthetic beliefs, directly connected with the things we want to say, and the way we want to say them … We'll take a stand against the present distribution-exhibition policies. There is something decidedly wrong with the whole system of film exhibition; it is time to blow the whole thing up. It's not the audience that prevents films like *Shadows* or *Come Back, Africa* from being seen but the distributors and theatre owners. It is a sad fact that our films first have to open in London, Paris or Tokyo before they can reach our own theatres.[7]

The Film-Makers Cooperative had considerable impact distributing non-commercial films to cinematheques, film festivals, universities, and art institutions, but the New York filmmaker who would have the most impact, John Cassavetes, was on the periphery of the group, and he was about to move to L.A. *Shadows* had attracted enough attention to spark Paramount's interest in him; his next picture, based on a script he had co-written about a jazz musician, *Too Late Blues* (1961), was for the studio. "That was a great lesson," Goldoni says. "He thought he could do a movie in Hollywood, but he couldn't. He had to do his own movie. There [in the studio system], there's a certain kind of demand: You do it my way. So many changes were made that the script was really not the script that he wrote or intended to do." Cassevetes' foray into studio filmmaking proved deeply unfulfilling. "The problem is, they don't know what it is to make a movie," Cassel says. "John couldn't work under that system; he had to have freedom. He had to have casting rights because he wanted to use people he loved. He loved actors more than any director I've ever worked with."

Cassavetes followed *Too Late Blues* with *A Child Is Waiting* (1963), a United Artists release set in an institution for mentally handicapped children, starring Judy Garland and Burt Lancaster. Again, Cassavetes' casting instincts were impeccable. "He took Lawrence Tierney and put him in *A Child Is Waiting*, and Larry was a huge drunk," says Cassel. "He would tear a phone off the goddamn wall. I mean, he was wild, though he was a great guy and a great actor. John said to him, 'If you take one fucking drink, I'll beat the shit out of you. This is the best part you've had in a long time and you get twelve weeks of pay. Don't drink.' And I started laughing and had to turn away because Lawrence Tierney was seven inches bigger than John and heavier. I knew John was kidding, but he was intense; you believed him when he said something."

Cassavetes found working with a studio-partnered independent producer even more wanting than his experience with Paramount. His actor-driven improv approach clashed with *A Child Is Waiting* producer Stanley Kramer's more conventional methods, and the two fought during post-production. Cassavetes was removed from the project and dissociated himself from the cut that was released. After *A Child Is Waiting*, Cassavetes would produce his own films, taking roles in pictures he didn't care about and pilots he knew wouldn't sell to finance the movies he wanted to make. "That's why he did *Shadows*. He didn't like the way people told him what to do when they didn't know what they were doing," says Cassel.

Cassavetes and the making of *Shadows* would later inspire the entire independent movement, but at first few directors could see options beyond the studios and their producers. Jack Garfein, who cast Cassavetes' friend Ben Gazzara in *The Strange One*, recalls running into the director in L.A.

> I was walking down Wilshire Boulevard and there was Cassavetes. He said, 'Jack! Why the hell aren't you making movies? What is the matter with you? I'm telling you, no one got the performance out of Gazzara you got.' I said, 'Listen, I admire you because you get $100,000 or $150,000 for acting in a film, and you put it into something that you want to make. It's absolutely great, but I can't get any money. No one will give me the money to do it.'
>
> Next day my phone rings and it's John. He said, 'Jack, I've got all the cameras for you. I've got all the editing equipment. You've got it all. You don't pay anything. Make a movie.' I said, 'John, I've got to get film. I don't have basic money. What do I do?' I still needed to pay for film, for the crew, you know. But it was wonderful; he called me like that to say, hey, do a film.

‡

After the lessons of *Too Late Blues* and *A Child Is Waiting*, Cassavetes created a string of inspired independent, self-financed films from *Faces* (1968) to *A Woman Under the Influence* (1974) to *The Killing of a Chinese Bookie* (1976). Cassavetes provided roles of a lifetime for an acting ensemble that included his wife Gena Rowlands, Peter Falk, Gazzara, and Cassel. Actors confined to character roles for other directors were stars to Cassavetes. Cassel, for example, could be a leading man in a Cassavetes movie (*Minnie and Moskowitz*, 1971) and a supporting-actor Oscar nominee in *Faces*.

*Faces* was Cassavetes' first movie after the studio debacles. "It took me eight months to shoot, cost $40,000, and took three years to cut and find a distributor," Cassavetes said.

> I had to beg, borrow, and steal. I can be a killer when I believe in something! I conned my friends. I got bank loans without collateral. My salary from *Rosemary's Baby* helped, too. *Faces* got off the ground because I'm such a big mouth. Whenever I'm interested in something, I can't stop talking about it. I hadn't done a film of my own since *Shadows* ... one of the happiest experiences of my life. It kept haunting me all the time I was trying to make like a big Hollywood director. I've since learned I'm just not temperamentally suited to that kind of ball game. I can't fake anything.[8]

Loaded with devastating performances (from Rowlands, Cassel, John Marley, and Lynn Carlin), *Faces* is a tough, harrowing look at an upscale America in which lives are so empty that even the laughter rings hollow. The affluent but defeated middle-aging characters are almost in constant motion, thanks to frenetic hand-held shooting and overlapping voices. Before delivering his performance, Cassel worked cameras for nearly three months in the small *Faces* crew. Cassel says the sudden move from crew to cast wasn't much of a jolt because he was among friends and Cassavetes encouraged actors' input. "Even if he explained the scene or he had the scene written, we'd take off from there. It was the best way of working." Still, when Cassel turned to acting, Cassavetes shut down the shoot early for several days until he nailed his character. "I was so anxious to act that I over-acted. He saw that I was tense. I wasn't going to be loosey-goosey the way he liked actors to be. John didn't like to see you act it; he liked to see you *be* it." Finally, Cassavetes knew Cassel had it, and the shoot resumed. Cassel plays the hippie-ish, happy-go-lucky party-animal Chet, who walks face-first into the disintegrating marriage of an L.A. couple (Marley and Carlin). Chet comes home from a club with married Maria, then proceeds with a long, intense, often hilarious, late-night/

early morning session complete with serenading. When bedtime with Maria is interrupted by her husband's sudden return home, a partially dressed Cassel jumps out a second-storey window and races away down a wooded hillside. "We walked over to the window and John said to me, 'Can you make that jump?' I said, 'Can you?' He said, 'I don't have to.' So I jumped. He thought this was funny and then he had me do it about eleven times."

*Faces* featured veteran character actor Marley more than rising to the occasion, as did newcomer Carlin in her shattering turn as the barren Maria. "When John wrote *Faces,* he was across the hall from [Robert] Altman at Columbia. Lynn Carlin typed his script, and that's how she got the part," Cassel says. "When Bob fired her, she came to our office to say goodbye to Johnny. He says, 'What's the matter?' She says, 'Bob fired me. He says I'm a lousy secretary.' John says, 'Fuck him. You do Maria, you know the part—you wrote it.'" Carlin, who had earlier acting experience at the Pasadena Playhouse, was nominated for an Oscar for *Faces.* She continued acting afterwards but, as for many in Cassavetes' movies, nothing she did came close to that performance.

‡

"He loved working with people he loved," Lelia Goldoni tells the audience that's crowded the Billy Wilder Theater in the Westwood area of Los Angeles for a screening of *A Woman Under the Influence.* Those who comprised Cassavetes' extended cast-and-crew ensemble have a continuing bond. Long after his death, they find ways to work together, meet for lunch, share a panel. Several of Cassavetes' accomplices have taken the stage following this 2009 screening to field questions from an audience so moved by what they have just seen on screen—an exasperating look at a working-class couple (Gena Rowlands, Peter Falk) dealing with a spiraling mental illness that's creating havoc in their already desperate lives.

This panel and audience share a satisfying certainty that the work is as good and as pure as it can be. Editor David Armstrong remembers a conversation he had with Cassavetes about the distribution of the film. "It was the same way John did everything. He was fearless. He said, 'Why don't we do it ourselves? There's no one to stop us.'" Mike Ferris became a cameraman on the movie after running into Cassel in L.A. Ferris noted the naturally lit close-up on Rowland's nervous hands that reveals her character. "John just picked the stuff that made you feel

*Gena Rowlands, John Cassavetes, and Peter Falk during the shooting of* A Woman Under the Influence. © *Faces International / Photofest.*

like you were seeing something real life," Ferris says. "What you saw tonight is what happens when you don't formalize the photography … Peter Falk said it best. He said, 'John saw the dawn before anyone else.'"

"That's because," adds Cassel, "he was up all night."

‡

Since their earliest days, studios relied on stars to sell movies, so their movies were identified by actor, not director—*Casablanca* was a Humphrey Bogart movie, not a Michael Curtiz one—and a studio screenwriter who turned out a successful Jimmy Stewart vehicle might be asked for another. Contract directors moved from star to star, genre to genre, at the whim of the studio. The studio/independent producer alliance was star-centric, too. *Shadows* marked a turn. It was a movie identified with its director, not its no-star cast. The French emphasis on the director as a movie's author was realized in America by Cassavetes, and it would become a vital part of the independent sensibility. The naturalistic acting style of the US method and France's New Wave made possible, even inevitable, low-budget, high-quality, character-driven independent filmmaking. No one understood this better than Cassavetes. His roots in acting provided him with an acute sense of what it takes to develop character; his movies were actor-driven, not star-driven.

Goldoni married and divorced her *Shadows* co-star Ben Carruthers between the completion of its original shoot and its opening. Of the cast, only Cassel, Goldoni, and Rupert Crosse had longevity as actors. Still, the cast and crew that worked on *Shadows* maintained a bond that carried on through the decades. "It was very special," says Goldoni. "Whenever we saw each other, it was always like the big family getting together."

When Lelia Goldoni walks alone down neon-lit 42nd Street in *Shadows'* opening sequence, there is no doubt this is a woman, and a movie, willing to take on danger. And the urgency never quits—the racial conflicts are raw without platitudes, the sexuality real (after Lelia's first time: "I didn't know it could be so awful"), the New York actors and street-life and night-life an organic mix. All of this comes from the rich characters created by Cassavetes and his cast. As the 1960s unfolded, it was *Shadows* that defined the choice for filmmakers: Cassavetes' independence or dependence on a Hollywood studio. *Shadows* was startlingly new when it first screened, and a half-century later it is still astonishing.

Before French documentarian André Labarthe set out to interview legendary US studio directors for the TV series *Cinéastes de notre temps*, he turned his camera on Cassavetes, a then little-known filmmaker in the middle of editing his "free film" *Faces*. Labarthe asks Cassavetes how he will make money from *Faces*. "How will we sell it? Well, we made it first to like it ourselves, then hopefully somebody else will like it. You know, if they do, if they don't, if we sell it, if we don't—we've made it. Our fun is in making the picture, not in the glories that come from making the picture. We're not making it for the *Cahier* you know ... not for Stanley Kramer or Metro-Goldwyn-Mayer or Columbia. We're making it for ourselves ... We make ourselves happy and we can enjoy the picture that we made and see the performances come alive."[9]

## CHAPTER SIX

## New Hollywood

WITH OPENLY LEFT-WING actors, directors, and writers in exile in the 1950s, the studios had been willing to tolerate the new rebel actors and social-issue directors, as long as it was profitable. "Rebel actor" once meant John Garfield appearing at a rally for the striking CSU; now it meant James Dean scratching his ass in public. Despite their surliness toward Hollywood brass, the Actors Studio alumni, true to Strasberg's teaching, were mostly focused on the self and psychological angst, unlike the earlier crop of Stanislavski-steeped actors out of the Group Theatre, who had seen their anxiety through a class prism. While the studios saw the new personalized rebellion as safe, albeit crude, it represented more of a challenge than they knew. The method mainstays were determined to find truth in their art, a revolutionary endeavor in an era defined by lies. This determination (and the times) would draw everyone from Brando to Newman to Jane Fonda to activism and into the streets. Soon all of the festering personal alienation would merge with a new radicalism, and the combination of the personal and the political would result in rebels who, like those in the 1940s, challenged the system and, like those in the 1950s, challenged themselves—arriving full-blown in the late 1960s when the beat subculture morphed into the much larger hippie movement and James Dean met John Garfield and grew his hair.

This was the first left-wing generation in Hollywood since the blacklist, and its films, like its politics, were rooted in the counterculture.

‡

There was a time when Laurel Canyon, the wooded wonderland between Hollywood and the San Fernando Valley, was one of the hippest of hippie enclaves along the West Coast. In 1968, Seymour Cassel left his home in the Canyon, loaded up a camper with camera equipment, and drove to New Orleans to help shoot *Easy Rider* (1969).

"I knew [Dennis] Hopper and I knew [Peter] Fonda and I knew the other cameraman. Everybody was high all the time, which was all right, but I remember telling Dennis, 'You got to take a shower.' He said, 'I can't, man, I'm making a masterpiece here.' I said, 'Dennis, you can't be in the camper, man. It stinks.' He said, 'Don't fucking bother me with that, man.'" Despite this, they stayed friends, and in the heady days after *Easy Rider*, Cassel was invited to partake in Hopper's next movie, *The Last Movie* (1971). "Dennis wanted me to go down to Peru. I said, 'I don't want to go to fucking Peru. I got a movie that's coming out, and we got to finish that.' That was *Faces*."

Henry Jaglom did briefly go to Peru for *The Last Movie*. "I acted in it, then I split." He had also worked on *Easy Rider* as an editorial consultant, and was more than surprised ("stunned," he says) by its success.

> I thought it was a piece of crap. Peter Fonda and Dennis had been doing these Roger Corman biker movies that were nonsense. I wasn't interested in them, and I thought the original storyline—I was there when Dennis and Peter read it to Bert Schneider—was like a bike movie. I thought it was a bad title. Because I loved comic books, I thought it should be called *Captain America* after the character Peter Fonda played. It was very much Dennis Hopper's film, but we all contributed a lot to it and the contribution gave us the opportunity to make our own movies. I didn't think it was going to be such a smash-hit cultural touch-point.

Funded to the tune of $340,000 by Bob Rafelson and Bert Schneider's Raybert Productions and distributed by Columbia, *Easy Rider* would make $60 million and cause a studio stampede to the counterculture.

‡

Message movies of the 1950s often idealized American individualism, their band-aid liberalism no threat to studios, which happily distributed them. There were stories about facelessness in white-collar corporatism (*The Man in the Gray Flannel Suit*, 1956), race relations (*The Defiant Ones*, 1958) or "juvenile delinquency" (*Knock on Any Door*, 1949), but these productions stopped far short of the critique of capitalism in pre-blacklist leftist films such as *Force of Evil* (1948), *Body and Soul* (1947), and *Monsieur Verdoux* (1947). In the early 1960s, between the Beats and the hippies, there had been a moment of pre-hippie hipness featuring an easily bemused generation that liked *Rebel* and Bogart, Lenny Bruce, folk music, Holden Caulfield, the French New Wave, the civil rights movement, women like Julie Christie and Lelia Goldoni, and guys re-

*Dennis Hopper, Jack Nicholson, and Peter Fonda get a taste of southern inhospitality at a diner in* Easy Rider. *© Columbia Pictures / Photofest. Photograph: Peter Sorel.*

sembling Dustin Hoffman; they were looking for something real, not the "plastics" in *The Graduate*.

There had been movies about youth (*Beach Blanket Bingo*, 1965), even hippies (*The Trip*, 1967), before *Easy Rider*, but it captured the spirit of the counterculture like nothing else. Peter Fonda's Wyatt and Dennis Hopper's Billy were Brando's wild ones on Kerouac's road but with the new hippie sensibility, passing through communes and altered states and hateful local yokels. While there was a script for the film (Fonda and Hopper with help from Terry Southern), it was largely improvised. Laszlo Kovacs' camera work captured the wonder and freedom of the landscape and the counterculture, rainbow hues passing over Fonda and Hopper as they rode to a rousing soundtrack of psychedelic standards.

The overtly countercultural *Easy Rider* rocked the stodgy studios. Like the New Yorkers hired for the talkie technology of the 1920s, New Hollywood filmmakers were signed by studios confused by the times and desperate for talent. Not all of these filmmakers were hip-culture freaks or even young, but they had a similar anti-authoritarian bent and combined to create the last great era of studio filmmaking. The studios opened the vault to directors they believed might reach *Easy Rider*'s audience. Had these filmmakers been perceived as individual mavericks, without the demographics of the counterculture audience to back them up, studio doors would not have been thrown open to them—but they were. With the discarding of the repressive Production Code in 1968, which opened studio movies to a "new permissiveness," the climate seemed right for a New Hollywood. Like the European auteurs who inspired them, their unpredictable films often combined the raw, the stylish, and the sexual, embracing a libertine attitude that sent shivers through Production Code loyalists. It was a period of artistic autonomy within the system that would last roughly from *The Graduate* in 1967 until *The Godfather Part II* in 1974, running parallel to the height of the hippie movement.

New Hollywood filmmakers of note included: Robert Altman (*McCabe and Mrs. Miller*, 1971), Hal Ashby (*Harold and Maude*, 1971), Peter Bogdanovich (*The Last Picture Show*, 1971), Francis Ford Coppola (*The Godfather*, 1972), William Friedkin (*The French Connection*, 1971), Henry Jaglom (*A Safe Place*, 1971), George Lucas (*American Graffiti*, 1973), Terrence Malick (*Badlands*, 1973), Paul Mazursky (*Bob & Carol & Ted & Alice*, 1969), Mike Nichols (*Carnal Knowledge*, 1971), Jack Nicholson (*Drive, He Said*, 1971), Bob Rafelson (*Five Easy Pieces*, 1970), Jerry Schatzberg (*The Panic in Needle Park*, 1971), and Martin Scorsese (*Mean Streets* 1973).

‡

Police began nightly sweeps of the rock 'n' roll haunts around Sunset Strip in 1966. The harassment came to a head in July when people were hauled from two restaurants frequented by the counterculture. A demonstration (attended by Peter Fonda, Bob Denver, and Sonny and Cher) staged outside a Sunset Boulevard club, Pandora's Box, to protest the raids was attacked by club-swinging police. "At the height of the conflict, things got nasty," recalled protestor Derek Taylor. "I saw my first police flying-wedge on Sunset Boulevard, saw how professional cops can always crush amateur freedomniks if they had a mind to, saw a sheriff's deputy spit on a woman, saw Peter Fonda in handcuffs, saw how bad things could be before they got worse."[1]

It escalated into four nights of rioting. If the new culture was making its stand, so were the police, who rioted enthusiastically. A routine was established in which riot police would clear a block and protestors would reassemble in another block, and, like their parents' generation on the Warner Bros. picket line back in '45, give as good as they got.

The headline in the *L.A. Herald* read "Long Hair Nightmare." This was the Sunset Strip rioting that inspired the Buffalo Springfield song "For What It's Worth." Stephen Stills recalled, "I came down Laurel Canyon Boulevard and was greeted by that riot. I sat down and wrote the song in fifteen minutes ... You had the immortal genius of the idiots that ran the LAPD, who put all of those troopers in full battle array, looking like the Macedonian army up against a bunch of kids."[2]

Once the street fighting receded, several clubs' licences were revoked, but others remained open, and the counterculture thrived in nearby Laurel Canyon, where you never knew who you might run into grabbing late-night munchies at the Canyon Country Store. While some residents worked in movies (Cassel, Hopper, Fonda, and Jack Nicholson), the Canyon was mostly rock 'n' roll: Jim Morrison, David Crosby, Graham Nash, Joni Mitchell, Neil Young, Carole King, Brian Wilson, Frank Zappa, Jackson Browne, Gram Parsons, Glenn Frey, John Mayall, Keith Moon, Donovan, and Jimi Hendrix, members of the Byrds, the Mamas and the Papas, the Monkees, the Rolling Stones, Canned Heat, and Fleetwood Mac.

The hippies instinctively knew their parents' generation had left something of value behind when, after World War II, so many left their downtown ethnic neighborhoods and assimilated into a new world of cul-de-sacs and shopping centers. Escaping to a safe suburban haven seemed an exercise in somnambulism to a lot of Baby Boomers, so they left bland suburbia and invented their own ethnic group, with its own neighborhoods (in L.A., Laurel Canyon and Venice), music (rock), cuisine (health food), look (hair), language ("That's groovy but it isn't far out"), and movies (*Easy Rider*). Coming of age during the Depression, their parents were, by necessity, focused on immediate bread-and-butter survival, but many within the Baby Boom generation—the first to enjoy relative affluence, college education, and free time as commonplace—turned their attention from necessities to desires, from *what is* to *what could be*.

Like the Beats before them and the later punks, hip culture had much more depth and diversity than media clichés suggested. A few shared traits defined the culture: opposition to the war; experimentation with marijuana and psychedelics; communal living; preference for a natural look with long hair and casual clothing; and disdain for consumerism. Yippies like Abbie Hoffman declared a New Nation ("as rugged as the marijuana leaf") that would grow to supplant the old, corrupt Amerika.[3] "I was trying to question an attitude," Hopper said of *Easy Rider*, "an attitude of a society that was a criminal society, that admired criminals

... Either you become a criminal or you change the society, and you have a choice."[4] The counterculture lived in Madison and London, Ann Arbor and Amsterdam. The West Coast of North America, though, was its heartland. While San Francisco's Haight-Ashbury has received much of the attention, hip-culture quarters dotted the coastline, from Vancouver's Fourth Avenue to San Diego's Ocean Beach.

‡

"Of course I was part of the counterculture. That was my culture," says Henry Jaglom in his crowded office over Sunset Strip. Jaglom arrived in L.A. on July 1, 1965. "Three days later I was staying at Tuesday Weld's house. She took me to the Fourth of July party at Jane Fonda's house—it has since become legendary—where the Byrds were playing. And this incredible community was there. It was really something. It was almost a changing of the guard." Partiers at the Malibu home that night included Jean Seberg, Andy Warhol, Darryl Zanuck, Warren Beatty, Lauren Bacall, Dennis Hopper, Sam Spiegel, James Stewart, William Wyler, Gene Kelly, Henry Fonda, and Peter Fonda. "I almost died that night. Bob Rafelson, Ron Rifkin, and I went out to smoke a joint. I borrowed Tuesday's Porsche, but didn't know how to drive a stick-shift car. I was from New York; I practically didn't know how to drive any car. We got stuck in the middle of the Pacific Coast Highway, with cars barreling down on us." Nevertheless, he recalls, "It was an incredible night. The greatest party, probably, I have ever been to."

Jaglom began the Hollywood rounds peddling *A Safe Place* (1971), a script adapted from a play he staged at New York's Actors Studio. While his script went nowhere, he found acting jobs on episodic TV. "I felt this was an absurd thing for a person to be doing—*Gidget* (1965) and *The Flying Nun* (1967). What am I doing here? Here's a script I wrote. Nobody's looking at it. And then, finally, Bert Schneider—BBS."

BBS—Bert Schneider, Bob Rafelson, and Steve Blauner—was the essential production company of the L.A. counterculture. "They had all kinds of people coming in preparing films," says Jaglom. "There would be no Scorsese, there would be no Coppola—none of those filmmakers" without BBS. "That's what created the possibility that studios saw—that films could be made creatively by artists for small amounts of money and make a lot of money. It was mostly because of this one guy, Bert Schneider." Henry Jaglom's link to BBS went back to Jewish summer camp in Maine where Schneider was his counselor. In L.A., Schneider was a rarity of rarities—a left-wing producer. Jaglom showed his edit of a short film to Schneider, who was impressed enough to invite him aboard *Easy Rider,* then a four-hour director's cut. "He said, 'We are having a little problem with the film. Do you want to come and work on it?'" That gave Jaglom his entry into the heart and mind of New Hollywood.

Schneider and Rafelson began their counterculture adventure with *The Monkees* (1966), the TV sitcom about a hippie rock band. Their comic feature starring the band, *Head* (1968), did well enough for them to finance *Easy Rider.* The BBS offices on La Brea Avenue became the pulsating creative center for counterculture filmmaking, where close collaborations were forged in friendship. "When I came here, I was lucky because I stepped right into it," Jaglom says. "It was there in the person of Rafelson, Schneider, Hopper, and Nicholson. It was an amazing decade from *Easy Rider* to, for me, *A Safe Place,* then *Tracks* [1977], and then *Five Easy Pieces* and *Last Picture Show* and all of that. I directed Jack Nicholson, he directed me. 'I'll be in your first movie, you be in my first movie.' I directed Dennis, he directed me. Even Orson Welles became like an honorary member of our group. I brought Peter Bogdanovich to meet Bert Schneider."

When *Easy Rider* struck gold, the studios decided to throw a bunch of hippies against a screen to see what stuck. Jaglom says, "Bert was handed a deal by Columbia—that he could make any film with anybody as long as it was under a million dollars. And he picked me as one of those people. Jack Nicholson did *Drive, He Said* [1971]; Bob Rafelson did *Five Easy Pieces*; and Peter Bogdanovich did *The Last Picture Show.* If it wasn't for that, nobody would have let me make *A Safe Place.* It's a completely abstract, poetic film." Like Jaglom, *A Safe Place*'s co-stars Nicholson and Tuesday Weld were New Yorkers relocated to L.A. Nicholson landed jobs in low-budget Roger Corman movies such as *The Cry Baby Killer* (1958) while studying at the West Coast version of the Actors Studio. In the 1960s, Jack Garfein formed Actors Studio West. He was its director and taught at the University of Southern California while trying to get movie projects off the ground. He also passed Nicholson's Actors Studio audition while others felt he didn't even warrant observer status. "At one point they decided that Nicholson was in cheap little movies and they thought he should not have the observership any more," says Garfein. "But I said, 'I see a real talent in this young man.' So he stayed."

Jaglom was an alumnus of the Actors Studio, and he had a character-driven approach that suited Weld and Nicholson to perfection. "My films are actor's films more than anything," he says. "I come from being

*Henry Jaglom (middle) on the set of* A Safe Place *with Tuesday Weld (far right).*
*Courtesy Henry Jaglom, The Rainbow Film Company.*

an actor. Whatever Orson Welles said, he was essentially an actor. I think there is a huge distinction between those who are actor-filmmakers and people who come from some other discipline to be a filmmaker, because the acting is the essential thing. I don't care if it looks beautiful or if it's a great written script; I care about human behavior and the face, the emotions and the reality of feeling that you can get from actors. If somebody asks me about being a director, I always say, start with acting class."

So Jaglom cast Welles and, in Weld and Nicholson, two of the better actors of his generation in *A Safe Place*. Early in the shoot, Jaglom found himself unsatisfied with a scene Weld and Nicholson were doing from his detailed script. "I did it six times and, even though it was good, it wasn't as interesting as I knew Jack and Tuesday to be. So the seventh time I said, 'Look, you know what's supposed to happen in this scene. Just forget the words, just make that happen.' It was magic for me, and I threw away my script." Weld was a remarkable but undervalued actress, who just missed the two transcendent roles that would have made her as famous as Nicholson: She turned down *Bonnie and Clyde* (1967) and was in the running for *Frances* (1982). In *A Safe Place*, she

peels off the interiors of a fragile woman drifting between her unresolved childhood, an unsettling present, and no future, climaxing in
a liaison with Nicholson while her boyfriend is present. Her character
must constantly choose between safety and freedom.

Bert Schneider sat with Jaglom when he watched the rough cut.

> First he cried, which meant he was emotionally involved,
> which I liked, and then he said: 'Listen to me. The only per-
> son more indulgent than you in making this film is me for let-
> ting you. I'm not going to try to cut it, I'm not going to try to
> change it, and it's not going to make a penny. It's going to be
> a disaster commercially.' But he gave me essentially final cut
> because he saw that it was an attempt at something that was
> not conventional, and he didn't know how to work it. He had
> been very involved in re cutting *Easy Rider* and in working on
> *Five Easy Pieces* and all those films that had big commercial
> potential. He figured my film was just too off the wall.

Jaglom's independence was shaped by his *A Safe Place* experience
and, unlike many New Hollywood filmmakers, when the studio funding stopped, he would continue making movies outside the system. *A
Safe Place* was dismissed by some critics as incomprehensible and sent
studio suits scurrying under their desks. "They looked at it at Columbia,
and they had no idea what it was," he says.

> It was actually a very worked-out film, but emotionally se-
> quential, not informationally sequential. Because of what was
> going on in Europe, I expected everyone to get it. Nobody
> got it. But Stewart Stern came to me after a screening out
> here and said, 'People are going to tell you all kinds of shit.
> They are going to wipe you out for this film. You are using
> the studio facilities for this poetic dream film. You are doing
> something very important. Keep doing it.' It was amazing for
> me. This guy, who had written one of the seminal films of
> my life, *Rebel Without A Cause*, came to me fifteen years later
> and validated what I was trying to do in film.

Stern was aware of the impact *Rebel* had on so much of the counterculture generation. "I think it hit on the longing they all have and
the fact that they couldn't depend on the vertical family, which is so

hypocritical," says Stern. The parents in the film never tell their son "the truth; they never told him who they were, and they never wanted to know who their children were." The children of that generation, the hippies "reached sideways and found their families. I think that whole emergence of *Rebel* and the emergence of Elvis and the emergence of Dylan were all akin."

Seymour Cassel, a big fan of Bob Dylan, discovered that Dylan was a big fan of *Faces*. "He said, 'How did you guys make it?' So I showed him the camera and how we shot it. Bob was interested in film too." Dylan co-wrote "The Ballad of Easy Rider" and his "Tom Thumb Blues" makes a cameo in Paul Williams' film about student radicals, *The Revolutionary* (1970), co-starring Cassel. "He gave it to us for nothing."

‡

Lew Wasserman established a youth division at Universal Pictures in 1969. His MCA had taken the reins at Universal in 1962, creating a new template for the studio system—a horizontal integration of movies, television, and distribution. While the old moguls loved movies, Wasserman just as easily loved a made-for-TV movie, a miniseries, or a Universal Studio tour. And if audiences wanted to see movies Wasserman didn't like or even understand, that was all right with him too. His youth wing produced *Diary of a Mad Housewife* (1970), *The Hired Hand* (1971), *Two-Lane Blacktop* (1971), and *The Last Movie*.

Dennis Hopper called on Stewart Stern, his old friend from *Rebel Without a Cause*, to work on *The Last Movie*, ostensibly about a horse wrangler working on a western movie being shot in Peru. "He had just won the Cannes Festival for *Easy Rider* and he came over with this idea. I said I would do it," Stern recalls. "He would pace and talk, and I would type, and he would come over and say, 'My god, where did that scene come from?'" Their treatment was well-received, but Hopper decided he didn't need it expanded into a script. "All during the development of this thing he was saying, 'I don't really need a screenplay, you know, I'm a genius. I work like Fellini. All I really need are notes.'" Just before Hopper left to shoot in a Peruvian village, he asked Stern for a script. "I sat down that night with the treatment and I wrote all through the night, all through the next day. I thought it was a really good job and so did he, but he didn't shoot it; he was improvising all these terrible, terrible scenes."

There are shoots like *Easy Rider* where a loose process works wonders—there was method to Hopper's madness and a strong storyline moved it along. And then there are shoots like *The Last Movie*. After it was over, Stern received a desperate call. "Dennis said, 'You've got to come and look at all this film. I don't know what to do with it.' I sat in that theater for three days trying to make sense out of this mess, which had such wonderful stuff in it but no coherence as a story at all, and no ending. And I didn't know what to do except cry. He read the gospel of Saint Thomas aloud. It was madness. I made a few suggestions, this and that." Somehow, the contempt audiences felt for *The Last Movie* didn't scuttle the uneasy relationship between the studios and the hippies. It wasn't even Hopper's last movie.

†

Not everyone making movies in 1970s L.A. worked in the studio system. Jaglom spent four years trying to get a second film made. "I was obsessed with the Vietnam War. I tried to make a film about a soldier coming back full of the insanity that had been fed him, that led to Vietnam, about America and the end of the American dream." With negligible backing for independents at the time, he slowly put together low-budget financing and a strong cast (Dennis Hopper, Dean Stockwell) to shoot *Tracks*, then took it to studios. "There was no independent distributor. I showed it to each one of the seven studios, and each one turned it down. I couldn't get distribution." Still, *Tracks* drew raves when he screened it for Vietnam Veterans Against the War and other anti-war groups.

Jaglom grew up idolizing Paul Robeson and attending Pete Seeger concerts, so when the new activism of the 1960s erupted, he was in the streets at the civil rights march on Washington and innumerable anti-war protests. "When I came of age in the '60s, I was already left-wing," he says. "I was so passionate about what was going on and so in the middle of it all. I was part of a group called the Entertainment Industry for Peace and Justice. Jane Fonda, Donald Sutherland, myself, and three other people were the organizing unit of this group, which was sending out anti-war shows to the bases to counter the Bob Hope shows." These FTA (Fuck the Army) shows found receptive audiences of young soldiers. "The whole atmosphere, the whole circumstances of those times, colored everything we did. I think certainly it was the most important part of my life."

‡

Among those making their way outside Hollywood's studios was Charles Burnett, who grew up in L.A. watching movies. "I watched loads of old Hollywood studio films on old black-and-white TV." The studios where they were shot were just a long walk away from his neighborhood, but to Burnett they may as well have been on the moon. "I never had any idea that I could become a filmmaker. That was a world that didn't exist for me." But there were other things going on closer to home that attracted the young Burnett's attention. On August 11, 1965, a young Watts resident, Marquette Frye, was arrested for drunk driving. A gathering crowd surrounded his abandoned car, and when the arresting officer refused to let Frye's brother drive it home, calling for it to be impounded, the rocks began to fly. They didn't stop for six days. Decades of racial indignity were being thrown off. When the rioting stopped, thirty-four people were dead, another 4,000 arrested. "People were angry, so they took it out on everything, any kind of structure that represented the establishment or authority. It started as an isolated thing between the police and this one particular person, and it escalated and escalated and spread all over the community."

That L.A., not the L.A. of studio lots, was Burnett's hometown. "I was in South Central, and I knew Marquette Frye. Something was bound to happen because the police were so oppressive. You couldn't walk down the street without getting stopped or arrested or harassed or something." He enrolled at L.A. City College, where he was drawn to film, then went on to UCLA. "Everyone was expressing themselves, and I perceived art as a means of social change. UCLA was an open forum in a sense, where anything goes. They gave you a camera and said, 'Here, come back with a film.' We had that kind of a freedom."

Burnett made a couple of shorts, then began preparation for *Killer of Sheep* (1977), a naturalistic look at life in Watts, revolving around a man who works at a slaughterhouse. Shot in 1972 and '73 for $10,000, it was sporadically screened, but wasn't actually distributed to theaters until 2007 because Burnett didn't have the rights to its music. Burnett captures L.A.'s black community without clichés or blaxploitation— not much violence or drugs, but a lot of sadness, some joy, and real struggle. Cars break down. Kids try to fill their days. Marriage carries on minus passion. Yet it's all absorbing. "That was the third film I made at UCLA, which, at the time, had very much an anti-Hollywood atmosphere about it. I wanted to make films about my community that spoke about its problems. I just took examples of what had happened and things I'd seen and put them together in some sort of chronological way to form the narrative. I wanted to do something that looked like it was a documentary, but that wasn't the case. It was scripted and story-boarded."

‡

Among the notable movies about the counterculture (and its political cousin "the movement") were *Wild in the Streets* (Barry Shear, 1968), *Joe* (John D. Avildson, 1969), *Alice's Restaurant* (Arthur Penn, 1969), *Medium Cool* (Hasell Wexler, 1969), *Getting Straight* (Richard Rush, 1970), and *Billy Jack* (Tom Laughlin, 1971). The best: *Punishment Park* (Peter Watkins, 1971).

Katherine Quittner was living in Venice in 1970 when suddenly it seemed that everybody in her house was going to be in Peter Watkins' *Punishment Park*. "I was in the theater school at UCLA writing music for a show, and my boyfriend, who was an actor, had an interview with Peter Watkins. I just went with him. It was totally random. I'm not an actress."

The Venice counterculture community in which she lived was "a product of not just the time we lived in but of the architecture of the area," says Quittner.

> Where I lived, they didn't have houses with streets in front of them. It had walk streets; a front yard with a fence three feet high and then a sidewalk and another three-foot fence and yard in front of someone else's house. We had alleys behind us where we drove or parked the car. Where I grew up in the valley, people would drive into their driveways and go into their houses. They never saw their neighbors. But in Venice everybody sat out in their front yards.

> It was magic. You knew every single one of your neighbors on the street well enough to go get *not* a cup a sugar but a joint or whatever you wanted. Children on the block would simply pick a yard to play in; whether you had any children or not, they played in your yard. And every day at sunset we all took our dogs down to the beach and smoked joints and watched the sun go down. You shared, in most respects,

a common lifestyle. The oldest people on the block were in their thirties. Before Thanksgiving, everyone came over to my house and got high because we had to go visit our parents.

Quittner was a child of post-war San Fernando Valley suburbanization. By high school, she was speaking out against the Vietnam War. "You were either for the war or you were against it. That was the defining feature of the time," she says.

After graduating from high school in 1969, she enrolled at UCLA and relocated to Venice. She wasn't long at university when an army of motorcycle police came on campus during a protest. "There was a two-by-two parade of cops on motorcycles, hundreds of them. One of our friends got banged over the head and ended up in the hospital. I still remember those police coming down Sunset Boulevard to the school. It was like being invaded."

At the *Punishment Park* auditions, Quittner wound up talking to Watkins. The director wasn't simply being friendly—he was looking to cast smart non-actors with political savvy. "I didn't know any of this at the time, so I just started talking to him about the war and politics and his movie, and then he said, 'Will you be in my movie?' I didn't know anything about this man. I didn't want to be in the movie, but I figured all my friends were going to, so I'll go too."

‡

Watkins cast from the counterculture, and *Punishment Park* is bursting with the passion and the lingo of the day. It takes place in a fascist America where young movement activists face a right-wing civilian tribunal, then are given the choice of prison or escape on foot through sixty miles of desert park where they encounter the National Guard and other deadly obstacles.

Before *Punishment Park*, the English filmmaker's documentary-like narrative films had caused a stir back home. In *Culloden* (1964), about the last battle fought on British land, and *The War Game* (1965), about a nuclear attack on Britain, Watkins meticulously and movingly showed social conflicts through the brutal impact they had on the lives of their casualties. It was these people who intrigued Watkins, not the politicians and princes behind the events. When casting, he wanted little-known actors and even non-actors. Although it won a best-documentary Oscar, *The War Game* was banned from being shown on the BBC, which produced it, for twenty years.

Watkins' real-life hippies and New Leftists came together with some actual rednecks for two weeks in August 1970 in the California desert town Adelanto—with no budget, no stars, no script, one Eclair camera, and eight crew members. "We wore whatever we had," says Katherine Quittner. "We didn't have wardrobe, we didn't have hair, we didn't have makeup." Watkins wanted the outspoken Quittner be part of the tribunal, so while her Venice friends shot desert scenes, she stayed in town.

> I thought I was going with my boyfriend and other friends, and we were going to have fun together for two weeks. I didn't know I was going to go alone on a different part of the movie and be surrounded by rednecks. I had to sit around all day in this place called the Lazy 3 Café with all these people. I was famous for getting into fights with the rednecks in that café. I wouldn't shut up. I was eighteen or nineteen years old and had no fear of danger. Everyone was drinking beer and getting shit-faced. The redneck people were annoying and it was hot and I wanted to go home.

By the time Quittner filmed her tribunal scene, she was ready to go toe-to-toe with the same rednecks who had been so bothersome at the Lazy 3. The resulting raw exchange reflected the stark divisions of 1970s America, the tribunal drawing on the recent highly publicized trial of eight activists charged with conspiring to riot at the 1968 Democratic Convention. Unlike characters modeled on Chicago Eight defendants Bobby Seale or Abbie Hoffman, Quittner was left to her own devices as a defiant singer-songwriter. "People started asking me questions and I answered the questions," she says. "He [Watkins] didn't give me lines or a character. I had no direction at all. He just said, 'Do whatever you want, say whatever you want.'"

The cast's authenticity was complemented by the black-and-white verité look. "This was like a documentary, except he staged it," says Quittner. "So I don't think it's even possible to compare *Punishment Park* and Peter Watkins' movies with any other movies at all." Watkins had an outline for *Punishment Park* and trusted the cast to take the movie where he wanted it to go. "He controlled every frame of that movie," says Quittner.

It may be improvised in parts, it may have been chaotic in

parts, but he absolutely knew what he was doing from start
to finish. He was the director, and for the most part he got
exactly what he wanted, whether his method involved using
actors or non-actors or semi-actors, by placing people with
contentious political beliefs in the same room.

He's a fascinating filmmaker and, in my opinion, entirely
overlooked because he did stuff nobody has ever done since.
I don't care how many jerk-offs with a video camera go make
somebody improvise—it's a completely different idea. He was
an extremely accomplished filmmaker.

Quittner hadn't yet seen *Punishment Park* when, as many were wont
to do in the early 1970s, she and her boyfriend and co-star Jack Gozdick
set out on a backpacking excursion through Europe. "We got on some
kind of boat going to Yugoslavia. I was playing chess against some
Swedish people and they knew me from the movie. All of a sudden,
these people thought I was famous or something. It was a very bizarre
moment." The movie played the Cannes and New York festivals and
was screened in North America and parts of Europe, but major distributors wouldn't touch it. While it had ardent admirers, it often came under attack, one reviewer urging that the film, "like his others, [be] kept
from the public's gaze ... it shouldn't be allowed to encourage impressionable adolescents."[5]

The counterculture still permeated Venice when Quittner, who
would eventually work as a composer and music editor in film, left for
Europe in the mid-1970s to study music. When she returned to L.A. in
1980, the counterculture had virtually disappeared. "I remember coming back from Berlin and realizing that everything had changed. Venice
had a lot of things that made it very special. The depth of the relationships with our neighbors was profound because in other parts of the
city, regardless how hippie anybody was, they didn't spend their time
in a yard in full view of all of their neighbors. But when the rich people
moved in, the first thing they did was build enormous fences. It was
like everyone had gone crazy and everything was about money."

‡

Counterculture filmmaking wasn't confined to the BBS group or L.A.
New York's Paul Morrisey, in collaboration with Andy Warhol, focused

on the culture's underbelly in *Trash* (1970) and *L'Amour* (1973). In *Pink Flamingos* (1972), Baltimore's John Waters, a "Yippie agitator" turned cinema subversive, show how pervasive hip culture was in the early '70s—virtually everyone in this $12,000 production looks as though they just stepped out of the Mud Family commune in Oregon, as society's outcasts compete for the title of world's filthiest person. Just another day in paradise for Waters, a mainstay of the Midnight Movie circuit. Its counterculture audiences popularized *Night of the Living Dead* (1968), *El Topo* (1970), *The Harder They Come* (1972), and *The Rocky Horror Picture Show* (1975).

Mike Nichols and Robert Altman arrived in Vancouver separately but simultaneously in 1970 to shoot *Carnal Knowledge* and *McCabe and Mrs. Miller* respectively. During those shoots, the two casts and crews cross-fertilized, with *McCabe*'s Warren Beatty and Julie Christie hosting a seemingly endless party at their rented home overlooking the sea. Altman's film, a western, was shot with the working title *The Presbyterian Church Wager.* "It was wet but I loved it," Altman said of the shoot. "We put together for that film kind of a family, a kind of hippie family. Most of those guys that built the town of Presbyterian Church actually were living there on the property ... They built a still up there which I had to have destroyed because I was afraid somebody would go blind."

‡

Some of the blacklisted writers, directors, and actors found the New Hollywood years an opportune time to come in from the Cold War. Screenwriter Waldo Salt returned to win Oscars for *Midnight Cowboy* (1969) and *Coming Home* (1978). Walter Bernstein challenged racism in *Paris Blues* (1961), celebrated trade unionism in *The Molly Maguires* (1970), and parodied the self-help business in *Semi-Tough* (1977). "That's the side of the street I work," he says. "Those are the things that interest me, that I try to write about. Social issues, you know, social scripts."

With Bernstein writing and Martin Ritt directing, *The Front* (1976) paid tribute to the blacklisted. "Martin Ritt and I were good friends and old friends, and he had been blacklisted also," says Bernstein. "We wanted to do a straight drama about somebody who's blacklisted. We could never get anybody interested in it, and then I came up with the idea of going at it sideways, of doing it about the fronts and making it a comedy." Producers wanted it to star one of the era's leading men. They suggested "Redford, Newman, Warren Beatty, Jack Nicholson. We said,

*Walter Bernstein with Woody Allen during the making of* The Front. © *Columbia Pictures / Photofest.*

'That's not who we want.' Then we came up with the idea of Woody Allen and sent the script to him and he said yes. And that made it possible. He liked the politics of it, and I think he liked working with Ritt. It's the best performance he's ever given as an actor." Blacklisted actors and their children (such as Zero Mostel and John Garfield's daughter Julie) filled out the cast. Emotions overwhelmed the set the day the shoot began. Bernstein says, "We were getting back at them. We were saying, 'Fuck you. We're still here. We're still working. We're still doing what we want to do.' It was a very, very happy experience for me."

Norma and Ben Barzman remained in France during the New Hollywood era, but with a new outlook after the student-worker uprising that shook the country in May-June of 1968. "It gave me a kick in the ass," says Norma. "I wanted to be part of it and I couldn't—we would have been thrown out of France—but three of my children were on the barricades." Norma wrote a play called *May '68*. "That's when I started writing again. I couldn't demonstrate, so I had to write about it. I guess it was an accumulation of all those years when we couldn't be political." In 1979, the Barzmans returned to California. Ben wanted to be a Hollywood screenwriter again. Together, Ben and Norma wrote the novel *Rich Dreams*, a parody of epic romance novels. And that was just the beginning for Norma Barzman.

‡

The New Hollywood ending came with *Jaws* (1975), *Star Wars* (1977), and *Superman* (1978). These movies established a studio blockbuster strategy that has been unending: action for young males, combined with merchandising tie-ins, media crossovers, and sequels. Besides showing unprecedented profits, this strategy was a comfort for studio executives, relieved to have argumentative New Hollywood directors out of their lives.

Declining revenues in the pre-blockbuster 1960s and '70s had made studios inviting targets for takeover. With MCA entrenched at Universal, Gulf + Western Industries—better known for auto parts and sugarcane—purchased a flailing Paramount in 1966. The last of the hands-on Warner brothers, Jack, sold the studio to the Canadian company Seven Arts in 1967. Two years later, Warner Bros. was sold again, this time to the Kinney National Services conglomeration—better known for operating parking lots and car rental outlets than for any of the seven arts. By the late 1970s, studios were falling like dominoes to corporatism. The blockbuster strategy generated a new confidence in "the industry," and corporate ownership piled on board, with studios bought and sold and changing their names more often than starlets on the old MGM lot.

The director who broke ground on the new blockbuster approach, Steven Spielberg, was a onetime citizen in good standing of the Laurel Canyon counterculture. His first feature *Amblin'* (1968) was about a couple of California hippie hitchhikers, and before that he was a production assistant on *Faces*. But Spielberg learned how to be loved by studio suits, in particular Wasserman who, after seeing the young director's made-for-TV *Duel*, a taut 1971 tale of a psychotic truck driver, hired him to direct *Jaws*. Costing $8 million, it grossed close to $500 million.

*Jaws* set the template for the post-New Hollywood era—start with a saturation ad campaign (on seemingly every TV show on every network), open on 500 screens (150 had been considered a big opening), and sell promotional tie-ins from shark songs to *Jaws* beach towels. MCA shares doubled. Studios in the blockbuster age concluded that massive advertising followed by massive distribution delivered enough profit on opening weekend to make a movie virtually invulnerable to bad word-of-mouth or critics. And in succeeding decades, new stadium-seating multiplexes provided the required screens. With distribution and financing offering a round-about vertical integration—controlling but not owning exhibition—the new owners focused on horizontal expansion. Their goal: capture the selling of every form of entertainment.

While the low point of the New Hollywood in 1971 was *The Last Movie, The Last Picture Show* was one of its highs. New Hollywood filmmakers loved old Hollywood and European new waves—Laurel and Hardy and Fellini. Peter Bogdanovich's film revealed a rural Texas with the wide expanse of John Ford, while creating characters with the small intimacies of François Truffaut. It is set in 1951–52, a transitional time when TV is replacing the picture show and young people in a harsh town are looking for ways out. You wonder if the characters who don't leave town are the ones harassing Fonda, Hopper, and Nicholson nearly twenty years later when they stop by a local café for lunch in *Easy Rider*. It's the last of an era as well as the last picture show. The last movie when the local theater closes: *Red River*.

Neither the counterculture nor the New Hollywood vanished without a trace. The counterculture subverted the mainstream as much as it was absorbed by it, leaving behind more gender equality, less respect for authority, some ecological awareness, and healthier menus. The great movies of the early 1970s would have an enduring impact on new independent filmmakers. But most New Hollywood directors weren't independent filmmakers themselves. They pitched their films to studios, were financed by studios, lived and ultimately died by the hands of the studios. They did, however, create a remarkable body of work while fighting the good fight within the system, restoring some of the quality lost when Hollywood sent its artists into exile. But with the new corporate climate of the late 1970s, few would have much staying power. In the long run, it was Cassavetes' example of working entirely outside the studio system that roused independents far more than the New Hollywood did. And just around the corner and across the continent, another generation of inspired filmmakers was about to make its stand.

## CHAPTER SEVEN

# New York Magic

THE COUNTERCULTURE AND THE 1960s hadn't been down for long when a new underground sneered its head. Punk rock played a formative role in the independent film scene that emerged from New York in the late 1970s and early '80s, armed with a do-it-yourself ethos that would quickly spread like contagious magic to young filmmakers everywhere.

Filmmaker Tom DiCillo came out of that scene, but on this fall morning in his New York apartment, having just wrapped a documentary about the Doors, he is ruminating on something that happened years earlier in L.A. The Doors' Jim Morrison returned from a long drunken spree to find that other members of the band and the president of the Elektra record label had licensed their song "Light My Fire" for a Buick commercial. "He went insane. But they said, 'Jim, we tried to find you. We thought you would like it. This is TV, a new medium.' 'Forget it,' he said, 'I'm not doing it.' The last line of the documentary I wrote is: 'And to this date, none of their music has been used in a car commercial.'" Morrison's stance is no less timely forty years later. "It affects the psyche, this whole commercialization of everything," says DiCillo, "because it just relentlessly pounds this idea into the culture that everything is for sale. You've got to fight it."

By the early 1980s, the New Hollywood was done and the studios were drawing crowds to blockbuster after blockbuster—*The Empire Strikes Back* (1980), *Superman II* (1980), *Raiders of the Lost Ark* (1981), *Star Trek: The Wrath of Khan* (1982), *Return of the Jedi* (1983), *Indiana Jones and the Temple of Doom* (1984). There were stirrings, though, in the resistance. A decade after the West Coast rumblings of the New Hollywood, DiCillo and his friends began to make their stand, finding inspiration in Manhattan clubs. Emerging first in London and New York, then in L.A. and elsewhere, punk bands didn't rely on the approval of the major studios' cousins, the major recording labels. "That was one of the best things that punk blew apart," says Jello Biafra, who fronted the San Francisco band Dead Kennedys. "From the beginning it was, 'Hey, we don't have to tone this down to get a record contract if we make our own records. We may not sell very many of them, but if we release our music ourselves we can do exactly what we want. You didn't have to play for ten years [until] Warner Brothers offered you a huge amount of money, most of which would be kicked back to the producer and the recording studio and Warner Brothers anyway. The revival of DIY is probably the best gift punk gave the world."

Punk's DIY code quickly permeated the New York film scene. "Punk opened up the idea of possibilities and the idea that if they can do it themselves, we can do it ourselves," DiCillo says.

> Many people feel they can't make a film unless someone allows them to. The rules perpetuate that. 'We won't give the money unless you change your script, unless you da da da.' Well, the punk movement said, 'Fuck that. No one is going to allow me to do anything. I'll do it if I want to do it.' The same thing then affected the idea of independent film. A lot of people were shooting features in Super 8 and projecting them on the walls in bars. It was just that feeling of, 'Don't tell me a film has to be a certain way.'

This new punk-fueled independence eventually included New York University students (DiCillo, Jim Jarmusch, Susan Seidelman), No Wave filmmakers (Amos Poe, Eric Mitchell, Vivienne Dick), the Cinema of Transgression (Nick Zedd, Richard Kern, Cassandra Stark), and assorted individuals such as Slava Tsukerman and Mary Harron. Seidelman recalls the collaborating and socializing that crossed Manhattan. "I knew Jim Jarmusch and his girlfriend Sara Driver. I knew Lizzie Borden—she did a good movie called *Working Girls* [1986]—Bette Gordon, and Alexandre Rockwell. Tom DiCillo was an extra in *Desperately Seeking Susan* [1985]; the camera pans along the bar at the Magic Club, and he's one of the extras sitting there. Amos Poe is in *Smithereens* [1982]. Richard Edson, who was the actor in *Stranger Than Paradise* [1984], is also in *Desperately Seeking Susan*. Richard Hell's in both of those movies."

Not all of these people identified as punks, but without the punk scene and its attitude, their filmmaking would have been far different. After Jim Jarmusch's *Stranger Than Paradise*, independent film would never again mean drive-in double bills. New York emerged as the North American capital of independent cinema, which was now attached to a street-smart bohemian cool. Infused with an oppositional ethos, the New Yorkers' anti-corporate outlook spread to film students and art houses everywhere in the late 1980s and early '90s, becoming role models for the uncompromising, their hipster DIY attitude help-

*Richard Edson, Eszter Balint, and John Lurie on a tragically hip road trip in Jim Jarmusch's* Stranger Than Paradise. © *Samuel Goldwyn Company / Photofest.*

ing to galvanize young filmmakers from Paris to Seoul. Bruce Sweeney would go on to be a mainstay of Canadian independent filmmaking, but in the late 1980s he and his friends were Vancouver film students infatuated with Jarmusch and his friends. "*Stranger Than Paradise* was a huge film for us. I loved it," he says. "You know, the popular fare in the '80s was really quite a turnoff. I was not a big *Raiders of the Lost Ark* fan."

The filmmaking out of New York in the 1980s was an acute expression of the place, but it wasn't as if Seidelman and her friends were introducing filmmaking to the city. New York had a long legacy of independents, and in Seidelman's era there were other talented NYU film students not as consumed by the punk aesthetic, such as Spike Lee and Joel Coen. "New York was interesting," says Seidelman, "whether it was the Scorsese version of New York in the '70s or the Spike Lee version of New York in the '80s or the Woody Allen version. It started changing once it got so stockbroker-yuppified in the late '80s when it became all about glitz and money. Before that, it was intellectually, culturally, just a cool place to live." So New York's place in independent film is secure even without the punk-influenced scene from which Seidelman emerged. That film scene, however, combined a determined auteur sensibility, emphasis on place, and sense of community and purpose that recalled France's New Wave, and it provided a seductive example for the upcoming American independent movement.

‡

In Slava Tsukerman's *Liquid Sky* (1982), aliens meet Alien Nation in sub-terranean Manhattan, circa 1980, a place where it's difficult to distin-guish aliens from punks, models, hippies, androgynous men, androg-ynous women and, ultimately, Soviet filmmakers (Tsukerman) from American filmmakers. "Aliens appeared in specific subcultures—punk circles," a character in the film explains. When another's punkish look is criticized ("some kind of phoney theater") by her ex-lover, an old hip-pie, she tells him: "So your professor wore a three-piece suit and blamed you for your jeans ... You thought your jeans stood for love, freedom, and sexual equality." Punk, at first glance, seemed an anti-hippie move-ment, but DiCillo, for one, drew inspiration as much from Jim Mor-rison as Joe Strummer. The counterculture and punk were bookends of the same Baby Boom generation. As the hippie movement faded in the mid-'70s, the punks were taking root, and many of them, especially the more politicized ones—from London's Strummer to members of Canada's D.O.A. and The Subhumans—had been hippies during the waning days of the counterculture.

When punk exploded with the Sex Pistols in 1977, suddenly any re-bellious kid who would have identified with hippies a year earlier was now a punk. Case in point: Jello Biafra. He grew up Eric Boucher in Boulder, Colorado. "My cynical attitude about the entertainment in-dustry and consumer culture came early from just watching my father alternate between laughing at commercials and getting angry at them." Soon Jello was on to Frank Zappa for his

> lyrics that weren't, 'I love you baby, sex, drugs, rock and roll, buy my record.' That was where my feelings about globaliza-tion came from. They've called it different things over the years, but even then it was known as corporate fascism, and I've never been a fan. I hate corporations and I hate fascism. What can I say? Everything they touch turns to dumbed-down shit. And that applies to food, art, architecture, infrastructure—you name it. I learned, even before I was in a band, that the commercial entertainment industry was the enemy of good art and good music.

Not only were the record labels just as intent on conquering the world as the movie studios, the two were increasingly doing it in tandem, sometimes under the same corporate umbrella. Decca Records, which purchased Universal Studios back in 1952, merged with MCA in 1962, thus owning both a major film studio and a major record label. Warner Bros. Records was founded in 1958. Columbia Records and Columbia Pictures were L.A. fixtures which had nothing to do with each other until Sony bought them both. The major labels' relationship with independent musicians and the counterculture was much the same as the relationship that major studios had with independent filmmakers. "Demographically, it was the Baby Boomer generation," Biafra says, "and major labels didn't know quite what to do about music. They just figured they'd let Bob Dylan say what he wants, let Steppenwolf sing about drugs and evading the draft, and let Jefferson Airplane and the Grateful Dead do what they want because they're selling more albums than we've ever been able to sell. So we don't quite understand it, but if there's money to be made, we intend to be the ones making it."

Young Biafra's disaffection wasn't confined to corporate culture. He closely followed the trial of the Chicago Eight, spoke out in class against the Vietnam War, and let his hair grow. But he soon noticed that the counterculture in his hometown no longer had much edge to it, and the music had evolved into arena hard rock and "adult" FM soft rock. "In other words, 'Now that the Baby Boomers are aging, we've got to mellow all these people out. We've figured out what sells. We'll still keep the psychedelic light shows but commodify it and call it disco.' People who were born just a little too late to really go all the way into the wild shit that went down in the '60s and the early '70s came of age, and suddenly it wasn't just the music that was disappointing—life and culture itself were too." But something new was breaking: punk rock.

> It shocked and annoyed people, and something inside me knew that, as much as I was a fan of this music, I was still a hippie and associated short hair with right-wingers, rednecks, and marines. But finally, in the middle of my one quarter of college in Santa Cruz, I was blasting the Sex Pistols out my dormitory room door and thought, 'This is it. The time has come.' I just cut off my hair with a pair of regular old scissors. Having hair spiked and crudely cut and that short gave me an instant element of danger that I hadn't felt, both projecting

and coming back at me, since I was the first person to grow
my hair long in sixth grade. It brought that back—that level
of shock and knowing you were the outlaw and everybody
knew it ... When punk came out, even the very sound of it
was offensive as hell, the attitude, and by the time the Sex
Pistols defined the look, of course the fashion did as well.
And I suddenly realized, 'Hey, I wasn't born too late.'

‡

Tom DiCillo did a lot of moving on as a child. "My father was in the
military, so I moved from base to base, usually in outskirts of small
towns across America. I couldn't really tell you I was from anywhere."
DiCillo enrolled at Old Dominion University in Virginia, wanting to
be a writer. "By complete accident I joined a film society and the first
film they showed, *La Strada*, blew my mind. I said, *that* is an art form I
would be interested in, so I applied to a couple of schools and got into
NYU graduate film school."

DiCillo arrived in 1976 with few romantic notions about New York.
"I knew nothing about it, and I was terrified at first. What drew me into
this crazy place was the desire to make a film—that gave me the courage
to come here. The first thing I did when I got here was accidentally take
acid. I had never taken it, and I dropped a massive amount that was in
some punch at a party. I staggered around the city awake for about forty-eight hours. It pushed me into the essence of what the city was. The
city was intense. I had seen *Taxi Driver*, and I had seen *Midnight Cowboy*." So, shortly after watching Rizzo and Joe Buck wander Manhattan
("One of the most powerful movies to come out of that era; I can't
even comprehend that that film won an Academy Award. It would be
banned today"), DiCillo found himself embracing the same streets.

As punk took hold in Manhattan, a collection of NYU film students
were regulars at punk venues such as CBGB's and the Mudd Club. It
was an incendiary mix: the students' cinephilia, the music scene's DIY
determination, and the gritty Manhattan of the times. "I don't want
to sound nostalgic, but there was a very human quality that was happening," Dicillo says. "The punk movement in America was one of the
most genuine musical movements. There was a tremendous power and
freedom in that."

‡

*Susan Berman in* Smithereens. *Courtesy Susan Seidelman.*

Susan Seidelman moved into the East Village in 1974. "There was a kind of a grungy quality in the East Village back then that was inspiring. In that period before punk turned into New Wave and became more commercialized—I would say '75 to '83—that punkness was reflected in the music and in the art and in the people making films. There wasn't a lot of money, but we didn't need a lot of money. People were making low-budget feature films for $3,000. You were doing it for the sake of art, not really thinking about selling it. It wasn't a product."

Before attending NYU, Seidelman wanted to be involved in movies, but living in suburban Philadelphia in the mid-1970s, she didn't see a lot of role models for female film directors. Instead, she studied fashion design at Philadelphia's Drexel University and took one film course, fell hard for the French New Wave and Ingmar Bergman, and applied to film schools. She got accepted at NYU.

After graduating, she started working on *Smithereens,* a punk *Breakfast at Tiffany's*, about a young woman who moves to Manhattan (in this case from Jersey) desperate to reinvent herself. With a crew of friends from NYU, the *Smithereens* shoot started on the streets of Manhattan in 1979 and didn't finish until 1982. Seidelman raised $10,000 and had another $10,000 her grandmother left her. "It was supposed to be for my wedding, but it was put to a better cause. And the rest of the money—the budget was about $40,000—was in deferred payments to the crew that I didn't have the money at the time to pay. But there was a salary on paper for everyone and the hope that if we ever did make any money, it would get distributed. Everyone did ultimately did get paid." *Smithereens* premiered at Cannes in 1982. "The response was amazing," Seidelman says. "New Line Cinema picked it up. It had a pretty good run in college towns and big cities. I think it had its finger on the pulse of something that was happening at the time, at least in the counter-culture, because the main character, like myself, was an outsider. It's about a girl from New Jersey, i.e., a girl from Philadelphia, who wants to be part of what she thinks is happening. It's about the drive to look for another kind of life, an alternative to the options you think you have."

‡

Inspired by punk and Cassavetes, Jim Jarmusch and his *Stranger Than Paradise* would win over audiences and award juries at Cannes and Sundance, and in the process reaffirm the new New York hipster cinema introduced two years earlier by *Smithereens*. The era's cool punky Manhattan permeates both films, although *Smithereens* was about going to New York and *Stranger Than Paradise* was about leaving it. Tragically hip New Yorkers Eddie and Willie decide to get out of Dodge, heading for the Midwest to visit Willie's cousin Eva, and the three engage in a low-end road trip highlighted by petty law-breaking and other misadventures shot minimalist-style, with long scenes delivered deadpan by musicians John Lurie and Richard Edson and all-round avant-gardist Eszter Balint.

"Most of the people just worked for free," says DiCillo, who shot the film.

> Wim Wenders had some leftover black-and-white 35 millimeter negative from one of his films, *The State of Things* [1982], and he gave it to Jarmusch. Once we were shooting in a motel room and the characters were coming in from outside. My assistant said to me, 'Tom, there's great light outside. When they come in, it's gonna be completely blown out.' When they came in, it looked like they were coming out of a blizzard. There was just a sense of, so fucking what? Otherwise, we would've had to put all the gels on the windows, balance the light so that the inside was more properly exposed to the outside. That's one simple example. It affected every aspect of making the movie. Some independent films from that era are pretty stupid. Just because something is independent doesn't mean it is well thought out or has any profound, engaging idea. The ones that did were very effective. *Stranger Than Paradise* was one of them.

Jarmusch grew up in Ohio and fell in love with movies during a summer in Paris's Cinémathèque Française. After enrolling at NYU, he became a regular at punk clubs. "You could live in New York cheap," Jarmusch recalled.

> You could find apartments for $175 a month, so there was an influx of younger people that had artistic intentions. It was a really lively scene in New York. You could go to CBGB's or Max's and see the Ramones, Television, or Patti Smith. There was the very young Jean-Michel Basquiat painting on the streets all night under the name SAMO. There was a group of people on St. Mark's Place making movies called the New Cinema—Eric Mitchell, Beth and Scott B—then people like Charlie Ahearn and Susan Seidelman ... They weren't worried about how much money was behind it or how many people it would reach or how refined a product it was or whether you were an experienced virtuoso with your instrument. It wasn't about that; it was about the spirit of expressing something.[1]

DiCillo would go on to direct a string of independents, including *Living in Oblivion* (1995) and *Johnny Suede* (1991), but he started out as a cinematographer on Jarmusch's student film *Permanent Vacation* (1980) and Eric Mitchell's *Underground USA* (1980). Jarmusch, who did sound on *Underground USA*, was hired by director Nicholas Ray, then an NYU instructor, as his personal assistant during the making of the Ray/Wenders documentary collaboration *Lightning Over Water* (1980). When Jarmusch set about making *Permanent Vacation*, he had the support of Ray and Wenders and DiCillo, but none from NYU, which refused to grant him a degree. "Hooking up with Jim Jarmusch was a cool experience," recalls DiCillo. "We were friends. We both felt the only thing that matters is doing what is true to you. The teachers [at NYU] were morons at that point. I can't tell you how many of them said to me, 'Why do you want to do that?' And I'm going, 'Wait a second, this is a school; I thought we were supposed to be able to try things.' Why follow a formula?"

*Stranger Than Paradise* and *Smithereens* weren't the only breakout American independents in the early '80s. There were the Coen brothers' *Blood Simple* (1984), Spike Lee's low-budget *She's Gotta Have It* (1985), an engaging tale of a Brooklyn woman juggling suitors, and Gus Van Sant (*Mala Noche*, 1982), Wayne Wang (*Chan Is Missing*, 1984), Alan Rudolph

(*Choose Me*, 1987), and Abel Ferrara (*China Girl*, 1984). And just over the bridge in Jersey there was John Sayles.

‡

Nancy Savoca grew up working class in the tough Southeast Bronx of the 1960s. Her first high school had a lot of *Blackboard Jungle* going on, but she was drawn to other movies: "I was obsessed with Brando and Dean." Her next school offered a film class. "That's when I found out what a director did, and I said to the teacher that I really want to do that. And she said, 'Go to NYU.'" After NYU, she volunteered as a gofer on John Sayles' *Brother from Another Planet* (1984). "I watched [Sayles] and learned a lot. Maggie Renzi, his partner, was producing, and I remember watching how they set this incredible tone of collaboration and family on the set—no prima donna thing happening. He financed that movie on his own." Sayles had helped to set the tone for the later East Coast DIY breakout with *Return of the Secaucus 7* (1979)—a movie about a reunion of New Left students released while Ronald Reagan's so-called New Right was in ascendance, the New Hollywood was history, and independent filmmaking was virtually invisible. Ignoring the inhospitable atmosphere, Sayles made the film with his savings and distributed it on his own—traveling the country theater by theater. Driven by some of that self-starting 1960s' idealism, Sayles, who attended anti-war protests while at Williams College in Massachusetts, wrote, directed, edited, and acted in *Secaucus 7*. The film precisely captured the experience of Baby Boomers disconnected from their recent pasts and unsure of their futures, and marked the start of a low-budget art filmmaking that would find an audience in the 1980s.

Sayles wrote for Roger Corman (*The Howling*, 1981; *Piranha*, 1978) to raise money for *Return of the Secaucus 7*, and would continue to fund his own work (including *Matewan*, 1987; *Eight Men Out*, 1988; and *Lone Star*, 1996) by scripting or script doctoring movies for other directors. In *City of Hope* (1991), an ensemble piece set amidst the corruption and despair of a New Jersey town, actress Barbara Williams plays a single mother dealing with a bad-cop ex-husband. "John's a very down-to-earth straightforward guy," she says. "Everybody had equal importance on the set. The caterer was Maggie, John's wife and producer, and all the actors were paid the same." At the time of filming, Williams was commuting from L.A. to New Jersey for the shoot while going through a marriage breakup. "He said, 'Stay here, learn to be a grip or something.' You really felt like you were part of the family. He's definitely got the right ideas about movie-making."

Set in New York, *The Brother from Another Planet*—about a black extraterrestrial who escapes slavery in his world only to find himself on earth—is a look at the universal alien, who slowly learns to fit in. During the shoot, Savoca handed Sayles and Renzi her first draft of *True Love* (1989), a raw look at personal interactions in the buildup to a Bronx Italian wedding. Six years later, he asked about that script she had shown him. "Nobody wanted to make it. We had no cash. People reading the script said it was too ethnic. So it was going nowhere. John said, 'Well, if you want to do it really down and dirty, I will be the first investor.' Then Susan Seidelman and Jonathan Demme became investors. We were able to then go out and get the rest of the money to shoot. I was ecstatic."

†

While music and film scenes co-existed in several cities, there was more interaction between the two in New York. "They were all the same people," Gus Van Sant says. "Some of the ones in bands were actually filmmakers who had turned into punk rockers or vice versa." The No Wave, a set of punky avant-garde filmmakers in the East Village, included Amos Poe, who directed *The Blank Generation* (1976), the first film about punk, and *The Foreigner* (1978), with Deborah Harry and fellow No Waver Eric Mitchell. Jello Biafra was still with the Dead Kennedys when he started landing roles in independents such as Bill Fishman's *Tapeheads* (1988). "In San Francisco, it's rare that you find musicians talking to poets talking to filmmakers talking to painters talking to journalists," he says. So Biafra was taken aback when he played New York for the first time in 1979 and was approached by a filmic punk couple—filmmaker Nick Zedd and actress Donna Death. "Nick was clearly a very intense, intelligent person, but he said right away, 'I'm not a musician, I'm a filmmaker.' And sure enough, he came out to San Francisco a little later and showed his film called *They Eat Scum* [1979]. It was a no-budget film with amateur actors but had flashes of brilliance and John Waters-level sickness and dementia, which drew me right in. He later pronounced himself part of a new rabble-rousing, punk-attitude film underground out of New York called the Cinema of Transgression."

Zedd wrote the Cinema of Transgression manifesto. "We propose that all film schools be blown up and all boring films never be made again," it declared. "We propose that a sense of humor is an essential element discarded by the doddering academics and further, that any film which doesn't shock isn't worth looking at. All values must be challenged ... Since there is no afterlife, the only hell is the hell of praying, obeying laws, and debasing yourself before authority figures, the only heaven is the heaven of sin, being rebellious, having fun, fucking, learning new things and breaking as many rules as you can."[2] Says Biafra: "That to me was the most direct use of punk attitude and tactics crossing into film that I ever saw; it was so completely underground, completely DIY, and the material those people created was completely offensive to everybody else who had anything to do with film. And they were very proud of that."

‡

In light of the positive response to *Smithereens* and *Stranger Than Paradise*, the studios were curious about this punky New York scene, and like they did in the New Hollywood era, producers came bearing offers, albeit more subdued ones than Dennis Hopper had attracted. Punk gave independent filmmakers some freedom within the system for a short while. "Once *Smithereens* got out there, I started getting calls from some agents and studio people," Seidelman says. "I had heard horror stories about people who made an interesting independent film and then got lost in Hollywood because they made the wrong choice. I didn't want to make a film in which somebody else was going to control what I wanted to say. I got a bunch of bad scripts submitted to me. I had to read about twenty in order to find the one that had the core of the thing I was looking for."

*Desperately Seeking Susan* (1985) was perfect for Seidelman because it read like something she might have conceived, and she worked with its writer Leora Barish to shape something that captured a down and gritty and often wonderful New York. Its Roberta (Rosanna Arquette) is living proof of the fine line between the suburban mainstream and urban bohemia. After losing her memory, she is as comfortable being an alternative New Yorker as she had been as a New Jersey housewife. "For me, there was a basic theme about who you are on the outside and who you are or want to be on the inside. You know, the suburban housewife who settled into a complacent, nice, but somewhat boring life, who wants a bit of an adventure. It was not that different from, in some ways, the

*Susan Seidelman in 1982. Photograph by John Clifford, courtesy Susan Seidelman.*

world of *Smithereens*. It was still partly set in the East Village, and the other part was set in a suburbia I could relate to, having been a suburban Philadelphia girl."

Produced by Orion Pictures, *Desperately Seeking Susan* was small by studio standards ("I think the budget was somewhere between $5 and $6 million"), but on the heels of *Smithereens*, it felt mega-budget to Seidelman. The film drew large crowds across North America and Europe. "I don't think anyone expected it to get the response that it got. Part of it is about timing, let's face it. Madonna suddenly burst onto the scene. The movie helped her but she certainly helped the movie, having her huge *Like a Virgin* album come out at the same time." Seidelman drew out Madonna's best performance—by far. "She was not famous at the time, and I knew her because she lived down the street and because I knew what was going on in the downtown music scene; it was the right timing and the right part for the right person."

The film tapped into something authentic in the culture that a studio can't understand. "It made a lot more money than the studio thought it was going to make," Seidelman says, and they fast-tracked her next film into production. "They wanted to get it out quickly because the studios want to capitalize on the success of the thing that went before." *Making Mr. Right* (1987) had an okay premise—a guy can be so emotionally dead that an android is more appealing to be with—but it didn't move audiences like her earlier work.

The low-budget studio offers to Seidelman were the sort successful independent filmmakers had attracted since Cassavetes made *Shadows*. That would change after Steven Soderberg's *sex, lies, and videotape* hit Sundance in 1989. The film drew, for the first time, the corporate film industry en masse to Park City, and they (unfortunately) would never leave. It was, in its way, as much a movie about the movies as *Sunset Boulevard* (1950) had been, only its movie was the new video kind a young drifter makes out of women's sexual lives. Just as *Easy*

*Rider* opened doors to the counterculture in 1969, *sex, lies, and video-tape*—with its smart combination of sexuality, new media, and a compelling title—marked a sea change for independents twenty years later (although the bulk of its $1.2 million budget was financed by Columbia). It defined Sundance, established the "studio indie" era, and was a Palme D'or winner that would make nearly $25 million at the box office. In the 1980s, the heart of American independents was in New York, but by the end of the decade, *sex, lies, and videotape* had moved the focus to Sundance.

The year the studios showed up at Sundance, Nancy Savoca's *True Love* won the festival's grand prize. It was also the year the United States Film Festival changed its name to the Sundance Film Festival. "So we were there at exactly the right time," she says. But she wasn't there. "I was in labor the night I won." Savoca returned home from the hospital with her new son to find flowers from every major studio. "They had their eye on the indie movement. That's why they inundated me with stuff. John Sayles didn't get that, you know what I mean? I was literally there when this wave hit." It was almost as though the New Hollywood was back in the studios' good graces. "It came around again with Sundance in '89," Savoca says. "Miramax walked away with *sex, lies, and videotape* and came into their own. Within a few years every studio had its classic division. They made studio films really cheaply and labeled them 'independent.' I always find it dangerous when something outside the mainstream suddenly becomes mainstream. How did that change it?"

Among the studio offerings, Savoca found a project from Warner Bros. that combined her interest in relationship stories and subculture. *Dogfight* (1991) is about a bohemian woman (Lili Taylor) and a straight-laced soldier (River Phoenix) who meet in San Francisco just before it was transformed by the counterculture. Phoenix's character is torn between the tradition he knows and the new consciousness Taylor represents. When Warner Bros. did a test screening of the film at a mall in Pasadena, the audience liked the comedic parts but had problems with the complexity of the relationship, and that meant studio execs now had a problem with it too.

> It was a very low-budget film for them, but still they wanted
> it to appeal to everybody. They were very excited about it
> when they saw it, but then they tested it. They came up
> with this idea to just change the last scene, so that audi-

ences would leave satisfied. They offered me a lot of money to re-write the ending. I said, 'I don't even have a clue what I could do to help you.' What are you going to say to the studio? You have to stay true to your film. They went to a couple of other writers and paid a lot of money to get the ending re-written. Then they took it to River, who called me and said, 'So, you're not going to do this re-shoot that they're asking me to do?'

I said, 'I didn't know there was a re-shoot—they're probably going to get another director.'

'I'm not going to do it if you're not doing it,' he said.

I said, 'River, don't do anything for my sake. Do what you have to do.'

He said, 'No, I don't agree with what they're doing anyway.'

And he didn't do it.

The movie's most memorable image comes near the finale when Phoenix runs off into the distance down a San Francisco hillside as a brilliant sun rises in the crisp early morning. "That was not planned," Savoca says. The final day of shooting ended with an all-night marathon at City Lights bookstore:

We were done. They were wrapping up to leave and everyone was in a sad mood because the shoot was pretty special. Our gaffer suddenly looks down the street and says, 'Oh my god, the sun is coming up. This is going to look amazing in a minute.' So we yelled at the crew to get everything back up. And then it was: 'What are we shooting?' I remembered the scene where Phoenix said goodbye to Taylor and ripped up her phone number." It became a moment of pure movie-making, when any film-industry nonsense was left in the dust of a run for freedom. "I said, 'River, just start walking down the street, and he started walking, and then I said, 'Run, River, run. Just run.' He started running and he didn't know why. He didn't know what part of the movie this was, he just took off. 'Run, River, run.' That was the last shot of the movie.

Savoca's woes over *Dogfight* were no different than those independent-minded directors have always faced with studios. "If we're going to talk about the independent movement of the late '80s and '90s, Warner Brothers would not fit in," says Lili Taylor. "I mean, *Dogfight* would not fit into that. We had a studio head bothering us the whole damn time."

*Smithereens* is a cinematic New York time capsule. It's the pre-gentrification Manhattan of the '70s and '80s which, regardless of how much garbage littered its sidewalks, was a magnet for America's refugees and fugitives. Susan Seidelman's characters have come to the city from Montana, Ohio, and New Jersey. Paul (Brad Rinn), like Joe Buck, is a small-town guy who finds something irresistible about the ultimate big city. So does Seidelman, who takes us down its tough streets and into its frenetic clubs and vacant lots. It's a shot-on-the-run-without-permits Lower Manhattan that's vibrantly colored and covered in graffiti and posters. Wren (Susan Berman) is often an unsympathetic character—a wannabe artsy type on a relentless mission for fame, or at least survival. Still, Seidelman, a female director when they were almost non-existent in American film, creates unpredictable, three-dimensional women: the self-centered Wren, who also cares enough to drag her friend from a bad bubble bath with an unappetizing man, and the thoughtful prostitute who shares her lunch with Paul. "Everyone's a little weird these days," says Wren. "It's normal."

"I think there's a real, undeniable correlation between how you get the money—the means of making the film—and the content," Seidelman says. "In the beginning of the independent movement that I came out of, there was no thought about how the film was going to be marketed, what elements you needed, i.e., stars or production values, in order to get distribution. We were thinking, 'I want to make this movie. It's about a subject matter I feel passionately about.' But by the early '90s, independent film became about putting together a package that an independent film distributor could sell, hence you needed someone like Gwyneth Paltrow in your movie to make it appealing overseas. It changed the dynamic of how you were putting your films together."

## CHAPTER EIGHT

## Studio Nation

THE TURNING POINT FOR independents came when *Stranger Than Paradise* and *sex, lies, and videotape,* in comparison to *Pulp Fiction,* looked like failures. "The prime example of success for an independent film was *Stranger Than Paradise*," says Tom DiCillo. "It grossed $2 million. That was huge. What do you think happened when *Pulp Fiction* came out? It blew that shit right out of the water. Two million. No one was going to make a movie that only grosses $2 million." Made for $8 million, *Pulp Fiction* made more than twenty-five times that worldwide. "When [Quentin] Tarantino became the Elvis Presley of film directors, when the amount of money became so unbelievably overwhelming, all the rules became exactly like Hollywood."

By the time Tarantino's *Pulp Fiction* premiered in 1994, the studios had long understood that blockbusters, with special effects and stars, inspired repeat viewing. Now, an "independent" movie, with star casting—John Travolta, Uma Thurman, Samuel L. Jackson, and Bruce Willis—inspired repeated viewing. There had been a proliferation of small production and distribution companies during the 1980s, then *sex, lies, and videotape* attracted industry players to Sundance, and five years later *Pulp Fiction* moved the "independent" goal-posts again. Whether *Pulp Fiction* actually was independent is debatable (Disney owned Miramax by the time of its release), but it played Sundance and was perceived as independent. So when it was released into 1,100 theaters and topped the box office on its opening weekend, the studios set about absorbing independent film under the "studio indie" brand.

The term "independent" came up from the underground as, one by one, the studios established "specialty divisions." This inversion (to borrow the Weather Underground's term when it surfaced) didn't occur over night. Before there were studio indies, there had been "minimajors," film production companies that were smaller, well-financed versions of the studios, including Miramax, New Line, Samuel Goldwyn, Newmarket, Lions Gate, USA Films, October Films, and Artisan. Disney bought Miramax in 1993 for $80 million, and founding brothers Harvey and Bob Weinstein stayed on to run the company within a company. Fine Line was purchased by the Turner Broadcasting System, which was purchased by Time Warner. USA Films was bought

out by Universal, then morphed into Focus Features, the indie arm
of NBC-Universal. Rather than buying out a mini-major, sometimes a
studio would turn a mini-major, such as Orion Pictures, into a satellite
contractor. More often, studios would simplify matters by building
their own independent subsidiary from scratch. Sony unveiled Sony
Picture Classics, 20th Century Fox had Fox Searchlight, Paramount
had Paramount Classics, and Warner Bros. had Warner Independent
Pictures.

Miramax set the tone for the big-business "indie" era—first as an
autonomous company, then as an adjunct to Disney—eventually ac-
cumulating some $4.5 billion in grosses and 249 Oscar nominations.
The major studios' blockbuster strategy had provided an opening for
smaller companies that produced lower-budget films. Much of what
Miramax now financed or picked up might have been studio movies
in an earlier Hollywood—*sex, lies, and videotape* (1989), *My Left Foot*
(1989), *The Crying Game* (1992), *Reservoir Dogs* (1992), *The English Pa-
tient* (1996), *Good Will Hunting* (1997), *Life is Beautiful* (1997), *Shakespeare in Love* (1998), and *In the Bedroom* (2001). If Miramax's mini-
major films recalled the studios in better times, the company's boss of
bosses, Harvey Weinstein, was something of a throwback too—a mini-
mogul who took a hands-on approach from casting to editing and was
able to shout a decibel louder than almost anyone else in show business, especially come Oscar-campaign season. Miramax wasn't always
a winner. It bought Jim Jarmusch's *Dead Man* sight unseen in 1995 on
the strength of the name of its director and star, Johnny Depp. At the
first sign that *Dead Man* might not prove entirely popular, Miramax
dumped the western into theaters and it disappeared as though it had
been run out of town by Gary Cooper.

Although *sex, lies, and videotape* and *Pulp Fiction* encouraged the studios, Steven Soderbergh and Tarantino were hardly shills for corporate
Hollywood. Like the New Hollywood filmmakers before them, they just
wanted to make their movies and took the money being tossed their
way. But not always. Following *sex, lies, and videotape*, Soderbergh, to
his credit, chose to return to the independent fold. His follow-up, *Kafka*
(1991), was more a cinematic version of the title character's ambiguous
fiction than anything resembling a conventional biopic. And *Schizopolis*
(1996), a low-budget film directed by and starring Soderbergh, was the
movie Kafka would have made had he been an independent filmmaker.
In the '90s, some filmmakers such as Wes Anderson (*Rushmore*, 1998),
the Coen brothers (*Fargo*, 1996), David Fincher (*Fight Club*, 1999), Spike

Lee (*Jungle Fever*, 1991), Alexander Payne (*Election*, 1999), and Gus Van Sant (*Good Will Hunting*, 1997) were able to navigate the studios and their specialty divisions while retaining some independence.

These were a rarified few, however, and the difficulties faced by Nancy Savoca on *Dogfight* or Todd Solondz on *Fear, Anxiety and Depression* (1989) are more representative of the independent-minded director's studio experience with commercial-minded producers. Solondz's Polygram-backed film was so cut up by studio editors that he withdrew from filmmaking for several years. He made an auspicious return with the independent *Welcome to the Dollhouse* (1995), about the mundane hellishness of unpopularity in a suburban high school. By the late 1990s, even specialty-division hit makers such as Van Sant were dissatisfied with an independent formula as restrictive as the studio's—star casting, happy endings, few risks.

In 1999, Disney's Miramax was about to distribute Kevin Smith's satire *Dogma* (1999) but was scared off by religious protestors. Bingham Ray, a founder of the distribution/production outfit October Films, realized the studio independent world was fake shortly after his company was purchased by Universal in 1997. Universal refused to distribute Solondz's *Happiness* (1998), a movie about pedophilia and violence that had been acquired by October Films. "The dream of being able to work within the studio system as some maverick, autonomous independent—it was just total horseshit," Ray noted.[1] So much for "studio indies." Actual independents—practically everyone on the planet apart from the corporate studios—don't have guaranteed access to global markets. Sony Classics, Warner Independent, Fox Searchlight, and Paramount Classics were born with that access, and when film festivals and art-house cinemas bought into their definition of independent, it meant even less screen time for actual independents.

With Miramax and Sundance and a plethora of "studio-indie" specialty companies, suddenly "independent filmmaker" could be a job description and a lifestyle choice: "Includes free travel, festival passes, hip swag attire—independent thought not required." Take Edward Burns, who saw his independent film *The Brothers McMullen* (1995) as a calling card in trying to secure a studio deal. The problem was that he kept making the same movie. There was a similar trap for actors. "It got contaminated," says Lili Taylor. "Scoring an independent became a means to get a big Hollywood movie. All of a sudden it was cool for a star to do an independent movie, and you could get more work from it. The financiers were thrilled because then they could sell their movies.

That made it harder for some of the ones like me, who weren't the financiers' first choice."

Now the independent producers wanted *Pulp Fiction*'s stars. Gus Van Sant had a remarkable cast of non-professionals for his first feature, the independent *Mala Noche*, but found that unacceptable when he moved to studio-backed projects. "For the executives and the producers it's like: 'Why wouldn't you use a big-name actor? They're going to be doing it for scale. You're getting something for nothing.'" The emphasis on stars signaled a fundamental turn from the naturalistic acting of the method and the French New Wave that had helped to establish the tone of independent film. "I think one of the things that really distinguishes the early years was that big stars weren't interested in being in independent films," says Mary Harron. "There were no well-known independent film stars in *Stranger Than Paradise*. They might have had cultie people, but they weren't movie stars. Once big stars wanted to be in independent film, there was a huge pressure to get them."

When Harron made *I Shot Andy Warhol* (1996), she was excited to land Lili Taylor. "In indie film, she was a big thing," says Harron. "She had a reputation, and we felt very lucky to get her." When Harron read the SCUM (Society for Cutting Up Men) Manifesto by Valerie Solanas, known for her attempted assassination of Andy Warhol, she knew she'd found her first feature. The film revisited Warhol and the prolific bohemians of his Factory, and Taylor's unvarnished Valerie Solanas is the performance of a lifetime.

Harron took a roundabout route—through print and broadcasting—to get to filmmaking. In 1975, she was an aspiring journalist from Canada, working at the Manhattan film cooperative founded by Toronto filmmaker David Secter, when she landed face first in the brand-new New York punk scene. She wrote a piece on the Ramones for the first issue of *Punk* magazine and soon moved on to London as its punk scene was emerging. "I had always been attracted to the underground. I didn't see it so much as the rock 'n' roll thing. This is what people in Paris were doing in the 1920s and '30s. This is what I have been looking for my whole life—this art underground. I wasn't really a music person; I just fell into it because that is where exciting things were happening. Culturally it was interesting to me. I wanted to be a filmmaker."

By the time Harron started her second feature, *American Psycho* (2000), she found that the casting process had changed. "The pressure of casting was 100 times worse than it had been on my first film. It was a different world in which you are pressured to get stars in every

*Lili Taylor as Valerie Solanas in* I Shot Andy Warhol. © *Samuel Goldwyn / Orion Pictures / Photofest.*

single role, even small ones. I think this is what has probably damaged independent film more than anything else." The novel on which it was based, by Bret Easton Ellis, was filled with enough sexuality and graphic violence to leave many wondering how anyone would be able to film it, so there was already considerable controversy around the project when Harron insisted on casting then little-known Christian Bale in the lead role. "I had a huge battle over Christian," she says. "I got Lions Gate to agree to let me cast Christian even though he wasn't famous enough. I could cast him if I got bigger names in the film." Harron had Reese Witherspoon as well, but at the time she wasn't famous enough to satisfy Lions Gate's taste for stars. "I was trying to cast Wynona Ryder—'If you cast Wynona Ryder, then you can cast Christian.'"

Meanwhile, Leonardo DiCaprio read the script and wanted to do it. Harron opposed Lions Gate's decision to offer him the movie, saying she would walk off the film if Bale was fired. Lions Gate arranged for her to meet with DiCaprio. "I said I wouldn't, so they fired me off the movie. Everyone in Hollywood thought I was out of my mind for not embracing a huge star." DiCaprio is no less of an actor than Bale, but sometimes a director is convinced someone is perfect for a role. Harron was positive that Bale was the one for *American Psycho,* and so it became a battle over who decides casting—the filmmaker or the film financier. "I felt like the tone of the film was so delicate between what was offensive, what was satirical, and what was scary. If you got it wrong, it would just be a horrible mess." While production stalled on *American Psycho*, DiCaprio decided to take another film, *The Beach* (2000). "They called me and said it wasn't going to work with DiCaprio and [her replacement] Oliver Stone, and I could have the movie back, but I wasn't allowed to cast Christian." Harron prevailed and Bale played the lead.

‡

While "independent" became a marketing brand with an emphasis on stars to feed an increasingly celebrity-obsessed culture, DIY filmmaking would not be put back in the bottle. Charles Burnett, Jim Jarmusch, Tom DiCillo, and Henry Jaglom weren't about to change, and in the '90s they were joined by directors such as Julie Dash, Jim McKay, Hal Hartley, Sarah Jacobson, Alexandre Rockwell, Larry Clark, Vincent Gallo, and Harmony Korine.

Burnett's *To Sleep With Anger* (1990) is about the southern black diaspora to cities in the north and west. The impact of this "wave of movements"—virtually an immigration and assimilation within one country—is captured by Burnett, whose own family moved from Mississippi to L.A. after World War II. "When I grew up in L.A., everyone was from the South. It was a rarity when you found a black person who'd been born in Los Angeles." Danny Glover delivers a searing performance as the manipulator from back home who shows up in L.A. one day and disrupts the new world his old neighbors have carefully constructed. Burnett fought to keep his story intact. "I think you have only a moment to do what you can do, and express the things that only you have, that are uniquely yours," he says. "The problem with this is that it's a money proposition, so there's a lot of concern about how far you can go. When I first tried to do *To Sleep With Anger*, one of the people I initially approached for funding said, 'We're not interested in the folklore stuff. Just do the story about the black middle-class couple and the young couple.' But the story is about this cultural clash and all these other elements. They wanted to cut all of that out, so what I was left with was just another television drama about a family interested in materialistic things. There's nothing unique about that. That's the way the fight went."

Tom DiCillo's *Living in Oblivion* is one of the great movies about the movies, hilariously capturing the chaos of a low-budget shoot. Nick

(Steve Buscemi) is a put-upon Fellini wannabe meeting the demands of post-*Pulp Fiction* filmmaking by casting a movie star (James LeGros). But the star is only slumming in an independent because he thinks Nick is friends with Tarantino. "We were literally in a warehouse down on 42nd Street that no longer exists and shot the whole movie there," says DiCillo. "It started out with $35,000. My wife's cousin inherited some money—she plays the script girl—and she asked, 'Can we invest in your film?' I went, 'Yes, you can.'"

In preparation for Jim McKay's *Girls Town* (1996), about working-class high-school friends coping after one in their circle commits suicide, Lili Taylor did improv for a year. "Jim modeled it on the Mike Leigh model. We came up with a script that we loved, and we had no money. Shot it in fourteen days, on the fly. Everybody was there because they believed in Jim's vision. I love the collaborating and the pure creative desire—when somebody's got that idea or vision and wants to do it."

No one represented the resistance to the corporate takeover of "independent" any more than San Francisco's Sarah Jacobson. "Lately in the mainstream media, there has been lots of excitement over 'indie' films," she wrote in 1997. "But that excitement has turned into Indiewood with its own set of bullshit rules and limits. Not only do those pressures inhibit creativity, it's not what I want as a filmmaker."[2] Jacobson's first feature, *I Was a Teenage Serial Killer* (1993), is about a woman who kills sexist men. Jello Biafra appeared in her second, *Mary Jane's Not a Virgin Anymore* (1998). "It's about the best coming-of-age film for women I've ever seen," he says. "You know, none of the *Hollywood 90210*-cast-the-pretty-girls-and-have-a-little-bit-of-anguish type crap at all. This one is painfully real and shot mostly with people who were not trained actors, and she toured the film just like a punk rock band would tour, contacting the same kind of below-ground venues and just driving around with her mother in a station wagon to show the film. Unfortunately, she died of cancer before she could make another film." *Mary Jane's Not a Virgin Anymore*, which explores a young woman's (Lisa Gerstein) awakening on innumerable levels following her first sexual experience, was a festival favorite and cemented Jacobson's reputation as a pure practitioner of DIY. Biafra recalls, "She just said, 'Okay, if you improvise your lines, she'll do the same and we'll just see what happens.'"

Alexandre Rockwell's *In the Soup* (1992) is a low-budget look at the passions unleashed by filmmaking when a novice screenwriter joins forces with the minor mobster who's funding his film. When Rockwell took Sundance's grand jury prize, Hollywood came calling. "We were staying at this hotel, and morning after morning, hot chocolate chip cookies would arrive from one agency or the other trying to woo him," says its co-star Jennifer Beals, who was married to Rockwell. Among the offerings: future Oscar winner *As Good As It Gets* (1997). "He read it and said, 'I don't believe Jack Nicholson as this character.' And he turned the movie down." Beals was making independent choices long before Rockwell introduced her to the New York scene. Just out of high school in Chicago, she landed the lead in *Flashdance*, the dancing-will-set-you-free picture that became a cultural phenom in 1983. Many actors would have succumbed to the industry pressure to head for Hollywood, but Beals opted to study literature at Yale University. After graduating, she joined Rockwell in New York. The *In the Soup* shoot began unexpectedly. "We weren't supposed to start shooting for a couple months," says Beals, "then all of a sudden it started snowing in New York, and the snow was so beautiful that he just grabbed a camera and said, 'C'mon, we're going to go up to the roof and shoot a scene.' So we went up. It's exciting to be a part of something that's so alive and so organic."

There was an ample supply of talented New York actors in the 1990s who, like Beals, were excited about independent work, including Lili Taylor, Adrienne Shelley, and Steve Buscemi. "The moment I saw Steve, I said, 'I want to work with that guy,'" says DiCillo. "He was doing these bizarre plays in bars and clubs down in the Lower East Side. There was a community of people doing odd things. It was a great pool to choose from."

Lili Taylor grew up in Chicago suburbia and, after roles in *Mystic Pizza* (1988) and *Say Anything* (1989), settled in New York just in time to be "nicely rewarded with the great independent scene in the '90s." She became an independent headliner with an engaging everywoman presence that couldn't help but light up a screen. Besides *Girls Town*, *Dogfight,* and *I Shot Andy Warhol*, there were roles in Savoca's *House-hold Saints* (1993), Robert Altman's *Shortcuts* (1993) and *Prêt-à-Porter* (1994), Alan Rudolph's *Mrs. Parker and the Vicious Circle* (1994), John Water's *Pecker* (1998), and the collective (Rockwell, Tarantino, Allison Anders, Robert Rodriguez) *Four Rooms* (1995). Taylor recalls that it was "any means necessary" on independent productions such as Abel Ferrara's *The Addiction* (1995). "We had a camera hidden in the van to get around permits—did night shooting, stealing shots, incorporating New Yorkers into the scenes because you can't control the crowds. We did all that great stuff."

‡

Julie Dash's strikingly original *Daughters of the Dust* premiered at Sundance in 1991. "What I'm still pushing for is authentic African-American films," says Dash, "and that's why I dared to do *Daughters of the Dust*. I don't want to see stories that have nothing to do specifically with our culture but just have black people in them."

Dash grew up in housing projects watching foreign films such as Satyajit Sanjit Ray's *Apu Trilogy*, *The Battle of Algiers* (1966), *A Man and a Woman* (1966), and *Battleship Potemkin* (1925). The screenings were part of the Cinematography Workshop at the Studio Museum of Harlem. "The Workshop began as a result of the riots in Harlem in 1964," says Dash.

> The first subtitled film I saw was either *Potemkin* or *Jules and Jim*. I enjoyed them much more than the films that were out at the time. The film experience was supposed to be that you go into a darkened room, and when you come out you know something more. You've taken a magic carpet ride. But with American studio films that's not the case; too often you know what's going to happen. When the big blockbusters started coming out, if you saw a black person in the early part of the film, you knew that black person was just there to be the first one eaten by the monster.

Besides immersing herself in film, Dash was intensely curious about the social tumult around her. "My sister and I tried to find out more about the Black Panther Party. It was the beginning of something back then—no one knew where it was going. It was also very exciting." The BPP had near-mythological status within the black community and the New Left, with other organizations adapting variations of its militancy and alternative institutions (including a breakfast program for children), its look and language and ten-point program. Dash was introduced to Panthers while attending City College of New York. "Yuri Kochiyama was a Japanese-American activist. Her daughter Aichi went to school with friends of mine and I met her. They lived in a project on 110th Street. We used to go up to Yuri's house, and there were Weather Underground people there, Black Panthers, people from the Asian resistance group I Wor Kuen. People were cooking and talking and typing pamphlets. It was an amazing time."

*Julie Dash filming* Daughters of the Dust *on South Carolina's St. Helena Island. Courtesy Julie Dash.*

She pauses. "Do you remember the Panther 21?" In 1969 twenty-one members of the New York Panthers were charged with conspiracy to commit guerrilla warfare, but acquitted in 1971 after a widely publicized political trial. While living in Harlem, Dash was part of their support network, during the trial and its aftermath. She intertwined her passions for politics and film. "There are valuable lessons about life to be learned and shared. That's pretty much been my mission as a filmmaker. I don't want to do anything that doesn't take us to another level in making the world a better place for everyone, in some small way." After graduating from CCNY with a degree in film production, Dash, who had been focused on documentary, headed for a new life on the West Coast, but her work would be deeply rooted in her past. "I came out to L.A. because I wanted to learn how to make narrative films. I got a scholarship to the American Film Institute, but I wanted to go to UCLA because I read about Haile Gerima and Charles Burnett and Larry Clark who were doing dramatic films there. It was a breath of fresh air for me to move out here." Her fellow New Yorker Spike Lee was also influential, having followed his low-budget breakout *She's Gotta Have It* with other stereotype-smashing depictions of urban blacks, from *Do the Right Thing* (1989) to *A Huey P. Newton Story* (2001). "He continues to make movies and he's an inspiration because he still has an independent voice," Dash says. "Sometimes, I just like the effort. It's like, 'You threw that ball out there—thank you.' It's for us to pick it up and continue."

First at AFI then UCLA, Dash directed shorts, including an adaptation of Alice Walker's story *Diary of an African Nun* (1977). "It took a long time to get *Daughters of the Dust* financed because people kept expecting me to do *Sounder* [1972]. I love foreign films, and so I wanted to do an African-American film that appeared to be foreign because it was so deeply into a specific culture. It wasn't the Mississippi or Alabama, Montgomery type of African-American situation. It was the Sea Islands."

The Sea Islands' Geechee Gullah culture has always been with Dash. "I knew that my father's accent was different because our friends would say so. Geechee Gullah was almost like a secret culture within a culture. We grew up in the projects, in Harlem, but our family was very different. The food we ate was different; we had fish for breakfast, we had rice every day. My friends and their families were eating French fries. I didn't want to be different." Her parents made the trip north in the post-war years, and Dash was born in New York, where her father would work as a shipping clerk, her mother a clerical supervisor at Harlem Hospital. "When I was older I looked back and saw the most wonderful things that I was embarrassed about in my youth. By the time I was in AFI, I started reading about the Gullah culture and traditions. It was really intensely African still on those islands; things were preserved in a way that they weren't in Alabama and in the north. I had secrets, you know, and then I learned to appreciate those secrets."

Dash's *Daughters of the Dust* script was translated into Gullah, which the actors learned phonetically. "I had seen other films about the region, and they were using southern accents," but she knew "it wasn't accurate." She pulled together a strong, close ensemble, well aware that they were embarking on something remarkable. "I decided to cast it with people who had supported the independent film movement for many years: Alva Rogers and Tommy Redmond Hicks were in Spike Lee's films; Barbarao had been in Larry Clark's and Haile Gerima's films; and Cora Lee Day was in Haile's, Larry's, and Charles Burnett's. You're looking at the face of black independent cinema." Having grown conscious of their roots through the upheavals of the 1960s and '70s, these actors came together in this stunning, bittersweet spot at South Carolina's St. Helena Island. "It was a very emotional time for not only the actors but the crew as well. We were venturing into new territory, and as we were making the film, people were learning about the history of the place. They were on the land where—they call it the stepping stone—our ancestors went from the slave ship into the islands. We'd usually be on the set by five a.m. and the sun would be coming up. We'd be on the beach and everyone would just kind of settle down and watch the sun rise."

*Daughters of the Dust* turns over stereotypes, including the one about black filmmakers being men addicted to violent urban movies; the film is a non-linear, female-driven story about a largely unknown culture. "Someone at Sundance said, 'Well, it looks beautiful, but people don't know what to make of it,'" says Dash. In its own sublime way, *Daughters of the Dust* was as tough as any film being made in 1991.

> Yet there's no other filmmaker that I know of who has won something at Sundance—we won best cinematography—and never been able to get another feature financed. It's gender, it's race, it's the subject matter of my films. I want to do films that say something else, that look at things with a fresh eye, that introduce new things, and that's not what the people who traditionally finance films want. They want films they recognize. A lot of people felt threatened by *Daughters of the Dust*. I had a Japanese distributor once tell me that my film was not a 'real' African-American film. And when I was making a movie for television at a studio later, they joked: 'Just don't do *Daughters of the Dust*.' So I wear the banner above my head—'Beware she.'

It took nine months after the Sundance festival, but Dash did become the first black woman to get nation-wide distribution. Picked up by Kino International, *Daughters of the Dust* had long runs in New York and other cities, largely through grass-roots organizing and word of mouth.

> I thought it would be a lot easier for me to get my ideas financed and to get into production on another feature, but that didn't happen. The mini-majors and the studios took over the whole notion of independent filmmaking and made it their own: Get a star and a low-budget waiver. But really, they were studio films; they weren't films of independent thought and voice. I took a lot of meetings to try to raise

money for another feature and when that didn't happen, I
started doing music videos, television commercials, and movies of the week. You have to work, you know, and I was able
to do *The Rosa Parks Story* (2002), *Funny Valentines* (1999),
*Incognito* (1999), and *SUBWAY Stories* (1997). I got to work.
But ...

‡

Gus Van Sant might have been a part of the 1980s New York film scene,
but early on he got hooked on Portland, Oregon, and saved enough
money to leave New York just before its independents broke out: At
the Rhode Island School of Design, he studied painting but switched
to filmmaking. After graduating, he settled in L.A., shot the shorts *The
Discipline of DE* (1978), the longer short *Alice in Hollywood* (1981), then
set his sights on his first feature, *Mala Noche*, based on an autobiographical novel by Portland beat poet Walt Curtis. He raised money
to finance the film by working at a New York advertising firm. "I really
didn't like it, so I was going to leave after a summer, but I realized that
I had saved up so much money that if I just stuck with it I could have
some money to live on. And so I kept doing that and I realized I could
save up enough money to make a film."

With $20,000 saved, *Mala Noche* was Van Sant's ticket to Portland,
where he wanted to live, drawn by its close-knit film community. Besides, he was writing a movie with no future at a Hollywood studio: a
set-in-Portland story of relationships between a gay clerk in a skid-row
store and two younger Mexican illegal workers living in a cheap hotel
facing trauma generated by sex, race, and money. "I was thinking of
making the film in New York, but I realized that the subject of *Mala
Noche* was so specifically Old Town in Portland, Oregon, that New York
City wouldn't have been fair to the story. But also I had a lot of resources in Portland, I knew a lot of filmmakers."

Its milieu and no-star cast's natural performances, shot hand-held,
give *Mala Noche* an improv feel, but the cast followed Van Sant's script.
The bare aesthetic reflected the budget. "It was very Dogme," Van Sant
says with a laugh. "Dogme is just a list of things that you can do if you
have no money. Finding locations that have all the props in them is a
way to save a lot of money."

*Mala Noche* didn't have theatrical distribution, but its raw power
had festival-goers talking and it did introduce Van Sant to the studio

system. "I showed *Mala Noche* at the Los Angeles Lesbian and Gay Film Festival," says Van Sant, "and I found an agent that same day." Then he walked into Universal Studios with *Drugstore Cowboy* (1989). "The reason I was even meeting with people like this was because my agent knew them." Universal passed on his story but by the late 1980s there were alternatives to the big studios, and Avenue Pictures signed on. "*Drugstore Cowboy* started to get interest from these companies that are now subsidiaries of major studios. Avenue Pictures was a new one, but there were companies like Cinecom and independent releasing companies that were hooked up with video releases because, all of a sudden, video was a money-maker. So Live Entertainment would buy video rights for $1 million and then these companies would sell European television for a couple million dollars, and they would put as much as $4 million into a film. This was more standardized by the time they did *Drugstore Cowboy* in '88."

*Drugstore Cowboy* follows Matt Dillon and his pharmacy-robbing band in search of drugs in the Pacific Northwest of the early 1970s. Its box office generated interest for *My Own Private Idaho* (1991), a hybrid of Shakespeare's *Henry IV* and contemporary gay street life. While *Mala Noche* pre-dated the gay film wave of the 1990s, *Private Idaho* was in the thick of it. In the early '90s, the gay movement was dealing with AIDS and ongoing confrontations with the religious right. So it's no surprise that its long-festering cultural politics would explode in a New Queer Cinema, which included Derek Jarman (*Edward II*, 1991), Todd Haynes (*Poison*, 1991), and Rose Troche (*Go Fish*, 1994). Gregg Araki, as defiantly left-wing as any of the emerging gay filmmakers, kept his budgets bare and his characters tossing verbal Molotovs at "Republican fuckheads." In Araki's *The Living End* (1992), an intellectual finds he has AIDS and hits the road with a violence-prone drifter, doing things he'd never have done before.

As the '90s wore on, Van Sant promised himself he would find a way back to the pure independence of the *Mala Noche* shoot. Although *My Own Private Idaho* and *Drugstore Cowboy* were widely regarded as independents, to Van Sant every project he touched after *Mala Noche* was a studio movie, including *Cowboy*, *Private Idaho*, *To Die For* (1995), *Good Will Hunting* (1997), *Psycho* (1998), and *Finding Forrester* (2000). "The [producers at the] smaller companies had learned their craft at the studios," he says, "so they would influence whatever I was doing.

I was going along with it, but in the end I realized, 'Oh, the reason that we made this decision was because the producer or the executive producer or the studio head was a little bit nervous about the riskier, more exciting decision.' I eventually got used to this and I started to do the same thing.

There was an expected style in making a movie, like a template, and to deviate from it was highly suspect. That kind of sensibility was boring after a while. Whoever has the most credits always gets the job, no matter what—if it's the sound man or if it's the DP [director of photography]. Yet the guy who's never acted before may be the most exciting choice. You always made these a little more safe decisions because money was riding on it. I got tired of it.

As digital evolved, Van Sant contemplated a return to the creative autonomy that comes with no-budget filmmaking. "Before *Drugstore Cowboy*, I had never done a movie that I hadn't designed myself, like *Mala Noche* and *Alice in Hollywood*." In those early films, "there wasn't any money, so you could have just the sound man, the DP, one assistant, the actors, and me. You could all fit in a station wagon, pretty much. It's more fun when you have a smaller group."

‡

By the 1990s, the Motion Picture Association of America president Jack Valenti was the roaming ambassador for Studio Nation. Early in his administration, Valenti said: "To my knowledge, the motion picture is the only US enterprise that negotiates on its own with foreign governments,"[3] later adding: "I am really a small State Department."[4] As the audience for blockbusters spread, so did the studios' hold on the world's screens, the MPAA staving off quotas and other such irritants wherever they might arise, and bouncing local films from Seoul to Toronto to make way for their product. "[The studios] are huge, vertically integrated companies, public companies, whose main financial audience is Wall Street," noted former Writers Guild of America spokesman Michael Seel. "And what Wall Street likes, even more than five or ten percent more profit, is predictability of profit."[5] So if *Spider-Man* draws crowds, there will predictably be a *Spider-Man II* and *XXII*. While the studios dabbled in specialty divisions, their breadwinner remained the blockbuster, their audience so global now that any language was too local. The studios began to utilize the new image-generating technology to invent an unspoken language of explosions and crashes aimed at young males the world over.

At the beginning of the twenty-first century, the studio system and its power appeared more daunting than ever, its victory over local and international opponents seemingly complete. Valenti, Inc. had absorbed entertainment rivals (television, music), sent ideological rivals into exile (the Hollywood left, the New Hollywood), outsourced production to the lowest bidders, dominated the world's screens with its blockbusters and, for good measure, corporatized American independent film. How do you throw a picket line around Warner Bros. when it's just one piece of an omnipresent conglomerate that's everywhere? The original studios were buried inside an array of corporate tentacles. Twentieth Century Fox, for instance, shared its owner, the News Corporation, with such unappetizing enterprises as the UK's News of the World and the US's Fox News.

*Barbarao as Yellow Mary in* Daughters of the Dust. *Courtesy Julie Dash.*

*Daughters of the Dust* is a startlingly good movie. It's a moving look at generational change, set at the last gathering of a Gullah family before some members leave the island. It is lush in every way, from the beauty of its scenery to the depth of its connection to Gullah culture. Julie Dash and cinematographer Arthur Jafa studied the photographs of James Van Der Zee and other early chroniclers of black America, and the result is dazzling. "It's almost like you're turning a page in a scrap book, like people caught frozen in tableau," Dash says. "That was the thing I wanted to do, so it's branded into your brain." *Daughters of the Dust* is an overwhelmingly local story that can touch anyone anywhere for the timeless reasons that make the movies great.

At the beginning of the twenty-first century, there were new challenges to studio power. Some of them would come from digital technology. Some would be as old as the movies themselves—an enduring resistance handed down from Charles Chaplin and Orson Welles, John Garfield and Sylvia Sydney, James Dean and Stewart Stern, through John Cassavetes and Lelia Goldoni, Julie Dash, Jim Jarmusch, and Sarah Jacobson. It's a cinematic resistance that rises up when least expected.

In 1999, it was Norma Barzman's turn. That year the Academy of Motion Picture Arts and Sciences decided to give Elia Kazan a lifetime-achievement Oscar. "When I heard that Kazan was getting an Oscar, the first thing I did was go to the Academy, of which I am a member, and said, 'I don't think you should do this. Really, there will be a great outcry. He's got two Oscars for his work, and we'd be glad to see him get more for his work, but lifetime achievement—what is his lifetime achievement? The destruction of twenty-three of his best friends, the destruction of lives.' And they said, 'We're sorry, it's too late.'"

Norma knew she had to act for the many no longer around to do it. Her husband Ben had died in 1989. "I called [screenwriter] Bernie Gordon and a couple of other people and we all said, 'We've got to do something.' The plan was for every limousine heading to the big show to have a *Hollywood Reporter* or *Variety* magazine with a full-page ad urging: 'Don't applaud. Sit on your hands' when Kazan got his award. I must have called 4,000 people. But I raised the money for the ad. Every limo going to the Oscars did have the full-page ad in it."

The week before the Oscars, the Writers Guild called a press conference to announce it was retroactively giving credit to uncredited
blacklisted writers, including Ben and Norma. Warren Beatty, who had
gotten his screen start in Kazan's *Splendor in the Grass* (1961) and went
on to make *Reds* (1981), supported the honorary Oscar for the director.
Beatty approached Norma at the press conference. "I didn't know him.
He put his arms around me, kissed and hugged me, and whispered,
'I'm nothing if it weren't for him. I hate doing this, but I'm forced to.
I wouldn't be Warren Beatty, I wouldn't be in California, I wouldn't be
an actor, I wouldn't be anything. Forgive me.'" Norma, maybe for the
first time in her life, was speechless. "I was in shock. I couldn't think
of anything to say. And then the press started hurling questions at him
and at me, and that was it."

On Oscar night, Norma's friend Sophia Loren went to the show.
"From where she sat, she looked around and saw that seven-eighths
of the Academy did not stand for Kazan." Among those who remained
seated were Tom Hanks, Steven Spielberg, Ed Harris, Nick Nolte, Richard Dreyfuss, and producers Sherry Lansing and David Geffen.

Norma had been moved to action on behalf of dear friends such as
Morris Carnovsky and Phoebe Brand, whose Hollywood acting careers
had ended with the blacklist. "They were my Group Theatre idols from
when I was in high school. I later met them and loved them. So they
were my friends. People shouldn't forget. It shouldn't be just sloughed
off. Too many of us had suffered ... that's all."

# PART II

*And Why Are They So Good?*
*The Rise of Independent Film*

## CHAPTER NINE

## *France: The Impossible Is Realistic*

Aaron Barzman jumped on to the hood of a parked car. "Langlois," he shouted. "Langlois, Langlois!"

Along with several hundred other protestors, the young cinephile had taken to the streets in February 1968 when the French government fired La Cinémathèque Française's Henri Langlois. His screenings of European cinema and Hollywood classics had made the Cinémathèque a nurturing home to the founders of the New Wave. In response to his firing, letters poured in from Hitchcock, Kurosawa, Chaplin, and Fellini, and in Paris, the New Wave and its partisans—*les enfants de la cinémathèque* (Children of the Cinematheque)—staged demonstrations.

"I was outraged," Barzman says. "The Cinémathèque was Langlois and Langlois was the Cinémathèque. I saw everything there; American musical comedies, Russian films, English Free Cinema films. We went all the time." The French do two things better than anyone else—films and riots—and it was New Wave meets New Left at the protest outside the Cinémathèque. Jean-Luc Godard and François Truffaut were there, as were Daniel Cohn-Bendit, Claude Chabrol, and Jacques Rivette as well as Catherine Deneuve, Jean-Pierre Leaud, and Jean-Paul Belmondo. "It was just filmmakers who called for it, so they thought there would be thirty people," says Barzman. "Directors came first, but then other people started coming. When the cops tried to break it up, people held their ground. The cops started clubbing people. Truffaut was hurt. At the time, it seemed outrageous because they clubbed directors, but it was a very mild riot next to what came after that."

Future filmmaker Claire Denis was at protest after protest as the revolutionary fervor swept France that spring. "I was living on the Left Bank, and we were going every day, every night. It was the most important thing to do; there was nothing else to do." What started with a small protest outside a movie theater would, as other issues piled on, explode into a historic uprising—the May-June events of 1968. Everyone in France would be touched by the rebellion and general strike, with masses of students and workers occupying and collectivizing schools and factories, and building barricades across the country.

For Denis, a twenty-year-old student, it was a time for euphoria and coming to terms with her own uncertainty. "I was at all the protests,"

she says, "but I came from a different world." She grew up in French colonial Africa, where her father was a civil servant. "I carried in me a sort
of rage already about injustice. I felt a little bit ashamed—something
you might understand if you've read Doris Lessing. When she came
[to the UK] from South Africa, she had the guiltiness of growing up as
a white girl in an African country. The way she wanted to be a communist, I also wanted to be a communist. I felt insecure, but I wanted
to go as far as I could."

Like many of the protestors, Denis was a budding cinephile in the
1960s when innovative filmmaking seemed the norm in Paris. "Each
time I'm asked if I was inspired by the French New Wave I think I have
to say no; when I was twenty, the French New Wave seemed normal
to me. It was only ten years later that I realized that a movement like
that was not so normal—the collision of those personalities and that
moment in the century."

‡

In 1956 a young Parisian, Jacques Rivette, borrowed a camera to shoot
a short called *Le coup du berger* (*Fool's Mate*, 1956). Filmed mostly in
Rivette's apartment, with a minuscule budget, it was written by his
friend Claude Chabrol and features, as actors, Jean-Luc Godard and
François Truffaut. While the film is unremarkable, the group Rivette
assembled wasn't. They would continue making films on a shoestring
and soon change the face of cinema—and not just in France. Their New
Wave, the *Nouvelle Vague,* played a defining role in what would become
known as independent film.

Paris had been the first city to publicly screen a movie—the Lumière
brothers' *La sortie des usines Lumière a Lyon* (*Employees Leaving the Lumière Factory*) was shown on December 28, 1895. By 1910 French studios produced two-thirds of the world's movies.[1] American studio power was on the rise, however, particularly after it won the race to sound.
France established a quota system (one in eight films screened had to be
French), and local movies drew audiences—including Abel Gance's *Na-
poléon* (1927), René Clair's *Sous les toits de Paris* (*Under the Roofs of Paris*,
1930), Jean Vigo's *Zero de conduite* (*Zero for Conduct*, 1933), and Jean
Renoir's *La grande illusion* (1937). Still, the French studios Pathé and
Gaumont were slow to invest in sound and, hit hard by the Depression,
declared bankruptcy. During World War II, the occupying Germans established a studio in Paris, and while some French nationals worked

there, many of France's finest, including Renoir, Clair, Max Ophüls, and Jean Gabin joined other Europeans in exile in Hollywood. In the post-war years, the French studios unleashed the "cinema of quality"— big-budget pictures drawn from literature, shot in studio, and utilizing costumed, plummy movie stars—such as Marcel Carné's *Juliette ou La clef des songes* (*Juliette, or Key of Dreams,* 1951).

Meanwhile, a new sensibility was emerging among young film-lovers. It was articulated by François Truffaut in a 1954 article—"Une certaine tendance du cinéma français" (A Certain Tendency in French Cinema)—in the magazine *Cahiers du Cinéma.* Truffaut vowed "no possible coexistence" with the French film establishment.[2] He challenged the artifice of the country's better-known filmmakers, contrasting their big-budget theatricality with films by auteurs—the authors of their movies no less than novelists were authors of their books. There had been earlier advocates of the auteur idea, including writer André Bazin, but Truffaut's article became a virtual manifesto for the French New Wave, reflecting the sentiments of fellow *Cahiers du Cinema* writers Jean-Luc Godard, Claude Chabrol, Eric Rohmer, and Jacques Rivette. As these friends became filmmakers, they would collaborate and be joined in the New Wave by others such as Alain Resnais, Agnès Varda, Chris Marker, and Jacques Demy. By *Cahiers du Cinema*'s count, 162 first-time feature filmmakers made their debuts between 1958 and 1962.[3]

The auteur theory would have been nothing more than a fine idea had the New Wave not been able to back it up with fearless innovation and talent. It went public with Chabrol's *Le beau serge* (*Bitter Reunion*) in 1958, followed at the 1959 Cannes Film Festival by Truffaut's *Les quatre cents coups* (*The 400 Blows*), Resnais' *Hiroshima mon amour,* and Marcel Camus' *Orfeu negro* (*Black Orpheus*) and, a year later, Godard's *À bout de souffle* (*Breathless*). Their simultaneous arrival created an international sensation. Something breathtaking had arisen in Paris. New Wave films often cast Paris as a character, as its naturally lit streets and cafés proved irresistible movie locations. In Truffaut's *The 400 Blows,* the cramped living quarters meant repression, while the endless streets of Paris meant freedom. It is the Dead End Kids, French-style, with Truffaut's cinephilia all over the picture, borrowing from *Zero for Conduct* and *Little Fugitive.* The New Wave was influenced by American noir and Howard Hawks, Italian neorealism, and Alfred Hitchcock. Godard's *Une femme est une femme* (*A Woman Is a Woman,* 1961) is a homage to the movies, including his own *Breathless.* In *Breathless* the characters played by Belmondo and Jean Seberg, while contemplating lives of crime and

*Parisian streets were irresistible movie locations in New Wave films such as* Breathless *with Jean-Paul Belmondo and Jean Seberg. © Films Around the World / Photofest.*

games of desire, take time out to consider Bogart, gender issues, and existential dilemmas as they talk and walk the city.

Early New Wave features shared some stylings—jump cuts, long tracking shots, and hand-held mobile cameras shooting on location in one take—with stories that were at once cool and poignant, cerebral and street-smart, realistic and existential, documentary and narrative, cynical and idealistic. In rejecting the theatrics of the cinema of quality, the New Wave allowed for the acting eccentricities of Jean-Pierre Leaud and others and, along with New York's method scene, popularized a new naturalism that would pave the way for generations of actors, creating such unconventional stars as Jeanne Moreau, Jean-Paul Belmondo, and Anna Karina, who were infused with the sensibility and sensuality of youth breaking free from a cultural straightjacket.

Shedding shackles sometimes meant finding ways to avoid the film school, L'Institut des hautes études cinématographiques (IDHEC), or the control of the Centre national du cinéma (CNC), overseer to a labyrinthine system of obtaining a director's card. "If you don't accept this system," explains François Truffaut's daughter Eva, "you can be totally independent, just like my father, and be somebody who never went to school, never had this card, never was an assistant to anyone, but does a movie." Chabrol summarized the New Wave attitude: "Everything you need to know to direct any movie can be learned in four hours."[4]

Although the New Wave was of its time, expressing the same hipness as John Cassavetes' *Shadows* or Milos Forman's *Loves of a Blonde* (1965), the excited international response to its movies was entirely unexpected. "In 1959, we were living a dream," said François Truffaut. "Everything was happening in ways that would have been inconceivable two years earlier."[5]

‡

The revolt of 1968 caught Aaron Barzman by surprise. "One year before, I had been part of this little group. We thought we were a fringe of a fringe of a fringe. We talked about revolution. And then one year later we're in the middle of this."

While the New Wave filmmakers were getting to know each other in the 1950s, it was an unsettling time in Paris for Barzman, who'd been born in France in 1949, the son of recent arrivals Norma and Ben Barzman. "One day Luli, my older sister, asked my parents, 'Why are we living here in France? We're American—you're American.' I was very young, but I can remember them saying, 'The day has come and we must tell you what happened.' They told us about the blacklist. That was a big revelation."

In 1959, the family moved to London, where Ben worked with Joseph Losey on the thriller *Blind Date* (1959). "They didn't have much money in the '50s," Aaron says. "So we had to move to England because there my father could find work. The big break was in 1961 with *El Cid*." The family bought a home in Mougins, near Cannes, in 1963, and Aaron, who wanted to be a filmmaker, would take the eight-millimeter camera that his parents gave him into the streets to shoot. "My dad was interviewed by some French movie journals. That's how I started looking at *La Revue, Positif, Cahiers du Cinema*. I devoured them." Aaron rebelled against the quiet way his parents went about their politics. "They said, 'Hush, hush, we'll get thrown out of the country.' I was, 'Fuck it, I'm French. I can do whatever I want.' I withdrew from being a documentary filmmaker. I was so overwhelmed by the Vietnam War. I joined youth groups. At the beginning, it was a communist youth group, but it became Trotskyist, Guevarist, and surrealist." When he arrived in Paris in 1967 to study history, Barzman was told his address meant he would have to attend suburban Nanterre University. "And Nanterre was where the whole student thing started."

‡

On her childhood visits to France, Claire Denis sensed that the world she knew in Ivory Coast and Cameroon was unimaginable to her Parisian cousins. But when she was nine, she saw, in a Paris theater, what film could be: Satyajit Ray's *Apur Sansar* (1959), about a Bengali boy's coming of age. "I was terribly moved. I felt something. I knew I existed—that the world was larger than my own world. A little Indian boy was just like me."

Denis was fourteen in 1962 when her family moved back to France, and she became a dedicated movie-goer. "I didn't fall in love with Godard; I was irradiated by his films." She married at eighteen and lived in suburbia, loving film but not contemplating work in it, when her then-husband mentioned an upcoming entrance exam for the IDHEC. "After the exam, I came home. The summer went by, then I moved, and one day a letter came from the school. 'Where are you? You are in, but we have lost you.' I was so surprised."

Like Aaron Barzman, Denis was drawn to the new youth culture taking hold in France. "It was most important for me—the political aspect of hippie culture." In the wake of 1968, the situationist movement, which helped set the imaginative tone of the revolt, was active at IDHEC. "Our two years in school was a giant happening with situationists." After graduating in 1972, she became Jacques Rivette's assistant. "Little by little I entered the world of filmmaking through very independent films by Jacques." She would go on to be assistant to some of the more doggedly independent filmmakers, including Wim Wenders and Jim Jarmusch. Wenders encouraged her to be a filmmaker, and while traveling across the US during the filming of his *Paris, Texas* (1984), she was overwhelmed by memories of her childhood in Africa. "I knew I had to make *Chocolat*."

*Chocolat* (1988) is a powerful, poignant look at a white family from France in French-colonial Cameroon in the 1950s. "It is very autobiographical, but it is my analysis of memories. My mother was not exactly like that, my father was not exactly like that, and I had a brother and a sister." Funding does not come easy for independent cinema anywhere, but Denis was able to tap into the CNC's support system. Since the 1940s, the CNC has banked eleven percent of each movie ticket sold to fund features. Later it introduced the *avance sur recettes*, cash advances that needed to be paid back only if the films made a profit. Says Denis, "In the world of today, it's more difficult to convince people who make laws that cinema is important for a country—to have an image of your own world, of your own cities."

‡

Aaron Barzman stops by a courtyard at the Sorbonne. "I attended meetings here, and we occupied it." On this brisk walking tour of sites related to the May '68 events, Barzman explains that he barely had time to register for classes at Nanterre before joining a student occupation there too. "I was part of the March 22nd Movement, which was a student coalition of all the groups—the situationists, the anarchists like Daniel Cohn-Bendit, the Trotskyists like Daniel Bensaïd and me. We knew about Berkeley—the sit-ins—and we did that in Nanterre." After weeks of student empowerment, authorities closed the university, and the Nanterre movement took its protest to the Sorbonne. "And then it's Paris, May '68."

The wide street where Rue Gay-Lussac meets Luxembourg Gardens is now lined with pricy cafés and shops, but it's also where the "Night of the Barricades" played out after the Sorbonne rector ordered the university closed. "We settled here and gave them an ultimatum: Re-open the Sorbonne or we will not move. There was no answer, so people built barricades. The police attacked around two in the morning. You will notice now there are no cobblestones. After 1968, they covered it up with pavement. Like wild fire, it became a general strike." While the protests at the Cinémathéque and Nanterre were the precursors to May '68, this revolution wasn't about Langlois or student power or Vietnam or workers' self-management—it was about everything and crossed every line. Having experienced the relative affluence of the post-war years, its participants weren't satisfied with the bread-and-butter economistic demands of earlier revolutions. They disdained the capitalism of the West and the Stalinism of the East, and challenged every repressive relationship, from the workroom to the bedroom to the barricades. The writing was on the walls—"It is forbidden to forbid," "Be realistic, demand the impossible," "Power to the Imagination." On a banner outside the football association building: "Football belongs to the people."[6]

Says Barzman: "It was mind-boggling, actually. There was a moment of suspended time here in '68. I don't how long it was—a week or maybe two weeks or four days. Time had stopped. The whole country was on strike. The government wasn't able to control things anymore. People and time weren't structured by work or studying; it was just open. We didn't know what was going to happen. You approached people in the street and just started talking, exchanging." His sister Luli and brother John were also involved, but it wasn't for the young only. When Norma and Ben saw the French Communist Party opposing this bottom-up revolution they supported, it confirmed their growing disillusionment with Old Left ideology, although they remained socialists. "It shook them up. Something incredible happened and they were part of it—voilà—'68 reconnected them with politics."

The New Wave filmmakers were never more unified than in 1968 when Truffaut and Godard took the stage at Cannes and called for the festival to be shut down in support of the May-June rebellion. Godard, angry at someone who wanted Cannes to go on, snapped: "We're talking solidarity with students and workers, and you're talking dolly shots and close-ups."[7] The political stance of the New Wave filmmakers was far from uniform. While Truffaut had never been as directly political as Godard, he had supported the left more often than not. ("For years the right had told us: it is us or chaos. I always thought chaos would be preferable," he later said.[8]) After the revolt, Godard increasingly turned to non-narrative filmmaking and revolutionary politics, distancing himself from others in the New Wave. Taking a collective approach, he co-created the left-wing Dziga Vertov filmmaking group, directing *Tout va bien* (*All Is Well*, 1972) with Yves Montand and Jane Fonda. Asked in July 1969 about his relationship with other New Wave filmmakers, Godard said: "No, we don't see each other much anymore. They're going in their direction, I'm following ... my path. My road. I wouldn't say avant-garde, who is ahead and behind, just different direction. There's nothing in common."[9]

The revolt ended when the government called for new elections. As the first general strike in an advanced capitalist country, it showed what could be, and it became the touchstone for future generations of rebels. "Many people who lived through that had trouble adapting afterward," says Barzman. "They had a taste of honey, a taste of this incredible atmosphere. This was not happening just in a commune; it was the whole fucking country that had this taste that social relations can be different." What happens to an individual after experiencing such a thing?

‡

What happens to filmmaking after experiencing the French New Wave?

Every few years, some headline anoints a new New Wave, imagining something will restore Truffaut's magic touch in French cinema.[10] The initial phase of the French New Wave, so fresh and raw, didn't survive its formative years, but the individual filmmakers continued to make films. And French independent film didn't stop with the New Wave filmmakers. While some later French directors made a point of distancing themselves from the New Wave, its auteur stance also inspired innumerable others and became the way of going about filmmaking for many.

Maurice Pialat tossed his script away part-way through shooting *A nos amours* (*To Our Love*, 1983) and the result was an independent classic—with Sandrine Bonnaire in a stunning debut, dealing with painfully real family dysfunction, repressed sex, and not-so-repressed sex. Other post-Wave arrivals included Claire Denis, Chantal Akerman, Bertrand Tavernier, Claude Sautet, Marie-Claude Treilhou, Paul Vecchiali, Bertrand Blier, Claude Miller, and Catherine Breillat. F.J. Ossang mixes punk rock and auteur filmmaking. "To me, poetry and music and cinema have always been intimately connected. For music, of course, the DIY is foundational. Regarding cinema, I discovered the do-it-yourself when shooting my first short." His first feature, *L'Affaire des Divisions Morituri* (*The Case of the Morituri Divisions*, 1984), focuses on a futuristic youth rebellion with a punk beat. More recent arrivals to the independent French filmmaking scene include Bruno Dumont, Jean-Pierre Jeunet, Anne Fontaine, Éric Zonca, Jacques Audiard, Julie Delpy, Eugene Green, Olivier Assayas, Mathieu Kassovitz, Arnaud Desplechin, and the filmmakers around the magazine *La lettre du cinéma*.

Eva Truffaut is active as a short-film director, producer, and actress in France's current micro-budget filmmaking scene, appearing in Pierre Léon's *L'adolescent* (2001), Jean-Paul Civeyrac's *Toutes ces belles promesses* (*All the Fine Promises*, 2003), Judith Cahen's *ADN* (2005), Vincent Dieutre's *Fragments sur la grâce* (*Fragments of Grace*, 2006), and Serge Bozon's *L'amitié* (*The Friendship*, 1998). Born into the New Wave, she appeared in her father's movies, but those didn't trigger acting aspirations. Later, however, she was drawn to independent filmmaking when she became involved with the group around *La lettre du cinéma*. "Grab a camera, get some film wherever you can, take your friends with you, and do it," she says. "I mean, it's just as simple as that."

‡

Axelle Ropert sits across from me in the noisy Sarah Bernhardt Café on a spring Paris afternoon; she is back from Cannes where she drew raves for her first feature *La Famille Wolberg* (*The Wolberg Family*, 2009), a family story revolving around a small-town mayor. It received "a good reaction to the point that I didn't expect it, the emotion invoked by the film." It's not about her family, although her mother's name was Wolberg and her grandfather was in the Polish government in exile in London during World War II.

After high school, Ropert enrolled at the Sorbonne, where her focus turned to cinema.

> Meeting two major cinephiles who were my own age really brought me into the scene. The first was Serge Bozon. We were at the same school, La Femis. The second one was Fabrice Barbaro, who was a fan of Jacques Rivette. I liked Truffaut and Rohmer. Without the New Wave, I never would have gotten into film. They inspired me—what they accomplished by cutting ties with the classic form. I discovered the idea of directing in the writings of the New Wave. It was very attractive but terrifying at the same time. What's important to me is that the New Wave is not just movie-making, but the process by which movies were criticized, something that went against the mainstream, something that criticized what is.

Like the New Wave at *La Cahiers du cinéma*, Ropert, Bozon, and other future directors—including Leon, Dieutre, Cahen, Civeyrac, Sandrine Rinaldi, and Jean-Charles Fitoussi—wrote reviews and profiles for *La lettre du cinéma*. "For me, writing and criticizing films was a better school than film school itself," says Ropert. "The films that we were able to make are less well-known than those of the New Wave. We also didn't have the will to work together, have the idea of a unified team. Pierre Leon, yes, he's a friend of mine. Serge Bozon, of course. But the group is very diverse." Still, it's the closest thing to an independent film scene in France, and the actor-directors often appear in each other's films. Ropert wrote Bozon's first three features—*The Friendship*, *Mods* (2002), and *La France* (2007)—and her own *Étoile violette* (*Purple Star*, 2005) and *The Wolberg Family*. She has also acted in several of the group's films.

Ropert is inspired by some American cinema while wary of the im-

*Filmmaker Axelle Ropert emerged from the group around* La Lettre du Cinema. *Photograph by Claire Nicol, courtesy Axelle Ropert.*

pact of studio movies on French culture and filmmaking. "The American cinema does have that tendency to be a tyrant, and one has to be careful that it doesn't eat up everyone. In France, American films are incredibly popular. I teach kids who are twenty-two, twenty-three, at a film school, and what I see is that the young generation is no longer interested in the history of French film, the French actors. I find this very upsetting and depressing."

Bozon stops by the café. He was among the first of the *La lettre* group out of the directing gate. "We worked together for more than twelve years, and now we are all trying to make movies." Then he scans the list drawn up by Eva Truffaut of this particular New Wave. "Serge, Pierre, Axelle, and Anne are all movie buffs. Vincent [Dieutre] is much more rooted in the experimental '70s video art. And Judith [Cahen] is also experimental." Their influences and styles differ; some of their films screen at museums; others, such as *La Famille Wolberg* or *La France*, received CNC funding. Their work is disparate but bound by dialogue-driven narratives and no pretense. They work mostly with no budgets, no distribution, and no audience in France, but are welcomed regulars on the festival circuit from Rotterdam to Vancouver.

When Serge Bozon was at the Vancouver International Film Festival with his World War I story, *La France*, I spoke with him. His thoughts raced from Russian film directors of the 1930s to French films of the 1950s to punk bands of the 1970s, then jumped to the new millennium. Bozon self-produced his first feature, *The Friendship*, financing it with loans, his savings, and friends' contributions. "Nobody was paid, of course. Still, I had very long debts. I like the do-it-yourself. There's a song 'The Medium Was Tedium' by the Desperate Bicycles, an English group who produced themselves, and the chorus is: 'It was easy, it was cheap, go and do it.'"

‡

May '68 was neither the first nor last time French filmmakers would turn activist. To eliminate its debt after World War II, France signed an agreement with the US to open its markets; this was especially good news for American studios with their backlog of movies produced during the war. The Committee for the Defense of the French Cinema was formed, and on January 4, 1948, thousands of people took to Parisian streets in protest. During the blacklist era, Simone Signoret and Yves Montand were denied entry to the US, having signed the 1950 Stockholm Appeal, which called for a ban on nuclear weapons. In 1959, Signoret, Truffaut, and Resnais were among the signatories of a manifesto opposing the Algerian War and calling for civil disobedience. A 1971 declaration written by Simone de Beauvoir and signed by 343 women stated they had undergone abortions and demanded free choice and access to birth control. It was signed by acclaimed director Agnès Varda and a number of French actresses, including Catherine Deneuve, Bernadette Lafont, Jeanne Moreau, Marie Pillet, Marie-France Pisier, Delphine Seyrig, and Anne Wiazemsky.

Then there was the showdown with GATT. Founded in 1947 to advance free trade between markets, in the mid-1980s the General Agreement on Tariffs and Trade finally got around to cementing an exhaustive international agreement that was to reduce barriers to the exchange of everything from toothpaste to cultural products. As the talks at GATT headquarters in Geneva approached their December 15, 1993 deadline, France was under pressure from the US and some European countries to drop its opposition to including culture. "For us, films and other cultural works are not like common goods," said France's Minister of Culture Jack Lang. "Each work is in itself rare, fragile and precious, and merits attention and protection."[11] Jean-Paul Belmondo, Gerard Depardieu, and most of their friends in the film community rallied to the cause.

Hollywood, Inc. was not amused by France's intransigence. But having watched as other European film industries shriveled, France saw that including cultural products would threaten its system of subsidies and quotas. Although France was the only film industry in Europe yet to be buried by Hollywood studio movies—the US share of European screens was eighty-one percent in 1991[12]—American culture had entered French life in a big way, from Disneyland to McDonald's to its blockbuster movies.

Jack Valenti made the GATT agreement his personal mission, vowing in a March 1993 *La Monde* interview that the US would refuse to sign an accord without culture. Finally, in December, 1993, the US government, determined to finalize the agreement and realizing that France would not buckle, signed on minus the cultural provision. The *L.A. Times* noted: "Executives differed over the financial impact of the GATT defeat—some seeing Armageddon, others only a setback for an expanding industry. But there was wide agreement that it was one of Valenti's darkest hours. The silver-maned movie lobbyist treated the trade negotiations as a personal crusade, only to be undone by the uncharmable French on the issues of quotas and subsidies."[13] The year after France's successful holdout on culture, GATT was dissolved. It was renamed and replaced by a new global body: the World Trade Organization.

‡

When *Chocolat* premiered in Cannes to standing ovations, instead of grabbing the first offer from Hollywood, Claire Denis decided to start on the documentary *Man No Run* (1989). "Just to forget that I made a film, I went back to Cameroon and I made a documentary about musicians. *Chocolat* was a big thing in America. I was offered, like, *Chocolat Two, Chocolat Three*." Denis has considered studio offers. "I always found, after a month or two of hesitation, that I was not able to do it." She was attracted to the risk, but decided that was not enough. "There is something missing inside the story. I always felt my only strength, my only independence, was to be honest with my work, to never make it more shiny or attractive than it is."

Denis' *Chocolat*, with its combustible mix of race and sex in a colonial setting, is a preview of her continuing exploration of sensuality through body movement and the experience of the outsider. Culture clash, which she first examined in *Chocolat* and continued to consider in *S'en fout la mort* (*No Fear, No Die*, 1990), has been the dominant theme in Denis' work. *No Fear, No Die* is set in a sordid cock-fighting milieu, focusing on two immigrants from France's black colonies. "I was in a restaurant in Berlin that was owned by a French guy. His cook was black. I heard the way he was talking to the guy, and I recognized the sound of that language, the sound of orders. The story [for the film] came easy; stories are all over."

Her third film, *J'ai pas sommeil* (*I Can't Sleep*, 1994), was about immigrants from Lithuania; her celebrated *Beau Travail* (1999) about Foreign Legionnaires in the Gulf of Djibouti, and for *White Material* (2009) she returned to a post-colonial Africa of child soldiers and Europeans under siege. *Vendredi soir* (*Friday Night*, 2002) was a departure for Denis; it's about characters rooted in Paris who meet randomly during a traffic jam and spend the night together. It avoids every romantic cliché. The relationship is female-initiated and the sensuality, strong as it is, is more imagined than depicted. "I felt this was the way to approach the sexuality between this man and this shy woman who doesn't know she's beautiful," says Denis.

Women filmmakers have emerged in France as in no other country. (The first female filmmaker anywhere, Alice Guy, directed more than 300 movies after debuting in 1896 with *La fée aux choux* [*The Cabbage Fairy*]). Denis says women's position is enhanced by the *avance sur recettes* process. "When I meet the producer he will think twice before saying, 'Oh no, I don't want you to direct a film,' because the story belongs to me, and I'm coming along with this amount of money that could be a third of the budget." Agnès Varda pioneered with the engaging *Cleo From 5 to 7* (1962). "I was a lone woman director in the French New Wave," says Varda. "Now there are fifty women making feature films. The evolution has been earth-shaking."[14]

Before imagining gender bias has vanished from France, however, consider Virginie Despentes' *Baise-moi* (*Fuck Me*, 2000), about two women going on a violent spree against men after one of them is raped. It was pulled from some French theaters after a right-wing group's protests. "The hostile reaction made us stronger," Despentes said.[15]

‡

If any French filmmaker embodies the May '68 graffiti "It Is Forbidden to Forbid," it is Catherine Breillat. "I think that all artists, and I consider myself an artist, always have to go past the boundaries of taboos and constantly have to expand the territory of what's available and what can be dealt with," she says. "Everything that's forbidden, everything that's taboo in a society—it's important to understand why it's a taboo. We're not supposed to examine taboos—just accept them. No one explains why there are taboos. That is really the goal of the artist. It is only they who can do this, and that's why they have always been seen as subversive and dangerous elements."

It's not surprising that Breillat's first film job was on Bernardo Bertolucci's taboo-busting *Last Tango in Paris* (1972). She began as an actress, landing a small role in the film. "I became a director because at age twelve I saw my first movie, and it was [one of Ingmar] Bergman's. I understood then that the only world I want to live in is the world which cinema invents." Her first novel, *L'Homme facile* was published when Breillat was seventeen, but was banned in France for readers under eighteen. Starting with her directorial debut, *Une vraie jeune fille* (*A Real Young Girl*, 1976)—an adaptation of her novel *Le Soupirail*, about an adolescent female's sexual awakening—Breillat's films have pushed boundaries, often with eroticism or violence or combinations of the two. Her exploration of female sexuality without exploitation riles the censors; close-ups of actress Charlotte Alexandra's vulva in *A Real Young Girl* caused the film to be banned in several countries. Breillat's anti-romantic *Romance* (1999) was banned in Australia. In *Fat Girl* (2001), Breillat captures that sudden shift from adolescent innocence to sexuality. "The whole obligation of the parent and the law is to preserve the girl from herself, and precisely by carrying out that role, they provoke the worst," says Breillat. "We're still in the nineteenth century. There's still the same puritanical hypocrisy today. Our moral values are based on success in industry and financial success, and that came with the rise to power of the bourgeoisie and rise of industrialization. There is a sense of extremism, religious stupidity, and fundamentalism that's extremely frightening. The forces of ignorance believe we were created in the manner of Walt Disney flicking his wand to suddenly create Snow White's yellow dress. So you have the rise of ignorance, the rise of hypocrisy, but we advance through knowledge."

‡

The French movie-going audience is huge and passionate; domestic box-office records were broken in 2009 and 2010, and French films regularly top the box office. The audience for local films is the largest in Europe, accounting for about forty percent of tickets sold. (The number fluctuates depending on what's showing.) Broadcasters are obliged to put ten percent of revenues into French film. More than 500 production and distribution companies are located in the Île de France. Among the twenty-first century hits in France are *Coco avant Chanel* (*Coco before Chanel*, 2009), *Entre les murs* (*The Class*, 2008), *Partir* (*Leaving*, 2009), *Un long dimanche de Fiançailles* (*A Very Long Engagement*, 2004), *La piscine* (*Swimming Pool*, 2003), *Bienvenue chez les Ch'tis* (*Welcome to the Sticks*, 2008), and *Un prophete* (*A Prophet*, 2009).

So you might think that if any country could survive the Hollywood studios' onslaught, it would be France. But France's auteurs face some of the same challenges as independents everywhere. French producers increasingly reach outside their market with English-language films such as Luc Besson's *The Transporter* (2002), Pierre Morel's *From Paris With Love* (2010), and François Ozon's *Angel* (2007), and it's not always a smooth transition. "We thought it would be easier because it's in English, but then we realized the English and Americans didn't get the film," says Ozon. "Americans first wanted to be involved in *Angel* because [Ozon's] *Swimming Pool* was successful in America. But when they read the script, they said, 'We want a happy ending, we want a big movie star, and François has to work on the script and change many things.' I realized this was not possible, so we did a co-production in Europe."

In 2010, France's film unions declared war when the conservative government wanted to divert CNC funds from ticket sales to help pay down the country's deficit. The CNC is under increasing pressure to make commercial choices. *A Very Long Engagement*, produced by Warner Bros.' French subsidiary, was approved for CNC funding (a decision later overturned in court), although the likes of Eric Rohmer and Alain Resnais were refused. Broadcasters are also focusing on mainstream, star-driven vehicles. "In France, more and more we're trying to make films that are like American films," says Breillat, "'and it's becoming more difficult for independent films to be shown on screen.

> The myth was that the rise of multiplexes and the huge number of screens was going to allow a diversity in the types of cinema that would be shown, but in fact they attract and project always the same cinema. The films open on Wednesday and by six p.m. that night they've tallied the results and made predictions about how a film's going to do. The following Monday, they're cutting back on the number of screens

certain independent films have because they haven't met box-office expectations. It makes it harder and harder for a film to reach an audience and to find its own place.

‡

The French auteurs would arouse a worldwide independent-film movement, with everyone from Mike Leigh to Nagisa Ôshima to Jim Jarmusch giving a tip of the hat to France's New Wave. Perhaps the most fitting tribute to this first of the new waves is that it was not the last, inspiring often brilliant communities of filmmakers in Britain, Czechoslovakia, Poland, America, Germany, Mexico, and Romania. The actual New Wave has been a persistent and prolific bunch: Eric Rohmer's last film was *Les Amours d'Astrée et de Céladon* (*The Romance of Astrea and Celadon*, 2007), Claude Chabrol's was *Bellamy* in 2009, and there are Jean-Luc Godard's *Socialisme* (2010), Agnès Varda's *Les plages d'Agnès* (*The Beaches of Agnès*, 2008), and Alain Resnais' *Les herbes folles* (*Wild Grass*, 2009).

Despite its woes, French cinema endures. There is an enthusiastic audience, diverse national and regional funding, and a filmmaking heritage that inspires new generations of independent-minded directors. "France is one of the best countries to make films if you're a young filmmaker," says Axelle Ropert. "You're part of this New Wave tradition that has existed. The separation between those who want to make art and those who want to make money is not as extreme as it is in North America. There's a certain amount of respect given to those who want to be an artist."

In *Wild Grass*, daily life takes on fantasy, where all expectations are off the table—the stalker becomes the stalked, passion comes out of nowhere, a little girl is a cat, grass grows through concrete—and it's all beautiful and frightening and thrilling. Years after Alain Resnais' entrancing *Hiroshima mon amour* and *L'année dernière à Marienbad* (*Last Year at Marienbad*, 1961), time for him remains a jumble, but in 2009, as in 1959 or 1968, he shows that the impossible is still realistic.

After 1968, Aaron Barzman would become involved in the Parisian counterculture for a time, then go on to write movies and television, occasionally pausing to reflect on the revolutionary days when the weight of everyday living suddenly lifted. "Oui, you felt light. There was just a moment," he says. Across town, in another café, Claire Denis recalls that, as the years passed, she would return on occasion to the movies of the New Wave. "In the '70s, when I slowly realized the world was already changing and the feast was over, I realized the *Nouvelle Vague* was a miracle. Only then."

## CHAPTER TEN

## Great Britain: The Ideological Is Personal

IN THE FINALE OF Lindsay Anderson's *if...* (1968), student rebels take to a rooftop and rain war upon every vestige of British authority. "We made it in Cheltenham, and three months later they did the same thing in Paris—for real," recalled Stephen Frears, a young assistant director on the film. Assistant editor Ian Rakoff recalls Anderson coming into the cutting room with the morning's *Daily Telegraph*, which had a photograph of helmeted French students making revolution from a rooftop, staring down all authority with a mix of disdain, determination, and idealistic certainty. "It was 8:30 in the morning," Rakoff said, "and we just looked at this ... It looked like that end shot of the film. It almost gave us the chills just to look at it."[1]

‡

A working class anti-hero *is* something to be. At least it is in British cinema. "Culturally, it's a great English tradition," Mike Leigh tells me. "You go back to Hogarth, Dickens. I've often been in France promoting films, and they say to me, 'How is it you depict working-class lives and we don't?' Of course, it's not entirely true that they don't—you can find it. But nevertheless it's just the tradition in England to look at working people." Leigh continues the tradition with richly character-driven stories such as *Life Is Sweet* (1990), *Naked* (1993), *Secrets & Lies* (1996), *Vera Drake* (2004), and *Another Year* (2010). Besides reflecting England's class-ridden society, Leigh says such films are "a reaction to the staid conventions of some movies and television dramas" and provide a "look at people who didn't otherwise have stories told about them."

Other European countries have workers' movements with roots as deep as England's, and the filmmakers of France or Italy also tend to be leftist. But in England, class—like race in America—has been the predominant conflict in public discourse. Nowhere else has it been more clearly demarcated, so it's no coincidence that England would give rise to everything from Diggers to dockers, from William Morris's *News from Nowhere* to Friedrich Engels' *The Condition of the Working Class in England in 1844*. Early films set in working-class milieus include John Grierson's *Drifters* (1929), John Baxter's *Love on the Dole* (1941) and *Let the*

173

*Malcolm McDowell (right) contemplates insurrection with David Wood (left) and Richard Warwick in* if... *© Paramount Pictures / Photofest.*

*People Sing* (1942), and Humphrey Jennings' *Fires Were Started* (1943). This class divide is reflected in firm ideological divisions, with many of the country's finest filmmakers taking an overtly left-wing stand, identifying with socialism and its variants (Marxism, anarchism, and social democracy). The blacklist, had it occurred in the UK rather than the US, would have nearly shut down the entire film industry.

The British New Wave that just preceded Leigh's arrival was a film movement steeped in class-consciousness, its material adapted from plays and novels set in the North of England and featuring pre-Beatlemania angry young men and women. "Virtually all of those films, with one famous exception, were secondary material," says Leigh, "and one of the things that I was very exercised by and excited by—and still am—was the fundamental principle of pure cinema—cinema that is original material expressed in film terms. The only film, in my view, that came out of that whole movement that was really original came after the movement was kind of over, and that was Lindsay Anderson's *if...*"

‡

*If...* was a movie exactly of its time. But its genesis took place years before when David Sherwin set out to write a script depicting the horrors of his private school experiences. Lindsay Anderson, another private school survivor, liked the concept and worked with Sherwin re-fashioning the script scene-by-scene. In early 1968, when Anderson started shooting the story of a schoolboy uprising, a series of historic uprisings were about to unfold from France to Czechoslovakia to Chicago. After taking a look at Anderson's finished product, the movie's distributor, Paramount, refused at first to release *if...*, and the British ambassador to France called it "an insult to the nation."[2] But when it was finally dropped into theaters, mainly to help fill the screen quota of the time, the public queued up. Then it won Cannes' Palme D'Or.

Anderson started out as a critic for the film magazine *Sequence*, which he co-founded in the late 1940s. "What is required," he wrote in an early piece, "is a cinema in which people can make films with as much freedom as if they were writing poems, painting pictures or composing string quartets."[3] Anderson's writings and a series of "Free Cinema" screenings—showcasing new European cinema—which he organized with filmmakers Karel Reisz, Tony Richardson, and Lorenza Mazzetti,from 1956 to 1959, were pivotal in the emergence of the British New Wave. Anderson and Mazzetti wrote the Free Cinema manifesto: "Implicit in our attitude is a belief in freedom, in the importance of people and the significance of the everyday."[4]

The Free Cinema filmmakers, having made their move from documentaries to narrative movie-making, formed the core of the British New Wave. Starting with *Room at the Top* in 1958, the wave would continue with *Look Back in Anger* (1959), *Saturday Night and Sunday Morning* (1960), *The Entertainer* (1960), *Hell is a City* (1960), *A Taste of Honey* (1961), *The Loneliness of the Long Distance Runner* (1962), *A Kind of Loving* (1962), *Billy Liar* (1963), *This Sporting Life* (1963), *The Knack... And How to Get It* (1965), and *Darling* (1965). Their characters existed in bleak northern industrial environs living lives handed down by their equally bleak parents, who occasionally turn from their chairs in front of the telly to express astonishment at the new generation's bad behavior. "My father [would] ... Turn over in his grave," portends Laurence Harvey in Jack Clayton's *Room at the Top*. The British New Wave was shot in black-and-white with the realism of the films being made in Italy and France; the acting was heavily influenced by the naturalism of Dean and Brando. While some of these movies are forgettable, others are inspired, such as Anderson's *This Sporting Life*, and Tony Richardson's *The*

*Loneliness of the Long Distance Runner* and *A Taste of Honey.*

*Long Distance Runner* features young working-class men landing in reform school, where—class dialects untouched (unlike Americanized British pop singers of the time)—the student inmates sing out "Jerusalem" in all its beauty and irony. "Don't like profit going to the bosses," one character declares. The cinematic depiction of English women was altered forever by the independent-minded, sexually active characters played by Rita Tushingham in Richardson's *A Taste of Honey* and Julie Christie in John Schlesinger's *Darling*. In *A Taste of Honey*, teenage Jo copes with pregnancy and poverty and her mother. Her closest relationships are with gay and black men, at a time when open portrayals of gays and black-white relations in the UK were virtually non-existent.

If the French New Wave produced hundreds of films, the English version—while creating some remarkable films—produced, at best, a score before quickly moving on to other genres or another country. (Richardson and Schlesinger, for example, moved to the US.) *If...* was a fitting postscript to the wave. Made by a British New Wave founder soon after its filmmakers had gone separate ways, the movie continued the movement's "angry young man" realism, but also contained bits of the experimental stylings that would infuse much of the next filmmaking generation. And while it continued the Wave's focus on class distinction, it also (like some of the era's New Left) assailed every other kind of domination. There is a moment early in *if...* when ringleader Mick (Malcolm McDowell) wonders: "When do we live? That's what I want to know." Every bit of preppy ritual, hierarchy, sexual inhibition, brutality, and prejudice is up for grabs here, with Anderson having none of it. It's one of the great cinematic assaults on authority. McDowell recalled: "I said, 'Lindsay, you're not Labour, you're not Conservative, what are you?' He just said, 'I'm an anarchist. I want to pull the whole bloody lot down.'"[5]

‡

While the Wave was being born, British movie-going was in a free-fall following the decline of Hollywood and the rise of television. From 1946 to 1960, ticket sales dropped from more than $1.6 billion to $501 million.[6] The last big slump had been in the late silent period when only five percent of films screened in Britain were domestic, resulting in the quota legislation of 1927. This prompted a surge of mostly underwhelming "quota quickies." Bigger-budget films were provided by

Alexander Korda's London Film Productions, whose *The Private Life of Henry VIII* (1933) became the first UK hit in the US. At Michael Balcon's Gaumont-British Picture Corporation, the focus was quality, and it produced Alfred Hitchcock's *The 39 Steps* (1935). With its studio system, theater circuits, and screen quota, Britain was soon the largest film producer in Europe. Filmmaking in the early 1940s featured wartime hits such as *In Which We Serve* (1942), directed by Noel Coward and David Lean, and Michael Powell and Emeric Pressburger's *The Life and Death of Colonel Blimp* (1943).

In 1947, the British government's attempt to tax imported films resulted in a short-lived boycott by Hollywood, but American films—and American filmmakers—would soon arrive in the UK in a big way. Established by the Cinematograph Film Act of 1957, the Eady Levy collected a portion of all movie ticket sales to help fund British film. US producers shooting in the UK could access the levy, so Americans such as Richard Lester, Sidney Lumet, and Stanley Kubrick came to work, joining blacklisted US expat Joseph Losey, who had emerged as the auteur he never would have been in America. In their confused state in the 1960s and '70s, American studios kept offices in England and produced more than British versions of Hollywood pablum. Warner Bros. backed *Performance* (1970) and *The Devils* (1971), and Paramount produced *if...* Later, they would bring their blockbuster strategy to England, shooting *Star Wars* and *Superman*.

British screen quotas would continue until 1983, when the Thatcher government ended their fifty-five-year run. Thatcher's Films Act of 1985 abolished the National Film Finance Corporation, which had provided loans to small companies producing films to fill the quota; and the Eady Levy, which was seen as too burdensome for exhibitors, was also eliminated that year. By the late 1980s, British cinema had a smaller share of the box office than at any time since the 1920s.

‡

There was a moment in the early 1980s when the future of British cinema regularly convened in a building at Greek Street and Soho Square in London. Mike Leigh was working on his feature *Meantime* (1984), Ken Loach on the documentary *Questions of Leadership* (1983), and Alan Clarke on *Made in Britain* (1982), and the three would lunch together in the square. Clarke made his mark giving the Thatcher era a dose of its own realism with the unrelenting *Scum* (1979) and *Made in Britain;*

he died in 1990 and left an uncompromising legacy. Leigh and Loach continued to display an enduring commitment to England's cinema and the depiction of everyday lives.

It's on the streets of London's Soho that you still find the unadorned workplaces of British film, the offices of libertine filmmakers and film censors in close proximity. At Ken Loach's Sixteen Films, his producer Rebecca O'Brien looks up from her computer in an office papered with posters. "As you can see, it's just a small, ramshackle office," she says. Down the stairway, I stop to look at a poster for Loach's *Land and Freedom* (1995) done up in the style of the exquisite posters from the Spanish revolution. "Tierra Y Libertad," it shouts.

Working-class politics are on the surface of Loach's movies, social ideas masterfully woven into personal stories—the ideological is personal. Where else but in a Loach movie could the most intense, memorable scene be a debate between radical socialists and reformist nationalists over the Anglo-Irish Treaty, as in *The Wind That Shakes the Barley* (2006). Loach's *Land and Freedom* protagonist David Carr (Ian Hart) leaves behind the daily grind of Depression-era England to fight the good fight, supporting the Loyalists against the fascists in Spain. The film features a mesmerizing scene in which Spanish peasants argue about whether to make the revolution now and begin collectivization or wait until the fascists have been defeated. "It's a story we've wanted to have a go at for a long time, really," Loach said. "If you've been in politics, particularly from the left, what happened in Spain from 1936 to 1939 was always like holy writ."[7]

Loach comes from a working-class family in Nuneaton, near Birmingham. After conscripted military service, he enrolled at Oxford University ("allegedly, I was studying law") where he joined a comedy revue, then worked in a repertory company. With the fading of the British New Wave on screen, realism's home was in television, and in the 1960s it wasn't so hard to be hired at the BBC. Loach turned heads in 1965 with the television film *Up the Junction*, which included an abortion sequence, then again in 1966 with *Cathy Come Home*, about a homeless mother whose children are taken by social workers.

Loach's first theatrical feature, *Poor Cow* (1967), was about a young woman who survives everything life throws at her, including marriage, prostitution, Terence Stamp, Malcolm McDowell (whose scenes were deleted), and music by Donovan. He followed *Poor Cow* with *Kes* (1969), the engaging story of an aimless boy who finds purpose training a wounded kestrel. Then, in Thatcher's 1980s, when industries were privatized, mines closed, unions gutted, and film funding cut, Loach largely retreated from feature filmmaking. His television work came under attack too, when broadcasters withdrew two of his documentaries, *A Question of Leadership*, about the union movement under Thatcher, and *Which Side Are You On?*, about the 1984 UK miners' strike.

With support from Britain's Channel Four Films, Loach returned to features with *Hidden Agenda* (1990), a spellbinding set-in-Ireland thriller about right-wing designs in the UK and then, in quick succession, *Riff-Raff* (1991), *Raining Stones* (1993), *Ladybird, Ladybird* (1994), and *Land and Freedom*. *Riff-Raff* is set at an unsafe work site in London, where old buildings are reconstructed into luxury housing. The film offers up relentless poverty, drugs, and violence that makes earlier British New Wave grit seem almost quaint and genteel. While *Riff-Raff* is compelling personal drama, Loach never lets you doubt for a moment who makes a profit out of all this. "A film's going to be political without talking about politics," he says. "You explore the medium and develop stories that you hope have some significance and characters that have some validity and conflicts that a lot of people share—and that will have some resonance."

Having ignored previous invites to shoot in Hollywood, Loach arrived in 1999 to shoot *Bread and Roses* (2000), about a drive to organize undocumented Latino janitorial workers. Paul Laverty, who's scripted other Loach projects, came up with the idea while living in L.A. As with his other films, Loach cast a mix of novices and professionals who, to heighten spontaneity, only saw their own lines and didn't know where the story was going. He enjoyed shooting the union story in the studios' back yard. "There was a kind of a wry subversive intent, really," he says.

‡

Social realism is not always the preoccupation of Britain's filmmakers. There is also magic and fantasy, as in the films by the team of Michael Powell and Emeric Pressburger, the nonlinear storytelling of Ken Russell and Nicholas Roeg, and the experimental narratives of Peter Greenaway, Derek Jarman, and Sally Potter. At a glance it might seem that their films have little in common with the British New Wave, but much of their work offers a simmering class conflict, often addressed through religious or cultural suppression. In Greenaway's *The Draughts man's Contract* (1982), for example, the act of turning artistic work into a business is shown to have its allure, but ultimately it is the artist's

downfall. Religious intolerance faces the wrath of Russell's nicely sac-
rilegious *The Devils*. Great dance and stylish camerawork mark Powell and Pressburger's *The Red Shoes* (1948), but it was also a cautionary
story about the artistic purity of youth being compromised and com-
modified. "Why do you want to dance?" aspiring dancer Vicky Page is
asked. Her answer: "Why do you want to live?"

Sally Potter's dancing alter ego in *The Tango Lesson* (1997) might say
the same thing. Potter grew up in London, deciding at fourteen to make
movies. "When I first got an eight-millimeter camera in my hands and
looked through the lens … I wanted to direct. By the age of sixteen,
I was watching—devouring, actually—enormous quantities of European new wave films and a lot of the structuralist independent and
underground films." She joined the London Film-Makers' Cooperative,
which had set up shop at the Arts Laboratory in Covent Garden. "There
was a cinema, a performance space, a café, and there were a couple of
rooms devoted to filmmaking, with a camera, an editing bench, and
a great big second-hand printer and processor. So you learned—either
from others or by a sort of self-teaching method—pretty much all the
rudiments of really, really low-budget independent filmmaking. I just
did it. I learned by making horrendous technical mistakes repeatedly
until I never made them again."

Like the rest of the western world, London in the late 1960s and early
1970s experienced a flowering of cultural creativity. "It was extraordinary, and there wasn't a center to it. It was amorphous and cropping up
all over the place and in all kinds of ways." Potter was as eclectic as the
London counterculture—a dancer and choreographer with her Limited Dance Company, a street performer in a guerrilla theater troupe, a
singer-songwriter in the Feminist Improvising Group, an experimental
filmmaker, and an activist attending conferences and protests.

> I grew up in a politically aware environment because my
> father called himself an anarchist, so I read Kropotkin and
> other philosophers. In a way, the broadly leftist politics,
> anarchist politics, continued to be my affiliation, but a huge
> turning point for me was the evolution of the women's
> movement. I went with a friend to the first-ever women's
> liberation conference in London, which I think was in 1971,
> and it was an extraordinarily eye-opening experience. The
> phrase 'The Personal Is Political,' which now seems so obvi-
> ous, was, at the time, truly revolutionary. All the aspects of

our lives that we had thought we were alone in feeling—and felt were perhaps our fault—were as political as class or race or anything else.

In the late '70s, Potter performed with the Film Music Orchestra and other bands touring Europe. She also completed a forty-five-minute film, *Thriller* (1979), a revisitation of Puccini's *La bohème*, which became popular on the festival circuit. "Film had always been my first love, but it was just so difficult to make films because of the money involved. I made *Thriller* in between music tours and editing, when I could borrow time in people's cutting rooms through the night. That made me think that I really have to stick with film and see what I can do."

Her first feature, *The Gold Diggers* (1984), made with a grant from the British Film Institute, starred Julie Christie on a Yukon adventure in search of her roots. Potter spent the rest of the decade as a performance artist, lyricist, and singer. "*The Gold Diggers* was such an anti-narrative, controversially received piece of work. It was very hard for me to get funded again. Finally, after enormous struggles, I managed, with the aid of many other people, to create a way of making *Orlando* [1992] as a co-production. It was a ten-week shoot, a four-month edit, and a nine-year preparation."

Potter had long loved Virginia Woolf's boundary-breaking, centuries-spanning novel *Orlando: A Biography,* about a man who awakens as a woman, and her adaptation would draw critical raves and awards. "*Orlando* opened the door for lots of other things that people wanted me to do, but I didn't want to do; Hollywood offers for this, that, and the other—mainstream stuff mostly. Some 'women's pictures.'" Potter faced the decision a suddenly popular independent filmmaker must make. ("Or repeatedly make, in a way.") She chose independence, and the result was *The Tango Lesson*, the semi-autobiographical story of a filmmaker who turns from her daily ordeal of raising financing for a lackluster thriller called *Rage* and focuses instead on a new passion for the tango. Potter's agents were not amused. "It seemed to them like a wasted opportunity to cross over into the big time. I think people just gave up telling me [about offers] because I said no to everything. I tortured myself about it as well and wondered. But it doesn't take long to remember that all the filmmakers' work that I've most enjoyed and respected over the years are people who have kept true to their own vision one way or another. On the whole, the more forgettable things are the ones that people seem to have done without really believing in them."

Like the character of Sally she portrays in *The Tango Lesson*, Potter has been a filmmaker whose dance lessons became a passion, but as a screenwriter she did research and added fiction to provide dramatic shape, and when it came time to shoot, the movie, like the tango, was one long dazzling embrace with turns and steps and character.

‡

Growing up in Salford, near Manchester, Mike Leigh was immersed in the arts—writing, drawing, performing, and attending the theater and movies. "When I was a kid watching movies, I always used to think it would be great if you could see a film where the characters were like real people as opposed to characters in films." When he came to London in 1960 to study acting at the Royal Academy of Dramatic Arts, he saw, for the first time, movies that weren't British or American—[Vittorio] De Sica and [Akira] Kurosawa and the *Nouvelle Vague*—and, he says, "it blew me away."

After studying at RADA, Leigh enrolled in art school. "And it was there that I had a clairvoyant flash." Sitting with other students in a silent room drawing a nude model, it struck Leigh that everyone was absorbed in what they were doing in a way he never experienced in acting classes. Couldn't actors be completely involved in the process that creates a work? "I suddenly realized that what we were doing as art students was looking at life and finding a way of expressing it in a way that we never did as acting students. Acting was all about learning the lines and not bumping into the furniture, basically."

Throughout the mid-1960s, Leigh was a working actor, then turned to writing and directing plays and teleplays such as *Abigail's Party* (1977). His goal, always, was to work in the movies. "From the late '60s to the early '80s, television was where British cinema was alive and well and hiding." Leigh sees his generation in the evolution of the Beatles—starting as rebellious teenagers in the 1950s and becoming hippies in the 1960s, radicalized by Vietnam. By 1970, Leigh was a veteran of street protests. He grew up active in a Jewish socialist youth group, marched for nuclear disarmament, and, on October 27, 1968, was at the battle of Grosvenor Square, where 200 anti-war protestors were arrested when they tried to break police lines to get at the US embassy. "For me, as for a generation, one became properly and totally politicized by the end of the decade," Leigh has said. "'By the beginning of the 1970s everything seemed possible."[8]

*Sally Hawkins in Mike Leigh's* Happy-Go-Lucky. © *Miramax Films / Phototest.*

Leigh's first feature, *Bleak Moments*, is British New Wave ten years after. This was, after all, 1971, and along with the sort of characters who might have shown up in a Tony Richardson film, there is a folk singer producing an underground periodical called *Open Family*. At times, *Bleak Moments* has the awkwardness of a first film, but hints of things to come from Leigh, especially when Sylvia and Peter endure the most excruciatingly non-communicative date in movie history. The film was set in the milieu Leigh grew up in, a working-class town where his father was a factory doctor committed to the National Health Service. It was also the opportunity for Leigh make a movie with the improv-driven working process he had been fine-tuning since his clairvoyant moment back at art school. "You create the thing organically, in pure terms, combining writing and rehearsing and exploring to arrive at the material and to do it."

The release of *Bleak Moments* was hardly a breakout moment that made everything easy for Leigh. He struggled on, mostly making BBC TV movies. Major notice came with 1988's *High Hopes*, a comic slice of realism about a feisty socialist couple trying to hold on to their beliefs in the face of new, crassly materialistic neighbors in Thatcher's England. There is no longer the "room at the top" of 1959, so the living quarters at the bottom have been gentrified. Leigh's next three films—*Life is Sweet* (1990), *Naked* (1993), and *Secrets & Lies* (1996)—established him as a funny, fearless chronicler of modern England.

The London that comes to life in a Leigh movie is nothing like any stereotype of proletarian life. "I'm always very specific," he says. "And in real life, people constantly challenge the general principles or general rules." In *Happy-Go-Lucky* (2008), Sally Hawkins is superb as the unsinkable Poppy, who seems blissfully innocent at first, but slowly, as the audience gets to know her, is seen to be an intelligent woman with as many complications as anyone else. "The truth is that the characters are already complex, but it's just how you've seen them," says Leigh, "and I think it's like real life. You meet someone for the first time and all you've got to go on is your preconceptions, and gradually as you get to know them they change because they become three-dimensional, and you start to understand them in a more thorough and rounded way. That's what happens in your relationships with the characters in my films."

Leigh has a habit of shining light on the invisible. A character who might be an extra in a studio movie is Leigh's protagonist; a character actor for another director is his star. In the Oscar-nominated *Secrets & Lies*, about a middle-aged woman (Brenda Blethyn) reconnecting with the child she gave up at birth (Marianne Jean-Baptiste), the actresses gladly accepted the roles because it was a Leigh movie. "People keep talking about the script," said Jean-Baptiste, "asking what attracted me to the role of Hortense. There was no role—what you're attracted to is the process."[9] Left to their own devices, smart actors tend to go where the good work is. When Leigh alumni Daniel Mays was offered a role in Eran Creevy's *Shifty* (2008), his agent told him that the good news was it was a lead role, the bad news was it was a bare-budget, three-week shoot. "She didn't want me to go anywhere near it, but the actors, and the crew, and everyone were paid the same—a fantastic leveller—and it produced an amazing sense of camaraderie, and it produced good work," Mays says.

Leigh's casting director Nina Gold scours acting schools for talent, which led to Mays being cast in *All or Nothing* (2002) and *Vera Drake*. Acting in a Leigh movie means a lengthy commitment. Leigh works individually with each actor, creating a character from childhood. The actor remains in the dark about characters being developed by other cast members. Slowly, each character evolves into someone real by the time the cast is brought together for improv-driven rehearsals. Leigh produces a script of sorts (scenarios without dialogue), and the improvisational shoot—the "actual work," Leigh calls it—is under way.

"All of his groundwork is just a process to get to a point where you go on location and you go in front of a crew and you make a film," says Mays, "and by the time you get to that point, you know your character inside and out; you've got a wealth of back history and imagery that's lodged into your brain, that you can draw upon. It's a completely brilliant and unique process, which is exclusive to him. You can try to apply it to other work that you do after his, but it never really fits. It's just his method."

Leigh has a broad definition of what constitutes politics ("everything"), but nothing he has done addressed an issue more directly than *Vera Drake*. The 2004 movie was a culmination of much of Leigh's work—a deeply personal family story, set in the working-class England of his childhood, which addresses the matter of abortion. "It was a threat and it remains a threat that there will be retrograde legislation that would outlaw abortion. I'm old enough to remember what it was like before the 1967 Abortion Act in this country when people had unwanted pregnancies and only illegal abortionists were what was available. I felt it was time to make a film that reminded us of what that was like and what that threat was." *Vera Drake* took three Oscar nominations, the Golden Lion award for best film at the Venice Film Festival, and best actress (Imelda Staunton) at the European Film Awards.

Despite the acclaim, funding is never simple for Leigh. He formed a production company, Thin Man Films, because he believes that the only way to get things done in film is to do them yourself. "It's about the means of production ... Of course, it still means we have to go with the begging bowl for each movie, but when we get the money we're in control of how we make the film."[10]

Leigh has had Hollywood offers and could be pool-side, making other people's scripts into studio movies, but he will continue to tough it out independently, without intrusive producers and financiers. "The thing that's made my films work, if they work at all, is the fact that they've been made with no interference whatever, at any stage of the proceedings." And how has he created such a large body of work while maintaining that independence? "Mainly by walking away every time there's the remotest glimmer of getting into a situation where that won't be the case. Look, it's very, very tough, and the real issue is that not enough filmmakers, particularly not enough young filmmakers, have access to funds. And when they do, there's too much interference. People aren't given the freedom to just explore."

‡

Potter's low-budget *Yes* (2004) and *Rage* (2009) were partially financed by the UK Film Council, which, along with Film4 and the BBC, has been a primary film-funding source since 2000. In July 2010, however, David Cameron's new Conservative government announced it was abolishing the UK Film Council. Although Tory governments have a habit of dismantling film programs, the assault on the council caught many by surprise, and it was denounced by Leigh and Loach and more than fifty actors, from *Secrets & Lies'* Timothy Spall to *The Young Victoria's* (2009) Emily Blunt. The Tories then turned on cultural funding, with cuts to the BBC and British Film Institute. While earlier reductions hadn't been so draconian, finding film money was a challenge during recent Labour governments (and some monies were diverted from film to help pay for the 2012 Olympics).

"Budgets have been squeezed and squeezed," says Potter. "So it's completely normal now, for example, for directors and producers to defer their entire fee. I've done that on every film I've ever made. I never get paid upfront; I always have to wait till the film is sold before I get any fee, if at all. I didn't get paid a penny for *Yes*, for example, and I never will—for four years' work." Adds Loach: "You see directors who will make one good film and then struggle for the next five or six years to get another one made. And then there are the ones who go to the States and become Americans."

Along with the American blockbuster muck of the Christopher Nolans and Tony Scotts, there is at least one British filmmaker who moved to the US without forfeiting an independent stance. Alex Cox faced the choice of continuing his film studies in London or moving to L.A. London never appealed to this Liverpudlian, so he went to UCLA, attending film classes and punk gigs. While trying to raise funds for his script *Repo Man* (1984), Cox met former Monkee Michael Nesmith, who loved his story of an L.A. punk repossessing cars. Nesmith wanted to produce and landed an arrangement with Universal, and *Repo Man* went from being a minimally funded, post-student independent to a studio picture. Then *Repo Man* nearly fell through the cracks following a regime change at Universal.

> Bob Rehme, who had been a head of the studio and had green-lit the picture, was fired. He was replaced by a guy called Frank Price, whose job was to make sure all the films that Rehme had green-lit would fail. If Rehme's films succeeded, why was he fired? Universal didn't want to bring it

out at all. So we had to take out advertisements in *Variety*, and eventually we were able to pit MCA records, the parent company of Universal, against Universal because the record album [which included songs by Black Flag, Circle Jerks, and Iggy Pop] had sold something like 55,000 copies without the film being distributed. Irving Azoff, the head of MCA music, called up Lew Wasserman or somebody at Universal and said, 'Hey, is there a movie to go with this record?' It was just a horrible battle. We got nothing out of it. And Universal, you know, hid money for many, many years.

Cox reached into punk again for *Sid and Nancy* (1986), then did *Straight to Hell* (1987), a western shot on the fly in Spain with Joe Strummer, Elvis Costello, Courtney Love, Dennis Hopper, Grace Jones, and Jim Jarmusch. *Walker* (1987), about American William Walker, who proclaimed himself president of Nicaragua in the 1850s, was backed by Universal, but the studio blanched at its politics and dumped it into theaters without promotion. And so the beautiful friendship between Cox and Universal came to a close. Newly resettled in Colorado, Cox's post-studio, low-budget features include *The Revenger's Tragedy* (2002), *Three Businessmen* (1998), and *Searchers 2.0* (2007). Through it all, Cox's politics remain defiant ("I am a socialist. I believe the state has an obligation to give everybody free education and free health care"), and his movies his own. "It is possible to get a message across—maybe," says Cox. "I don't know how many people I reach. I don't know how to reach them because we still have this great difficulty with distribution."

‡

British film has had its international moments since *The Private Life of Henry VIII*. There were, for instance, Lean and Hitchcock, and a brief period (1985-86) when *My Beautiful Laundrette*, *Wetherby*, *A Room With a View*, *Sid and Nancy*, *Caravaggio*, *The Mission*, and *Mona Lisa* were all released. In 2009, the British box office reached a record £944 million ($1.47 billion US) with "UK films," buoyed by *Slumdog Millionaire* (2008), taking 16.7 percent of domestic ticket sales.[11] That 16.7 percent is a misleading figure because more than half of it derived from UK films that had US studio funding.[12] Despite the talk of bigger, better numbers, the US studios dominate British screens—89.5 percent of movies released domestically in 2009 were American or American-studio funded.

The problem is that, in Britain, US studio products define the look of British movies. Since British producers can't afford that mega-budget look, US studios fund Harry Potter, James Bond, and Batman, taking the profits back to America. Too much studio domination of too few screens means actual British cinema and foreign independents, once allowed to stay in a theater long enough to build an audience, are quickly tossed, even from art houses, if they don't deliver.

The studio impact on England is particularly telling, its identity already shaken (along with its artificial abundance derived from empire) now that Britannia doesn't rule much of anything anymore, and with globalization promoting the disintegration of local culture. "England has, for a very long time, been in the shadow of the United States," Potter says. "It is a country that is now small and relatively insignificant—knows itself to be that—but not so long ago was the center of an enormous empire. It's a death-of-an-empire situation that North America is only beginning to face now, with China and so on. This is a huge part of the confusion of identity in the UK—the defence of the end of something and, at the same time, having the most commonly used international language in film."

British producers and funding agencies shoot for a global market with a range of imitation-Hollywood movies. Guy Ritchie's Tarantino-esque *Lock, Stock and Two Smoking Barrels* (1998) prompted a ripple of one-dimensional British gangster pictures, complete with cardboard-deep, almost always male characters—a bad example of style over substance. (If you like his ex-wife Madonna's music, you'll like Guy Ritchie's movies.) "I'll accept *Two Barrels* or whatever it was called, because it was the first," said director Richard Attenborough, "but to do that crap again for purely commercial reasons, to succumb to the pornography of violence because it is a prerequisite for commercial success, that I want no part of."[13] *Lock, Stock and Two Smoking Barrels'* British producer Polygram had made big inroads with the 1994 film *Four Weddings and a Funeral* (gross: $245 million), but soon disappeared into Universal, which disappeared into Seagram.

"So much does Hollywood dominate the marketplace, and so much is the punter in the street indoctrinated with the notion that a film is a Hollywood film, that we who make independent European films, or films from anywhere that are not Hollywood pictures, have got a battle getting our films on screens and getting people to be interested in them," says Leigh. Having international distribution or even winning the 2006 Palme D'Or (as Loach's *The Wind that Shakes the Barley* did) doesn't necessarily mean a British movie will reach a broad domestic audience. "It did okay at the festival, and there was a lot of editorial comment. We couldn't have asked for better notices by and large," says Loach, "but they still made only thirty-odd prints, which meant it couldn't even play all the art houses in one go. And it just didn't get into the multiplexes. As long as the cinemas are owned and programmed and controlled as they are, the independents are squeezed out."

Ken Loach's funding is a European patchwork.

> We've usually got three or four co-producers and four or five distributors who buy it at the outset. They make—all being well, touch wood—their money back plus a little bit; nobody has to make a huge investment, and we can go on and do the next one. We can raise money from European co-producers to finance films that are culturally specific to Britain, and we can cast them without interference; we can make them with real freedom. That's a massive good fortune, but the barrier is the access to screens. For us to develop in terms of getting an audience, there need to be cinemas that are programmed by people who like films rather than people who specialize in fast food, people who are tied to the American commercial industry. The cinema chains are locked up by those people, and the independent filmmakers have to start from scratch every time.

Despite the difficulties, there is no dearth of talent—from Andrea Arnold and Steve McQueen to Shane Meadows and Lynn Ramsey—to keep alive the rebel flame of Ken Loach, Mike Leigh, or Sally Potter. A tumultuous half-century after it was made, *A Taste of Honey*'s teenage Jo (played exquisitely by Rita Tushingham), at odds with her single, sexual mom, is now *Fish Tank*'s (2009) teenage Mia (played exquisitely by Katie Jarvis) in similar circumstances. Arnold's *Fish Tank* shows the raw reality today for a young woman coming of age in a council housing project, surrounded by broken relationships but determined to persevere. *Fish Tank* serves notice that the movies will also go on telling brilliant British stories in the twenty-first century.

‡

Potter's first digital picture, *Rage*, about a schoolboy who shoots an ex-posé of the New York fashion industry on his cellphone, was made available online and released in episodes on mobile phones. Putting together the funding for *Rage* was a course in advanced cobbling, as Potter explained in a descriptive blog that turned overnight into a kind of digital manifesto for independents, with debate raging about how low can low-budget go. "It is hard to imagine how it could have been made any cheaper," Potter wrote.

> When I started making films, we all worked for nothing, and
> I scrounged out-of-date film stock and free editing time in
> cutting rooms at night; I also printed my own early sixteen-
> millimeter films. *Thriller,* for example, cost about $3,000 to
> make this way. But there are only so many times one can
> ask for favors from friends. Crew members have rent to pay,
> families to feed … My hope was that *Rage* would, in its own
> way, encourage more money to go to more filmmakers if they
> could limit their budgets in a meaningful way. But perhaps
> more importantly, I hoped that one of the central themes of
> the film—the way in which the pursuit of profit impoverishes
> us all—might have its own subtle impact and do its work
> in the slow and strangely immeasurable way that art func-
> tions.[14]

## CHAPTER ELEVEN

## South Korea: Sympathy for Quota Vengeance

IM KWON-TAEK SAT CROSSED-legged and shaved his head. Other Korean directors—including Park Chan-Wook, Kim Ki-duk, Yim Phil-Sung, and Hong Sangsoo—were among the angry thousands of protestors, as were movie stars Lee Byeong-hun, Jeon Do-yeon, and Hyun Bin. They had suspended film work for the day to protest the South Korean government's plan to reduce screen quotas. Choi Min-sik, star of *Oldeubol* (*Oldboy*, 2003), would return the government's Og-gwan Order of Cultural Merit medal he had been awarded. "The government's decision to cut the quotas is equivalent to giving up our culture," Choi said. The sign he carried read: "No screen quota, no *Oldboy*."[1]

These protests in 2006 erupted after the government finally in order to close a US-Korea Free Trade Agreement (FTA)—acquiesced to longstanding American demands to cut the screen quota. Park Chan-wook held up the sign "Korean films are in danger" on the red carpet at the Berlin International Film Festival. At Cannes, Choi and directors Yoon Jong-bin and Bong Joon-ho—whose films *Yongseobadji mothan ja* (*The Unforgiven*, 2005) and *Gwoemul* (*The Host*, 2006) were the Korean entries—protested the cuts in front of the Palais du Cinéma. "This is my third visit to Cannes," said Choi. "The first two were joyful occasions, as films I was starring in were selected for competition, but today it is different for me. The situation is desperate and I feel like an orphan who has been deserted by his own parents."[2]

Filmmaker Whang Cheol-mean was at the Seoul protests. For Whang, a former director of the Korean Independent Film Association, the importance of film isn't the business of film. "For us, the most important thing is expression. We have the desire to express." In South Korean, the line for filmmakers is between what they call "independent" and "commercial." There is little doubt the screen quotas helped South Korea develop a huge domestic commercial industry. "It is not so important for the independent filmmakers, but we were against the FTA, and we don't like the neo-liberalism, so we fought against it," says Whang. "Through the FTA, the US forced us to cut [the quota]. Without the quota system, we can't defend ourselves against big-budget Hollywood films. In boxing, there is a rule—the two people fighting are the same weight. But in the film industry, you must fight with a big-budget film.

It is ridiculous. You can't. If you have money, you can easily influence the audience. It is the nature of the medium."

Kim Ji-hyen was at the protests too. Just out of film school, she was working as a script supervisor on Korean studio pictures when the quota issue exploded. "At the time, I was in the commercial industry. I agreed screen quotas were needed to protect the Korean commercial film industry, at least." Now, Kim's on the independent side of the line, which battles for screen time with or without quotas. "A pure independent film can't screen at the theaters in Korea," she says.

‡

In 1980, a protest in Gwangju against the latest military coup, which brought Chun Doo-hwan to power, was attacked by soldiers, leaving more than 200 dead, sparking a lingering resistance movement. There would be more protests and strikes and finally, in 1987, just as pro-Soviet regimes were about to fall in Europe, South Korea's pro-Western regime came crashing down.

From the movement of the 1980s, Whang Cheol-mean and his friends, including Park Kwang-su and Jang Sun-woo, created a New Korean Cinema that would lay a foundation for later independents. Jang, who had been jailed for his student activism, addressed the Gwangju slaughter in his film *Ggotip* (*A Petal*, 1996). The breakthrough was Park's 1988 debut *Chilsue and Mansu,* about the down-and-out lifestyles of a couple of billboard painters. An activist at Seoul National University, Park had made anti-government underground movies through the '80s and co-founded the Seoul Film Group, which set out to renew Korean film culture. "The New Korean Cinema arrived at a turning point for the film industry in Korea," Whang says. "The whole society changed. Before the 1980s, most people thought the purpose of movies was just to make a profit. In the 1980s, there was the big tragedy in Gwangju, and the students studying at the university at that time decided to change the world, change Korean society, by making films. The students were pretty left-wing at that period at a lot of universities."

From this student movement came the Korean independent film movement. Whang continues to keep his distance from commercial filmmaking. In his Internet-suicide road-trip *Woori, Jjongnaeja!* (*Let's Finish!!!,* 2007), Jaoquin (Jeong In-ji) joins two men she's met online for a joy ride that's supposed to end in death, but as life goes on, her plans spin out of control. "It was really low budget," he says.

Mostly, the industry's not interested in making that kind of story. It is not high concept. They don't see money in my film, so they don't produce my film. In this case, I need a strategy—how to make a film without money? There is a way; the technology is available. I write and I direct, I do camera and edit—so you can save money if you do many things. I think I can deal with producers, but they think I'm a difficult filmmaker—'He's very much stubborn.' They are not creative people, and they have very narrow opinions about what film audiences like. For us, independent film is free from capture.

‡

In the early twenty-first century, a wave of popular Korean culture—from movies to music to fashion—swept over much of Asia, including Japan. But a century earlier, after Japan invaded Korea, the Korean language was outlawed and Koreans had to take Japanese names. The best-known early filmmaker, Na Un'-kyu, who did two years in prison for his activism in the pro-independence March First Movement, created controversy with his first feature *Arirang*, made in 1926 when he was twenty-four; it's about class conflict and Japanese occupiers and focuses on a man driven mad by torture.

After World War II, as West and East fought over the spoils and Korea split into North and South, there was sporadic production. The first sustained filmmaking began after the Korean War, when South Korea exempted the movie industry from taxes. Following the Motion Picture Law of 1963, which increased state control over film, censorship intensified and production dropped, although filmmakers such as Shin Sang-ok and Im Kwon-taek persevered. Meanwhile, in North Korea, Kim Jung-il, the son of dictator Kim Il-sung, was a movie fanatic who authored *Theory of Cinematic Art* in 1973. A few years later, he ordered the kidnappings of a South Korean independent filmmaker and an actress, and instructed them to make propaganda films—one way to show government support for a domestic film industry. Actress Choi Eun-hee, on a visit to Hong Kong in 1978, was kidnapped by North Korean agents; when her ex-husband, director Shin Sang-ok, went there to investigate, he was kidnapped too. Their North Korean experience lasted eight years, until they finally made an escape at a Vienna film festival.[3] They didn't have much use for South Korea's pro-Western military dictatorships either, opting instead for Hollywood exile and returning to

South Korea only in the post-dictatorship 1990s. Many artists, like Shin and Choi, adrift between the capitalism of the south and the Stalinism of the north, found alternatives outside the two dominant ideologies of the day, in many cases more democratic or libertarian forms of socialism.

Director Im Kwon-taek was well-versed in East and West, having grown up in a Communist family in South Korea. In the 1960s, he was a genre filmmaker, but churning out meaningless product wore on him. "One day I suddenly felt as though I'd been lying to the people for the past twelve years," he said. "I decided to compensate for my wrongdoings by making more honest films."[4] The move to independence came with his 1973 self-financed *Jabcho* (*The Deserted Widow*) about a woman widowed by the Korean War, and he would go on to make more than 100 features. In *Chihwaseon* (*Strokes of Fire*, 2002), for which Im was named best director at the Cannes Film Festival, there's an exchange between Korean painter Jang Seun-up and his mentor that speaks to Im's earlier struggles between art and industry:

> Mentor: "Your skill is faultless. Nonetheless, it's time you created paintings of your own, infused with your spirit and soul."
>
> Jang: "I really want to change! I often wake up at night, haunted by it. It churns my blood. So often, having to paint to order, I feel ..."
>
> Mentor: "A picture that's painted for profit and instant fame is nothing but vanity. Stillborn!"

‡

During a flurry of censorious movie legislation in the mid-1960s, the insular government of General Park Chung-hee instituted a screen quota to further control content, resulting in a raft of forgettable quickies. After Korea's rule by a series of dictators finally ended with Chun Doo-hwan's fall in 1987, radical young filmmakers were among the first to see the potential in quota legislation and worked to enforce it. "You know, it is very ironic," Whang says. "The quota system was founded in Korea by the dictator. He wanted to control the film industry so he needed this kind of rule." Although introduced in 1966, it wasn't until import restrictions were dropped in the late 1980s that quotas became the local industry's first line of defence against US studios.

In 1988, as a result of American studios gaining direct access to South Korean movie screens, smoke bombs and feces were tossed inside theaters, snakes were let loose during screenings, street demos turned violent, and the manager of American studio distributor United International Pictures sought refuge at the US embassy.[5] Before, they had relied on local distributors licensed to release US movies. By the early 1990s, American films claimed some eighty-five percent of the Korean box office.

South Korea's audience for domestic movies, however, wasn't dormant for long, thanks in large part to the screen quota. The original quota legislation called for theaters to screen Korean films sixty to ninety days a year, and in 1985, it was increased to 146 days. This ensured screen time for films that would have been shunted aside by heavily promoted American studio movies, creating an audience for Korean at least commercial Korean—film. "The Korean screen quota system has been the driving force behind reviving Korean culture," director Lee Jun-ik said.[6]

Since the Coalition of Cultural Diversity in Moving Images was formed in 1993 to enforce the quota system, local films' box-office share grew from sixteen percent that year to thirty-six percent in 1999 to nearly sixty-five percent in 2006.[7] But US studios maintained considerable coercive power in Korea. In 1998, the studios' distributor UIP demanded Korean theaters, under threat of not getting Hollywood films, show Sony's *Godzilla*, which chased the popular domestic film, *Yeogo goedam* (*Ghost Story in Girl's High School*) off screens.[8] Still, South Korea's quota was enough of a local success story that the Motion Picture Association of America ramped up its campaign to end it. The MPAA looked to the Pacific Asian countries as prime new markets, but screen restrictions were an impediment, so as part of talks over a Korea–US Bilateral Investment Treaty, it declared quotas a violation of free trade. At an April 1998 meeting with Korean officials, MPAA vice-president William Baker promised to provide $500 million for the construction of twenty multiplexes if the quota was slashed. In July, at a meeting in Washington, DC, US officials told their Korean counterparts that no investment agreement would be reached unless the quota was addressed.[9] When Korea's minister of state for trade Han Duck-soo then called for the quota to be eliminated or reduced, actors, directors, and producers were outraged and another branch of the Korean government, the ministry of culture and tourism, distanced itself from him. "Until the local film industry acquires international competitiveness and sufficient infrastructure, the screen quota must be sustained," said culture minister Shin Nakyun.[10] Even the American Chamber of Commerce in Korea called on the MPAA to stop linking trade discussions with the quota, saying: "By eliminating the screen quotas from the BIT [Bilateral Investment Treaty] negotiations, we believe the current discussions can proceed to a rapid and successful conclusion."[11]

The newly formed Emergency Committee to Protect the Screen Quota System called for a one-day nationwide shutdown of production to protest threats to the quota. "The US persistence in trying to abolish the screen quota system in Korea is a sad reminder that human values and decency have no relevance when avarice rules," its statement read.[12] At the Berlin film festival in February 1999, directors Jean-Luc Godard, Agnès Varda, Wong Kar-wai, Ken Loach, and Roland Joffe publicly supported the South Korean quota.

Jack Valenti fired back after a meeting at the home of South Korean president Kim Dae-jung. He said Korean cinema was "in crisis" and called for reducing the quota to "a reasonable and commercially acceptable limit."[13] In exchange for "liberalizing" the quota, Valenti offered training programs and multiplex construction. After Valenti's incursion, 113 Korean directors and producers shaved their heads and went on a seven-day hunger strike. "Jack Valenti is saying [this] to ... every country. Give carrots first. It looks like carrots, but it's really poison," said filmmaker Moon Sung-keun.[14]

The MPAA's anti-quota initiative came as Korean industry was feeling vulnerable. It was in the throes of a financial crash prompted when the huge debt of chaebol conglomerates, along with evidence of corruption in high places, brought the country to near bankruptcy. Bank credit was tightened, stocks plunged, and the International Monetary Fund ordered chaebols to trim operations. The chaebols pulled back from their considerable entertainment investments, with Samsung, Daewoo, and other multinationals shutting down film divisions.

Following the crash of 1998, in the midst of the war on quotas, something unexpected occurred—South Korean film blasted off. In 1999, Kang Je-gyu's thriller *Swiri* smashed *Titanic*'s Korean box-office mark and changed audience preconceptions of Korean film. It looked as good as a Hollywood blockbuster, but played nicely on the natural drama of a split nation. The storyline spoke to South Korean fears of North Korea, with North Koreans in the south trying to steal a bomb while the two governments attempt reconciliation. Produced for about $6 million, it grossed $27.5 million in South Korea, and was a huge hit across Asia.

In the face of success, South Korea's film industry reproduced the structure of its American counterpart, down to its vertically integrated studios, stadium megaplexes, corporate ownership, and blockbuster strategy. Movie theater attendance climbed from 42.2 million in 1996 to 166.7 million in 2006. It crested that year when the domestic share of Korean box office reached 64.7 percent, with US films a distant second at 30.8 percent and Japan third at 2.4.[15] Korea's studios were in place—CJ Entertainment, Lotte Cinema, Cinema Service, and Showbox/Mediaplex. CJ Entertainment embodied the expanse of the new industry; it was the subsidiary of a conglomerate (CJ Corporation, at one time better known for its sale of processed sugar) that it could rely on for funding, and had its own subsidiary as the primary exhibitor (CJ GCV).

South Korea had the most diverse film financing in Asia, mixing Korean conglomerates, venture capitalist funds, government support, and broadcasters. With production budgets growing exponentially, export sales had a new urgency. Unlike the American studios, with their ancillary revenues, South Korea relied on box office. While *Swiri* drew audiences regionally, it didn't sell globally. So Korea's studios started shooting globally, co-producing with Europeans and North Americans. Having once shot their movies in Japanese, Koreans now shot in English, with Hollywood studios providing distribution for English-language action like Showbox's *D-War* (2007).

‡

Meanwhile, auteur independents continued to shoot in Korean. While some received Korean Film Council state money, most faced the universal problems of funding, distribution, and access to screens. Many Korean independents were underwhelmed by the film industry's fast expansion; so much of it was rooted in Koreanized versions of blockbusters. The independents worried, as production costs soared, that diversity would be the cost of so much profit from genre production.

Like the New Hollywood, some independent-minded filmmakers, including Park Chan-wook, Bong Joon-ho, Lee Jun-ik, and Yim Phil-sung, navigated inside Korea's new studio system. Blockbuster auteurs Park and Bong are rarities who deliver enough at the box office to maintain studio backing with considerable creative autonomy. "I think they are artistic directors, not independent directors. They have the power to put their own visions in films," says filmmaker Kim Ji-hyen.

They weren't the first Korean auteurs to find an audience. Im Kwon-taek, for example, was able to instil a popular *chungmuro* movie (the Korean equivalent of a Hollywood film), such as *Seopyeonje* (1993), with his artistry and local touch. *Seopyeonje* looked at the traditional Korean art of dramatic singing called *pansori*, a part of Korea's past that was being forgotten in the rush to adopt western culture; large audiences connected with the film's embrace of this cultural tradition. Some of Bong's *Gwoemul* (*The Host*) is computerized schlock, but there is also something more happening here—it's a box-office smash with references to colonialism and protestors and a "virus" that could be anything from North Korean totalitarianism to Hollywood studio films.

Park was a philosophy student at Seoul's Sogang University when a screening of *Vertigo* moved him to take up filmmaking. By the time he graduated, he was a cinephile willing to do whatever it took to stay close to the process of making movies. "I worked at a very small foreign film importer for about a year doing bits and pieces. I made press releases, designed posters, and even translated subtitles with my poor English. Robert Altman's *Vincent & Theo* (1990) was one of the films I worked on." But his sights were set on directing. In some ways, his box-office record breaker, *Gongdong gyeongbi guyeok* (*J.S.A.—Joint Security Area*, 2000), is the essence of the Korean blockbuster era—produced by a Korean major (CJ Entertainment), filled with relentless action, released with a substantial marketing campaign, and featuring a North-South storyline. Unlike other blockbusters, though, it had three-dimensional characters. Alongside action with black-humor wit, Park's Vengeance Trilogy (*Boksuneun naui geot* [*Sympathy for Mr. Vengeance*], 2002; *Old Boy*, 2003; *Shinjeolhan geumjassi* [*Sympathy for Lady Vengeance*], 2005) offered insights into family, sexuality, school ties, and history. *Sympathy for Mr. Vengeance* didn't feature your typical apolitical action figures. "Destroy the new liberalism that ruins the lives of the people," shouts one character who's handing out anti-globalization leaflets on the street. In *Sympathy for Lady Vengeance*, the cool Lee Geum-ja (Lee Young Ae), who is falsely convicted, is intent on settling scores while dealing with her haunting past. It's a great layered action movie for people who otherwise don't like action movies.

"The case of Park Chan-wook is special," says filmmaker Seo Won-tae. "He's very, very smart. The artistic context I can get through his films is amazing. He knows fine art, he knows film history, he knows many other cultural things, and also psychology, sociology, anthropology—that's why I enjoy his films. But without noticing that kind of context, a huge audience can enjoy his films."

Park is of the generation that came of age during dictatorship, took to the streets, and made movies in the wake of the regime's fall. "We are the generation with the most self-confidence in modern Korean history," he says. It's a complicated generation, he says, which spent its "adolescence and university years exposed to the daily violence carried out by the government authority, further mixed with witnessing the unprecedented economic growth and the consequent gap between the rich and the poor ... These conditions have forged our strength."

Like Bong, he is a member of the socialist Democratic Labour Party and was active in pro-quota demonstrations. "The US demanded, as a pre-condition to the FTA, a substantive reduction in the number of days included in the quota, and the government officials and the members of the press who are neoliberal advocates, teamed up to meet their demand," Park says.

> More than anything, the US system of multiplex cinemas and wide release brought about a fundamental change. Films are released with massive numbers of prints, and huge amounts of marketing expenses are spent, but if the film doesn't perform noticeably well during the first week, it quietly disappears from the market. Naturally, such a system has an effect on filmmaking itself. Directors try to make films of the type that cater to the system in order to survive in this market. Films that can grab attention at first glance, films that are loud, all glitz and no substance—films that have stars. It's the same old story you already know, since it's happening in every country.

Park's vampire movie *Bakjwi* (*Thirst*), where blood lust meets sex lust, beat out *X-Men Origins: Wolverine*'s box office when it opened in 2009. Although he has easy access to funding now, Park doubts that will last forever, but he knows there is life outside the system. "It's different for each individual project, of course. Right now, I'm experiencing hardly any difficulty, but I don't know if it will stay that way in the future. I am getting older, and the Korean film industry is on the downhill at the moment. So I think there will come a time when I will have no choice but to make ultra-low budget films and have them independently distributed ... I'm prepared for that day."

‡

Like his friend Bong Joon-ho, Yim Phil-sung is an indie-commercial hybrid who has been able to bring an auteur ethos to Korean studio films. "My taste, my point of view, belong to independent filmmaking, but my films are released industrially and commercially." He started independently, with four short films that drew acclaim at festivals and eventually pried open the door to Korea's commercial industry. His two feature films—*Namgeuk-ilgi* (*Antarctic Journal*, 2005) (scripted by Bong) and *Henjel gwa Geuretel* (*Hansel & Gretel*, 2007)—were studio-produced but haven't attracted the box office of Park or Bong. *Hansel & Gretel* was produced by Barunson, which was also behind the popular *Joheun-nom nabbeunnom isanghannom* (*The Good, the Bad, the Weird*, 2008) and Bong's *Madeo* (*Mother*, 2009). Yim updates the classic tale, and the result is sumptuous filmmaking and a horrific storyline, a *Beetlejuice* in the Bermuda Triangle: after a car crash, a young man finds himself stranded in a "House of Happy Children" in the midst of a dreamy forest.

Yim says the American studio system has had an overwhelming effect on Korean film culture, with producers involved in the editing process who dismiss anything smacking of reality. "They only like the light screenplays," he says. "They think they're the commercial ones." With a sigh, Yim adds: "I made movies my own way, my original way. It is more important for me, but now I'm really struggling because my two feature films are not much of a success at the Korean box office. The films are more successful in the European film market and festivals."

Yim and fellow director Kim Ji-woon (*The Good, the Bad, the Weird*) visited Iowa in 2005 to participate in a Korean film festival and discussions, part of a month-long college event featuring international artists. They decided to take a break from the program and check out the local custom of rodeo. "You know rodeo, right?" Yim asks. "A thousand white people were looking at us. We were just curious about rodeo, curious about their culture, but they laughed, and some guys talked very badly to us. They were a little bit drunk, and this was really funny, so me and Ji-woon thought, how about creating an Iowa zombie film? Most of the people are really kind and good, but they have some racists there, you know." In the American heartland, you'll find the good, the bad, and the very weird. "That's right," Yim laughs.

‡

The initial assault on the screen quota faded with the mass protests of the 1990s, but FTA proponents never gave up hope, and in 2006, South Korea halved quotas to seventy-three days. "This is a major shock for us, and we feel great shame that our government has truly accepted this insolent request from the United States," said Chung Ji-yoiung of the Coalition for Cultural Diversity in Moving Images (CCDMI).[16] The Coalition's Yan Gi-hwan said the "cultural coup d'etat" was in response to American concerns about a quota domino effect. "The United States fears that South Korea will set an example of a country that succeeds in maintaining its own film culture and that other countries will follow us."[17]

There's a reason why the US studios and their supporters are so agitated about the quota system: it works. But while the quota gave local films the space to build an audience without provisions to support independent films—a quota within a quota—it mostly benefited American-style Korean producers. Kim Ji-hyen, like many independents, would go into the streets again to support the quota, but dislikes its emphasis on commercial film. "The quota is very necessary in Korea," says Kim, a member of the New Progressive Party, which broke from the democratic-socialist party of Bong and Park. Both parties, however, support quotas. The CCDMI's Yan noted the need for specific quota provisions for independents. "One idea is to create a special fund for low-budget national films and art films and have them handled through a special distribution system. We know that screen quotas are not a perfect system, but I hate to imagine where we would be without them."[18]

While Korean box-office numbers deflate and inflate depending on particular movies, the overall downward trajectory—from 64.7 percent of box office in 2006 to 42.5 percent in 2008—was consistent enough that investors were disappearing. In the summer of 2007, ten Korean film organizations issued a declaration decrying the state of film production, noting the collapsed video/DVD market, increasing costs, and the reduced quota.

‡

Despite the commercial Korean industry's dominance at home, much of the international interest that Korean film attracts is in its eclectic independent cinema, with Hong Sangsoo, Kim Ki-duk, Jang Sun-woo,

*Actress Seong Hyeon-ah with director Hong Sangsoo during the making of his engaging anti-romantic comedy* Woman Is the Future of Man. *© MK2 Diffusion / CJ Entertainment / Photofest.*

Lee Chang-dong, Kim Gina, Lee Min-yong, and Kim Dong-won among the featured attractions at festivals.

Hong Sangsoo's 1996 debut, *Daijiga umule pajinnal* (*The Day a Pig Fell into the Well*), introduced the bumbling men fumbling through relationships who continued to populate his films. Hong grew up in Seoul in the 1960s and '70s, studied film at Chung-Ang University, then in Chicago, Berkeley, and Paris. Seong Hyeon-ah, who co-stars in his *Yeojaneun namjaui miraeda* (*Woman Is the Future of Man*, 2004), talks about being cast by Hong. "You two exchange silly pleasantries and have a drink at dusk. He keeps jotting something down. As you know, his handwriting is illegible; you can't make it out. But he seems to have read some part of me that even I'm not aware of … His characters are created little by little as we actually shoot."[19] While Hong's focus is on the relatively non-violent foibles of romantic modernity, Kim Ki-duk takes aim at the culture that developed in Korea in the twentieth century in response to occupation, war, dictatorship, and neoliberalism; his extremely troubled characters often react with extreme violence. Kim was born in rural northern Korea, but in the 1970s his family moved to Seoul, where he spent his teen years. Without formal film studies, he began writing scripts. While acclaimed at festivals and art houses worldwide, his films such as *Seom* (*The Isle*, 2000) and *Ben-jip*

(*3-Iron*, 2004) have failed to attract critical support or a mass audience in South Korea. Says Seo Won-tae: "If I travel to other countries, the film-goers usually remember Kim Ki-duk's name and sometimes even his actors and actresses. But in Korea, they regard Bong Joon-ho as the best because commercially he's very salable. Not like Kim Ki-duk, not like Hong Sangsoo—they are totally independent filmmakers."

Digital cameras have created a generation of no-budget Korean film-makers. "Korean independent film is very dynamic, and the number of films produced every year is amazing compared to the other countries," Seo said. Growing up in Seoul, he was a "Hollykid," but his first feature, *Synching Blue* (2008), was made for $15,000—$12,000 of which he received from the Korean Film Council and the rest from his own savings. "It was very guerrilla style. I was the production designer, editor, cinematographer, director, and writer. I'm an independent filmmaker."

Lee Sang-woo found the story for *Tropical Manila* (2008) when, on a visit to L.A., he stepped into the wrong phone booth. "Somebody put a bomb in the telephone. I was almost killed. I couldn't go back to Korea because I couldn't see anything for three months. My mom would die [if she knew, and] I didn't tell her. So when I make a film, it's all about the mom." In the film, a Korean man wanted for murder back home hides out in Manila slums working as a fish peddler. He longs to see his sick mother back home, but regularly brutalizes his Filipina wife. Lee was Kim Ki-duk's assistant director on *Time* (2006) and *Breath* (2007), and *Tropical Manila* is as rough and independent as early Kim.

Kim Ji-hyen's *Koyangi-deul* (*Cats*, 2009)—three vignettes about women in Seoul—was a collaboration with the feminist Unninetwork, which agreed to raise whatever minimal budget Kim could make do with. While studying film at Dankook University, Kim's independence kept her at odds with instructors. "I didn't like the system. I learned from the university that style is Hollywood style. Actually, I want to find my style." After graduating in 2005, she found work as a script supervisor. "I thought the only way to be a filmmaker is to work in the commercial film industry." Between Kim's graduation and the release of *Cats*, she learned something about herself: "I'm not a commercial filmmaker. I want to be an independent filmmaker. I can understand why the system exists, but I want to find another way to make films, because my dreams are to feel creative joy through making films. That's why I want to be a director."

‡

*Woman Is the Future of Man* (which sounds like a title of a 1960s Godard movie) takes its name from a line in a poem by Louis Aragon that Hong Sangsoo saw on a French postcard. In *Woman Is the Future of Man* old friends meet and fireworks ensue, but they explode or fizzle with an engaging naturalism. The unfulfilled relationships, the less-than-fatal attractions, and the failures to communicate form the telling details about these people and this place. Rarely has a director found so much to work with in the nuances of human attraction.

Nowhere else but in South Korea are the lines between independent and commercial more clearly drawn.

"Unless the Korean film industry begins globalizing through co-financing, co-production, and content sharing with Hollywood, it will continue its course of decline," CJ Entertainment's Seo Hyeon-dong said at a 2010 forum. "Our industry must come up with 'global films'—films that can be applicable to a world audience."[20]

For Whang, independent film is "an international movement, but we should fight in our own districts. The difficult thing is you must decide to make a film which is not for industry but for yourself. Everybody wants to become someone famous, but as an independent filmmaker you must forget it." He laughs. "I make the film I want every time, and that's it."

CHAPTER TWELVE

## *Mexico: Revolution and Hollywood*

THE MEXICAN REVOLUTIONARIES opened fire on the movie screen.

At the height of the Mexican revolution in 1914, the audience at the Convention of Aguascalientes, held to determine the future of the country, is shown a newsreel. When reformist politician Venustiano Carranza, then in a dispute with Pancho Villa and other radicals, comes on screen, there is pandemonium in the audience. Boos become an uproar, the uproar becomes gunshots, the bullets strike Carranza's image, shoot past people standing behind the screen, and are embedded in a wall.[1]

Such was the emotion when Mexico's revolutionaries met up with the movies.

‡

Revolution and Hollywood came to Mexico at the same time. Unlike earlier revolutions in France, England, or the US, this one was caught on-camera. When it came to being a media-savvy revolutionist, Pancho Villa was as determined to get himself in front of a camera as Abbie Hoffman was a half-century later. Villa saw the agitprop potential of moving images, so he stage-managed events for newsreels—even arranging for battles to be fought in properly lit conditions—after signing a $25,000 contract with the North American Mutual Film Company. Ultimately Villa, Emiliano Zapata, and others who believed that a sweeping redistribution of wealth should be part of the revolution lost out to generals with more restrained ambitions. The victors' National Revolutionary Party (later renamed the Institutional Revolutionary Party or PRI), which remained in power from 1929 until 2000, governed with an odd mix of nationalization (oil companies, railroads), protectionism, electoral corruption, and political repression.

Mexican filmmakers would continue the more radical revolution, challenging convention despite ongoing government guile and the neighbor to the north who told them they were on the wrong side of the border. While the twenty-first century Mexican government likes to claim it's fulfilling the tenets of the revolution, filmmaker Francisco Vargas is more interested in reality. Vargas's *El violin* (*The Violin*, 2005)

*Captured rebels under fire in* The Violin. *Courtesy Francisco Vargas, Cámara Carnal Films.*

is the ultimate guerrilla movie: about Latin American guerrillas, it was also shot and distributed guerrilla-style. Although it piled up festival awards (fifty-five at last count) and worldwide distribution, it was unable to find a Mexican distributor. "*El violin* is definitely a movie that would find an audience, and I really find it obscene that it isn't being distributed," director Guillermo del Toro said.[2] So Vargas and friends moved into action. "We are not distributors, but in spite of this we were forced to become our own distributors," he says. "We organized a sort of alternative distribution campaign." Instead of conventional advertising, they covered Mexico City as if they were organizing a mass rally, handing out thousands of leaflets, staging campus forums on issues raised in the movie, and spreading the catch-phase, "I saw *The Violin*, how about you?" Soon *The Violin* was in the news and word of mouth was widespread. "And we reached 400,000 spectators in the sixteen weeks the film was shown."

*The Violin* is a stunning movie without a moment of dishonesty. Set in a sumptuously shot black-and-white countryside, it's about an elderly violinist, who is forced to perform for a military commander, but works with the rebels. "The black-and-white aesthetic, along with the hand-held camera and the work of professional and non-professional actors gave the film that documentary feeling," says Vargas. The response to the violinist's dignified, uncompromising rebel stand was understandably overwhelming, starting at Cannes, then inspiring audiences everywhere it screened. "Many of us want and dream for a new world," Vargas explains. At the Centro de Capacitación Cinematográfica (CCC), he studied filmmaking, while taking a minor in street protests and sit-ins. "I was at the protests against the closure of the CCC and the neoliberal policies that the corrupt government in Mexico has been establishing in recent years," he says. He was determined to fuse his passions for filmmaking and social justice. "That was, and still is, the reason for my artistic work."

It took Vargas six years to raise resources for *The Violin* (IMCINE funds, CCC equipment, and individual contributions), so it was gratifying to see movie-goers' excitement. "When they see on the screen a reflection of their reality or of their problems, people are grateful and they support it and go to the movies," Vargas says.

‡

The advent of sound in the late 1920s spread confusion at the US studios, which at first made foreign-language versions of its films before finding that too expensive and sometimes unintentionally funny. "Members of the same [onscreen] family spoke with different accents, mixing Asturian with Argentine, Mexican, Cuban, and Andalusian accents," noted director Alejandro Galindo.[3] Hollywood quickly regained its foreign footing with dubbing and subtitles, but a more authentic Spanish-language cinema had arisen—a "Golden Age" of Mexican movies that lasted into the 1950s. Some non-Mexican filmmakers made their contribution to Mexican cinema during this era too, most notably Sergei Eisenstein, who directed the unfinished folkloric epic *¡Que viva Mexico!* in 1932, and Luis Buñuel, who lived and worked in Mexico from the 1940s to the 1960s.

By the 1940s, film was Mexico's sixth largest industry, with the Banco Cinematográfico, the only bank created for a national cinema, providing the capital for production. Along with ample production of melodramatic schlock, Mexico's "Golden Age" was infused with cultural nationalism—a search for the country's cinematic self—expressed most prolifically by directors Fernando de Fuentes (*El compadre Mendoza*, 1934 and *Vámonos con Pancho Villa/Let's Go with Pancho Villa*, 1936) and Emilio Fernández, whose *María Candelaria* (1944) won the Grand Prix at the 1946 Cannes Film Festival. "I dreamt and am still dreaming of a different cinema, of course, but Mexican, pure," said Fernandez. "Now I have this great desire to Mexicanize the Mexicans, for we are becoming Americanized."[4]

Mexico's Golden Age also featured movie stars such as María Félix, Cantinflas, and Lupe Vélez. Dolores Del Río was a star of two "golden" ages, the first in Hollywood, the other in Mexico. She had taken silent Hollywood by storm in the late 1920s and continued into the talkies, scandalously swimming nude in *Bird of Paradise* (1932) and dancing with Astaire and Rogers in *Flying Down to Rio* (1933). Del Río and Orson Welles struck up a relationship in 1940, and when *Citizen Kane* was targeted by the Hearst empire, she stood with him. She returned from Hollywood in the early 1940s to star in Fernández's *Flor Silvestre* (1943) and *María Candelaria*. Dismissed as a "Communist sympathizer" (her friends included Frida Kahlo and Diego Rivera), Del Río was denied permission to work in the US for a time during the blacklist era.

Mexican cinema was the largest in Latin America, and steps were taken to keep it that way. With American expatriate businessman William Jenkins buying up Mexican theaters in 1949, President Miguel Alemán Valdés' government enacted a screen quota that required theaters to show domestic films fifty percent of the time. The quota, however, was tied up in the courts and barely enforced, and Jenkins continued purchasing theaters and screening American studio movies. Shortly after social reformer Adolfo López Mateos was elected president in the late 1950s, he nationalized movie theaters and distribution, but it was too late for the Golden Age. Along with Jenkins' preference for US movies, competition had emerged from television, which was as adept at appealing to melodramatic sensibilities as the era's bottom-feeder Mexican movie producers, who left expensive production values to Hollywood and increasingly turned to making bare-budget movies with titles like *La Momia azteca contra el robot humano* (*The Aztec Mummy vs. the Human Robot*, 1958). In the 1950s and '60s, movie attendance in Mexico plummeted, although production reached a record 136 features in 1958.

There was also a small but persistent auteur filmmaking community in Mexico. Buñuel made more than twenty Mexican films between 1946 and 1965, including *El ángel exterminador* (*The Exterminating Angel*, 1962) and his great and tough look at Mexico City streets, *Los olvidados* (*The Lost Ones*, 1950). Neorealism with a touch of surreal, *Los olvidados'* Mexico is relentless and sexy; it's young people at their worst, Buñuel at his best. A "New Latin American Cinema" developed in the region in the 1960s and '70s, with Mexicans directors such as Arturo Ripstein (*El castillo de la pureza/The Castle of Purity*, 1973), Felipe Cazals (*Canoa*, 1976), and Alejandro Jodorowsky (*El Topo*, 1970).

By the 1970s, the government owned sixty percent of the country's movie theaters. The privatization of Mexico's nationalized cinema began in earnest in 1989 under the administration of free-market ideologue Carlos Salinas de Gortari; the state theater chain was sold to large American and Mexican companies. In 1992, when the North American Free Trade Agreement was signed, Mexico's congress passed legislation reducing the screen quota from fifty percent to zero over a four-year period. During talks for NAFTA—which joined Mexico, Canada, and the US as the world's largest trading bloc—the Mexican government didn't even argue for a cultural exemption, suggesting its local culture was strong enough to withstand free trade. Instead, as Mexico sunk into debt, state film funding was cut and production shriveled. There were 747 films produced between 1984 and 1994 and only 212 the following decade.[5] The Banco Nacional Cinematográfico was closed and state-owned distribution agencies disappeared, no longer having state-owned theaters to distribute to. In 1995, Mexico produced just five feature films. "With NAFTA, the Mexican industry was left in the cold to just be openly ravaged," director Guillermo del Toro said.[6]

‡

It was the arrival of a new group of filmmakers in the late 1990s and early 2000s that brought Mexican film more international attention than the Golden Age had at its peak, and with a new urban reality—the dog-fighting wars of Alejandro González Iñárritu's *Amores perros* (*Love's a Bitch*, 2000), the middle-class intimacies of Antonio Serrano's *Sexo, pudor y lágrimas* (*Sex, Shame and Tears*, 1999), the sexual exploration of Alfonso Cuarón's *Y tu mamá tambien* (*And Your Mother Too*, 2001). In 1999, *Sex, Shame and Tears* set a Mexican box-office record, taking in $12.4 million. Two years later, *Y tu mamá tambien* attracted $11.2 million, with leads Gael García Bernal and Diego Luna becoming Golden Age-style Mexican movie stars. *Y tu mamá* and *Amores perros* attracted most of the world's attention, but Carlos Carrera's *El crimen del Padre Amaro* (*The Crime of Father Amaro*, 2002) drew the largest crowds back home, bringing in $16.5 million to shatter *Sex, Shame and Tears'* record.

"There was a rush to produce after *Sex, Shame and Tears*," said Alta-vista Films' Federico González Compeán. "There was gold fever. But then we realized that it wasn't so easy."[7] Despite the occasional break-through, local films were hard to find. Mexicans purchased a record 164 million movie tickets in 2004, but fewer than eight million were for domestic movies. Even *Sex, Shame and Tears* couldn't stave off the US studios' insatiable appetite for screens; it opened number two at the box office in the nation and was still at number four in the second week when its screenings were cut back to make way for *Ice Age 2* (2006). Gustavo Loza's *Al otro lado* (*To the Other Side*, 2004), Mexico's candidate for the foreign-language Oscar in 2005, was fourth at the box office on its opening weekend, but half of its prints were pulled from theaters two weeks later to make way for *Batman Begins* (2005) and *Madagas-car* (2005), whose 650 prints apiece took up forty percent of Mexican screens.

"From the outside, it looks really good. There is this amazing gen-eration. But from the inside, it is the opposite," said Iñárritu.[8] It's near impossible for independents to recoup a film's costs because exhibitors take sixty percent of grosses from day one, while the studios keep 100 percent of opening weekend grosses. "It is very unfair," says filmmaker Mariana Chenillo. "Why do they keep sixty percent of the ticket if they don't make any investment at all, and they also sell popcorn and they have twenty minutes of advertisement before the film starts?"

‡

Vincente Fox vowed to increase Mexican film production during his 2000 presidential campaign to replace the tired, corrupt PRI. Film-makers welcomed a French-style one-peso (almost ten-cent) levy on ticket sales, which had been enacted in 2002 to provide funding for local productions. The law would triple the film-funding agency Insti-tuto Mexicano de Cinematografía (IMCINE)'s budget, but it was op-posed by exhibitors. Jack Valenti, never one to stay out of this kind of internal dispute, wrote Fox warning that the levy could jeopardize studio investment in Mexico and be a detriment to US-Mexican rela-tions. Much of the Mexican film community signed an open letter by actress María Rojo and producer Jorge Sánchez urging Fox to stand up to Valenti's "threats," noting: "Any support to national cinema, such as the peso levy on admissions which bothers Mr. Valenti so much, is vital for its survival."[9] The levy, though, would die in court after exhibitors and studios filed injunctions.

In November 2003, Fox took an axe to the arts, including the sale or closure of IMCINE, the Churubusco Azteca studios, and the CCC film school. The film community fought back: CCC students, faculty, and alumni staged a protest march at which director-graduate Carlos Carrera decried the cuts as "schizophrenic."[10] The Mexican Academy of Cinematic Arts and Sciences accused the government of planning to "exterminate domestic film production, privileging the interests of the US movie industry."[11] A letter opposing the cuts attracted signatories from France to Uruguay. Alejandro González Iñárritu commented: "It's incredible that right now, when Mexican cinema has caught worldwide attention, instead of saying, 'Let's support this industry more,' they would do the exact opposite. This is a move typical of a president who wears cowboy boots."[12]

‡

Mariana Chenillo was a student at CCC when Fox moved to close it. "They couldn't do it because all the film community just stood up. It was a very stupid proposal from the start. That school really helped create the Mexican film industry. Carlos Carrera and Ignacio Ortiz and Rodrigo Plá and Francisco Vargas came out of there. And Alfonso Cuarón and Guillermo del Toro, and many, many more." At first, Fox turned a deaf ear to the protests, but the president didn't win the majority he needed in congress to push his measures through. The Mexican film community had successfully served notice.

After university, Chenillo set out to make a feature based on her grandmother's repeated suicide attempts. Funding for her script, *Cinco días sin Nora (Nora's Will*, 2008), about a woman who kills herself to reunite her family, came together slowly, so Chenillo used the down time to visit the homes of older women to learn how to meticulously recreate the specifics of her grandmother's Mexico City apartment. Chenillo has a way with the details of everyday living. "I discovered that film was the perfect way to talk about things that were small—not small as in unimportant but invisible. And if you're making a film about one decision in one person's life, then you can magnify it and you can get into the details. That's what really excites me." A left-wing, non-religious Jew, Chenillo considered removing a storyline involving Jewish burial rituals, but decided such particulars about her grandmother's background would breathe truth into the film. "I thought that, being my first film,

*Mariana Chenillo at work on* Nora's Will. *Courtesy Mariana Chenillo.*

talking about where I come from with honesty and with the capacity to laugh about some things would make it a more articulate film." In *Nora's Will*, her grandmother's suite is the place where truth is pervasive and everything is questioned—the family, mental illness, religion, suicide, food.

Chenillo was caught by surprise that the animus to the notion of a female director lingers so strongly in the twenty-first century. "I don't think we are really considered as intelligent or as talented. We are girls, and we are supposed to tell 'girly stories.' If you say that you're a feminist, men are like, 'You should have been in the '70s.' I think the truth is that it's not an old-fashioned argument. Every day you have to wake up and convince everyone that you woke up intelligent again. I don't know how it is in other countries, but in Mexico it's a really big issue." An increasing number of female directors have beat the stereotyping, however, including Marisa Sistach, Dana Rotberg, and Maricarmen de Lara. Director María Novaro was active in Cine-Mujer, the first Mexican women's film collective, then went on to make more than fifteen shorts and features including the groundbreaking *Danzón* (1991). Not the typical dancing-will-set-you-free movie, the dance here is the starting point for the protagonist's examination of her entire life.

‡

*Nora's Will* was widely acclaimed everywhere and Chenillo took awards for best director at the L.A. Latino International Film Festival and the Moscow Film Festival. "We sold it in Europe and also in Latin America," she says. The film even enjoyed a limited release in the US. Back home, it won seven Ariels (the Mexican film awards), but faced the usual distribution difficulties. The film opened in thirty theaters and drew crowds, but to make room for studio products, it was cut back to one "artsy" theater after just three weeks. "I had my film go through that horrible commercial death; we just send them to die there on the screen. We have many, many screens and lots of teenagers that go to the theaters every weekend, so we are an important market for the American blockbusters. They say, 'If you don't keep this Sandra Bullock film that no one wants to see on your screens for three months, then we won't give you *Spider-Man* this summer.'" Rodrigo Plá also had exhibition problems with his first feature *La Zona* (*The Zone*, 2007). "The majors put 1,200 copies of the same [US] picture in theaters. There is no place to put our pictures." He's not counting on government to do something about it. "Not this right-wing party that is the government."

Plá's student short, *El ojo en la nuca* (*The Eye in the Neck*, 2001) won a 2001 student Oscar while he was attending the CCC. A US agent and offers followed, mostly American projects about Mexican subjects, or rather "what America thinks about Mexico. And we are nothing like that." Plá had his own stories to tell. "I said to my agent, 'Don't send me any scripts. We are going to send you our script, and that's it.'" His features *The Zone* and *Desierto adentro* (*The Desert Within*, 2008), provide a lesson in the two paths facing Mexican filmmakers. Set in the aftermath of a break-in at a gated Mexico City neighborhood, *The Zone* was sold to Columbia Pictures, then a large Spanish production company got involved and, with a $2.5 million budget, Plá lost creative control. "I had to negotiate. I lost the script. They wanted me to put more music in it than I wanted." *The Desert Within*, on the other hand, drew financing from IMCINE's fund for art-film production. Set during a rural religious war in 1920s Mexico, the movie shows, through one family, how destructive a self-prophesy religion can be, how a father who believes in ritual and superstition ends up killing his children. "This is an independent movie. I didn't have anyone imposing anything. The story we wanted to do is the story we thought was interesting, and we wanted to talk about religion, madness, and all that." His next film will also be independent. "I will do whatever I want ... maybe not use music."

‡

In the face of obstacles such as NAFTA, the government's attempts to shut down the film community, the absence of backing from major broadcasters, and exhibitors' scant regard for local cinema, many Mexican actors and directors have moved on. Drug wars and street violence have also taken a toll: Iñárritu, for example, was robbed at gunpoint while location scouting *Amores perros* and had to rely on street-gang protection to ensure the movie's completion. "As a result of the socioeconomic inequality and the corruption of the government ... to live in Mexico today is to live in fear,"[13] he said. While Guillermo del Toro is admired by many in Mexico, he received some criticism when his film *El laberinto del fauno (Pan's Labyrinth,* 2006), a magic-realist tale of a young girl who utilizes her imagination to combat fascism in Spain after the civil war, was Mexico's nominee for the foreign-language Oscar—even though it drew partly on European funding and was shot in Spain. "I don't have problems with people making their movies outside of the country," says filmmaker Enrique Begne. "The only thing wrong about that is to call it Mexican cinema. Mexican movies are the movies that we make in Mexico." Begne's passion for Mexican cinema doesn't stop him from considering non-Mexican options, too, having had a strong first film, *Dos abrazos (Two Embraces,* 2007), badly distributed. "Mexico's a very difficult [place in which] to make movies. You don't have real support. You have to use your own money. That is the only reason why I want maybe to make a movie in a different country, but always independent."

‡

At the 1991 Toronto festival with his first feature, *Sólo con tu pareja (Love in the Time of Hysteria,* 1991), Alfonso Cuarón was approached by Sydney Pollack. The American director-producer loved the film and invited Cuarón to L.A. to direct an episode of his TV series *Fallen Angels.* Cuarón stayed in the US and directed the features *A Little Princess* (1995) and *Great Expectations* (1998). While he was mentoring young filmmakers at the Sundance Institute, Cuarón was struck by how jaded he had become. "I was really taken aback by the complete faith and dedication these guys had about their work. That was when I said to myself, 'I really need to reconnect with what my work is about.'"[14]

So Cuarón stepped away from directing MGM's *Hart's War* to return to low-budget, Mexican filmmaking with *Y tu mamá también*, his tale of two teenage males taking to the Mexican road with an older woman. "He could do anything he wanted without having to consult with anybody—no studio, no producer, nothing," said Cuarón's repeat cinematographer Emmanuel Lubezki. "It was a totally freeing experience. He needed that. In *Love in the Time of Hysteria*, he tasted that fruit. And once you have tasted that freedom, it's hard to go back."[15] *Y tu mamá también* is an entrancing, freewheeling travelogue. Its characters are on a road to modernization, but they pass through the now-marginalized *campesino* culture along their way. In the midst of a brief scene involving a fisherman, it's noted that he will lose his livelihood when his beach is developed by a hotel chain. "For me, that is a perfect example of what's happening in Mexico," Cuarón said. "For the sake of economic growth, they have forgotten about keeping the integrity of the culture. But I love my country. The film takes a negative view of the system, but the people and the land are full of life."[16] The traveling shoot gave Cuarón an eyeful of the new-look Mexico. "You could see the damage modernism and liberalism have done to the country. You could see new construction and shopping centers, but things were as socially bad as before, if not worse."[17]

Cuarón, del Toro, and Iñárritu frequently collaborate. As with the New Hollywood filmmakers or Korea's blockbuster auteurs, the three Mexican directors play in the studio world, and arranged a collective $100-million five-picture deal with Universal that included creative autonomy. When del Toro's *Blade II* (2002) grossed $155 million, he had his pick of studio projects, but instead went to Spain to make *Pan's Labyrinth*. After Cuarón, del Toro, and Iñárritu accumulated between them sixteen nominations at the 2007 Oscars—for *Pan's Labyrinth*, Cuarón's *Children of Men*, and Iñárritu's *Babel*—they returned to Mexico to lobby for regulation of exhibition and distribution to prevent US studio domination of Mexican theaters. "There is a family of filmmakers in Mexico that is large and talented. What is alarming is that there is no industry," said del Toro.[18]

Cuarón left Mexico, in part, to avoid dependence on its broken funding apparatus. "I'd tell them I wanted this movie to be sold outside Mexico," says Cuarón, "and the bureaucrats would tell me—and these are the people who are supposed to be supporting Mexican cinema—

they said, 'Don't be arrogant. Nobody gives a shit about Mexican cinema in the world, not even in Mexico.'"[19] Cuarón plans to make a movie about the protests that turned deadly at the 1968 Summer Olympics in Mexico City. Iñárritu and del Toro continue to make films in Spanish. "Growing up as young filmmakers, we felt there should be no borders that define who we are, but there should be roots that define who we are," del Toro said.[20] They are internationalists from a country whose border has long been a theme of its movies, a way to distinguish itself from the giant to the north and shed light on Mexican culture.

In American and Mexican movies, this border, depending on the filmmaker's perspective, has been the line between civilization (represented, say, by El Paso, Texas) and lawlessness (Tijuana), between hardworking and lazy, between mundane and exotic, between exploiter and exploited, between modern and primitive, between legal and illegal—from Miguel Contreras Torres's *Hombre sin patria* (*Man Without a Country*, 1922), to Roberto Curwood's *La China Hilaria* (1939), Alejandro Galindo's *Espaldas mojadas* (*Wetbacks*, 1955), Orson Welles *Touch of Evil* (1958), Gregory Nava's *El Norte* (1983), Maria Novaro's *El Jardín del Edén* (*The Garden of Eden*, 1994), Steven Soderbergh's *Traffic* (2000), the Coen brothers' *No Country for Old Men* (2007), and Patricia Riggen's *La misma luna* (*Under the Same Moon*, 2007). Galindo's *Wetbacks* is a cautionary tale of the hostile reception that awaits a Mexican worker who illegally crosses into the US for work. At one point, a Mexican-American woman tells him: "I feel very alone and afraid … I'm not Mexican, I was born here. I'm a *pocha*. Mexicans don't like us. And the whites, well, you saw."

Some Mexican talent vows to never leave the country, such as actor-director-producer Gael García Bernal: "This is the place that excites me. I have a strong itch that keeps me here, to be a part of this place. I think that if I abandon it, I'll become just another actor, like all the rest."[21] For Chenillo, it's a matter of knowing the local color of Mexico City. "I wouldn't know how to write a screenplay somewhere else," she says. The notion of moving on to studio work in Hollywood seems ludicrous to director Carlos Reygadas: "I have sufficient money to live as I like. Why should I be there? Would you move to Kansas City to print a book if they paid you a million dollars? I like to do what I like. I don't want to be dogmatic—maybe one day I will run out of ideas for inspiration and I will just feel like doing it, but for the moment I'm very happy. I'm doing this because it's a need. Making movies takes a lot of energy from you, and to spend your life doing someone else's dreams would be a waste."

Born in Mexico City, Reygadas was a lawyer specializing in international conflict, having worked with the European Union in Belgium and Mexico's UN delegation in New York, when he decided to quit and become a filmmaker. "I realized that my life was being dictated by others, as if I were in the military," he says. In 2002, his first feature *Japón* was released. His second—*Batalla en el cielo* (*Battle in Heaven*, 2005), the story of a chauffeur for a wealthy young woman who turns tricks, with stops at sexuality, shame, violence, church, and state—opens with an oral sex scene, which was enough to create a Mexican standoff between its backers and film authorities. Despite the success of Reygadas's *Japón*, including Cannes' Camera d'Or Special Jury Mention, IMCINE refused to fund *Battle in Heaven* four times until it too was invited to screen at Cannes. Reygadas didn't much care what authorities had to say about the film, and trying to appeal to an audience doesn't interest him either. "You start seeing people as just consumers, so you ask about trends, and you finish by making products for the minimum common denominator, and that means the quality diminishes."

‡

Mexico's independent filmmaking is remarkably vibrant in the face of so little support. There has been a breakout of talented directors in the new century, including Reygadas, Plá, Chenillo, Vargas, Fernando Eimbecke, Gerardo Naranjo, Patricia Riggen, Amat Escalante, and Ernesto Contreras. Filmmakers such as Israel Cárdenas and Laura Amelia Guzmán, who co-directed the festival favorite *Cochochi* (2007), demonstrate the potential of no-budget digital. By the early 2000s, production spread beyond its traditional Mexico City habitat, with digital auteurs from Guadalajara to Monterrey.

‡

In 2007, Warner Bros. dropped its offer to release Mexican filmmaker Luis Mandoki's *Fraude: Mexico 2006*, a documentary about the rigged electoral "victory" of conservative president Felipe Calderón. The film documents the role played by Televisa, Latin America's largest media conglomerate, in the campaign against left-wing presidential candidate Andrés Obrador. Televisa is Warner's Mexican partner.

In 2009, Calderón announced a forty-six percent cut to IMCINE and a twenty percent cut to Efecine, a program that encourages film investors. Since the privatization of Mexican cinema, it's been one fight for survival after another. "First it was for one peso from the box office, then it was screen the films for a minimum of two or three weeks," says Chenillo. "Every year there have been two or three big moments where they're just about to do something about it, but ever since they sold the theaters, we haven't been able to do anything about it. They make a lot of money, and they're not willing to let that change. It's not an easy fight, but there is a film community that gets together and fights to make it better. Since it's very small, everyone knows everyone and it is supportive."

After speaking with me, Chenillo was going to spend her weekend finishing a short for the omnibus movie, *Revolución* (2010), which brought together ten of Mexico's best filmmakers to mark the 100th anniversary of the Mexican revolution.

In the striking finale of *Revolución*, Rodrigo Garcia's short *7th and Alvarado*, Pancho Villa's army, circa 1910, rides on horseback into Mexican Los Angeles, circa 2010. The proud, grizzled revolutionists, with their sombreros and bandoliers— as photogenic as the day Villa choreographed their newsreel— ride in slow motion amidst their urban American descendants who, armed with cellphones, go about their business oblivious to any need for revolution, then or now.

While Mexican audiences seldom shoot the screen today, the revolution lives on. The best of Mexican cinema lives on the margins, facing intractable obstacles, but it continues to take risks and speak truths. "It is because of this that my way is going independent, without being limited by content or form, and even though it is more difficult, it is exciting," Vargas says. "It is dangerous because there is a thin line that separates independent from marginal, and I am not interested in being marginal, only independent. As long as I can go on doing it this way, I will continue, and when I can't, then I will do something else."

## CHAPTER THIRTEEN

## Romania: Out of the Silence

ON ONE OF THE HOTTEST days of the year, director Bogdan Apetri has been sitting at a table outside a café in Bucharest and telling me how much he likes Fellini when four men in tattered suits, carrying a heavy coffin, come walking down the middle of the dusty downtown street, causing us to pause as the scene plays out. "Look at it," says Apetri. "Bucharest. Typical. These weird things happen in Romania that you don't see anywhere else, and people take them for normal."

Apetri left Romania in 2001 to attend film school at New York's Columbia University. "I felt that nothing is moving in Romanian cinema," he says. But when Cristi Puiu's *Moartea domnului Lazarescu* (*The Death of Mr. Lazarescu*) opened in 2005, "I said, okay, something is happening in Romanian cinema. Then Porumboiu came with *12:08: East of Bucharest*. I thought it was a masterpiece. Then *4 Months, 3 Weeks & 2 Days,* which I think is one of the best movies I ever saw. I knew that something big is happening in Romania." Apetri was back to direct his first Romanian feature, *Outbound* (2010). "I only came here because the company sent me the script and asked me to direct it," he says. "I didn't come because I said, 'Okay, I'm going to be part of the Romanian New Wave.'"

The Romanian filmmakers who comprise this New Wave caught the film world—even the small corner of that world that resides in Romania—by surprise in the mid-2000s. It's a country with a minuscule movie-going audience and almost without movie screens, but it has filmmakers, mostly anonymous at home, whose work resonates with movie lovers everywhere.

‡

Romanian filmmakers were silent for much of the twentieth century—a silence enforced first by fascists, then by Stalinists—and when filmmakers finally spoke, it was sudden and explosive, like the opening of Corneliu Porumboiu's *Polițist, adjectiv* (*Police, Adjective,* 2009). The film begins with a long silent tracking shot of a teenager being followed by an undercover cop who doesn't believe in the marijuana law that he has been ordered to enforce. When, in contrast with the lengthy dead silence that precedes it, the film's dialogue finally does begin, it feels heightened, a burst of cinematic language all Porumboiu's own.

When I meet him, the director sits in his Bucharest office, having recently returned from Cannes, where *Police, Adjective* won two prizes. His other feature, *A fost sau n-a fost?* (*12:08 East of Bucharest*), won the Camera d'Or for best debut at Cannes in 2006. Whenever Porumboiu leaves Romania these days, he finds a visceral enthusiasm for its cinema. "It's overwhelming. I feel it when I travel, when I go to the festivals. But when you come back, it's another thing because here you start to forget this, because here it's a small world."

‡

Romania's actual silent-movie era wasn't particularly distinguished, but the country did have 250 theaters by the 1920s. When fascist Ion Anonescu took power in 1940, his Axis government commandeered the country's production facilities for propaganda purposes. After World War II, the new Communist government nationalized the film industry, imported projectors from the Soviet Union, and opened theaters in the countryside. Much of the institutional side of the movie industry arrived in the 1950s,[1] including the I.L. Caragiale Institute of Theatre and Film (IATC) and the National University of Drama and Film (UNATC), and with Buftea Studio and other infrastructure in place, filmmakers were called upon to produce movies promoting president Gheorghe Gheorghiu-Dej and, from 1965, Nicolae Ceaușescu.

Most films shown were from other Eastern Bloc countries, but Romania continued its own long, if marginal, history of production, including historical epics extolling Romanian nationhood like *Mihai Viteazul* (*Michael the Brave, 1971*). Filmmaking wasn't entirely reduced to period versions of Nicolae Ceaușescu the Brave, however; although much of Ceaușescu-era filmmaking was as uncritical as the rest of the country's government-controlled mass media, some filmmakers found artistic expression in circumventing the censors. The most notable of these pre-Wave filmmakers was Lucian Pintilie, whose *Duminică la ora șase* (*Sunday at Six,* 1965) is about a couple torn between responsibility to the Party and their love, a premise—the individual inside an intrusive nation-state—that would be repeatedly revisited by New Wave filmmakers. His *Reconstituirea* (*The Reconstruction,* 1968) was shot verité-style as, one by one, its authority figures—lawyer, cop, teacher—help students recreate a drunken brawl. This relative freedom came to a crashing halt in the East-West tensions following the invasion of Czechoslovakia in 1968.

Pintilie went into exile in France, while Ceaușescu entrenched his cult of no-personality, convinced that he personified everything good about Romania. The dictator fought his fall a little harder than other Eastern Bloc leaders—his soldiers fired on protestors—when so many of their dictatorships were swept aside by uprisings in 1989.

‡

Cristian Mungiu's 2007 Palme D'Or winner, *4 luni, 3 saptamani si 2 zile* (*4 Months, 3 Weeks and 2 Days*, or *4, 3, 2*, as it's known in Romania), is a brave film dealing with abortion at a time when few filmmakers were willing to even mention the word. It's about a young woman undergoing a meticulously detailed, chilling illegal abortion in Ceaușescu's Romania; there's no melodrama but plenty of pure, raw storytelling. "He understood so well the woman's psychology," says filmmaker Ruxandra Zenide. "I was very impressed. I wouldn't think that a man could understand and show it so well as he did in his film."

Abortion was legalized in Romania in 1957 by the Communist government of Gheorghiu-Dej, but in 1966 Ceaușescu introduced an anti-abortion, anti-contraception law to reverse the nation's flagging birth rate. Births nearly doubled, but Ceaușescu had ironically enacted his own undoing. This massive generation would come of age in the late 1980s and, like earlier rebellious Baby Boomers in the West, take their youthful ideals into the streets, playing a pivotal role in his overthrow. So it's fitting that the benchmark film of the New Wave would be about an illegal abortion during the Ceaușescu era. The New Wave filmmakers, those in the streets at the time, and those who watched events unfold as children, were all deeply touched by the fall of Ceaușescu.

Romanians started to lose the movie-going habit in the 1980s when the government placed an embargo on Western films. A film culture grew outside of movie theaters, as people watched smuggled Hollywood movies on VCRs. "We used to go to people's places to watch films," says director Cristi Puiu.

> You could watch five or six films in one night. You paid fifty *leu* and you could see *Rambo*, *Terminator*, *Taxi Driver*, and *Once Upon a Time in America*. It started this pirate cinema; it was really the beginning of what is happening now. People just stayed at home to watch films. Cinema became less and less attractive. After the fall of Communism, businessmen

bought theaters from the state and turned them into bingo places and bistros, because they weren't interested any more in cinema. You stay at home, you drink your beer, and you watch the film. And now it is really, really difficult to convince people to go out to cinema.

Before 1989, when the Communist regime was ousted, twenty-five to thirty features were produced annually, but filmmaking became almost extinct by 1999—not one Romanian feature was released the entire year, or the next. By the early 2000s, the country's more than 600 theaters had been reduced to a dilapidated handful—estimates range from thirty-five to eighty (for a population of 22 million). Some cities didn't have one cinema. For Porumboiu's *12:08: East of Bucharest*, five prints were made and 13,000 tickets sold. "The problem is that, in Bucharest, we have just two multiplexes, so they keep it just three or four weeks," he says. "We don't have specialized cinemas for independent movies." Adds Apetri: "The percentage of the population going to cinema is the worst in Europe, the number of theaters the worst in Europe. It just collapsed after Communism. Nobody goes. I think there's even antagonism toward Romanian movies."

‡

At the turn of the century, there was little hint of the New Wave to come. Talk of Romanian cinema seemed to be mired in how to attract cost-cutting Western producers, the problems of piracy, and the run-down state of movie theaters. Then, at Cannes, seemingly out of nowhere, the Wave quietly arrived. Cristi Puiu's and Cristian Mungiu's first features, *Marfa si banii* (*Stuff and Dough*, 2001) and *Occident* (*West*, 2002), were acclaimed, and Cătălin Mitulescu's *Trafic* (*Traffic*), was selected best short in 2004. The perception of Romanian film would change when *The Death of Mr. Lazarescu* won Cannes' 2005 Un Certain Regard prize and was the talk of other festivals, then went into theatrical release from the US to Sweden. In 2006, there were three Cannes success stories for Romanian filmmakers, all set during the last days of Ceaușescu: Porumboiu's *12:08 East of Bucharest*, Mitulescu's *Cum mi-am petrecut sfarsitul lumii* (*How I Celebrated the End of the World*), and Radu Muntean's *Hartia va fi albastra* (*The Paper Will Be Blue*). Ruxandra Zenide's *Ryna* won top prize at the Valencia festival in Spain. In 2007, Cristian Nemescu's *California Dreamin'* was Cannes' Un Certain Regard winner, and Mungiu's *4, 3, 2* won the biggest prize of all, the Palme d'Or, and was picked up for worldwide distribution. "The success of Romanian cinema over the last three years has been a surprise for everybody," Thessaloniki International Film Festival programmer Dimitri Kerkinos said in 2007. "Romanian filmmakers have not had a lot of support from the state and little infrastructure, but there's so much talent, and I think the problems actually spark creativity."[2] The festival acclaim continued; Marian Crisan's *Megatron* was Cannes' best short in 2008 and Florin Şerban's *Eu cand vreau sa fluier, fluier* (*If I Want to Whistle, I Whistle*) took two prizes at the 2010 Berlin festival.

There were seven Romanian features produced in 2001, another seven in 2007, but thanks to the New Wave, one of the smallest producers of film in Europe was among the biggest winners at Cannes. On many levels, awards don't matter, but without a domestic audience they took on importance to the Romanians. "You're almost sure that here nobody's going to see your movie," Apetri says. "People think your only chance of survival is to get two or three awards and a limited distribution in Italy and France. And that's the best you can do with a Romanian movie. Here, economic reasons don't matter at all. You get half of your funding from the government; you get the other half from people who are already tax exempt, so you're not forced to generate any returns. You don't care about it. You take the money, you make the movie, and that's it."

Filmmaker Radu Gabrea, once a student activist who had gone into exile in Germany in 1974, came home after the revolution to find movie audiences had disappeared. He became director of the National Film Office (later renamed the National Center for Cinematography [CNC]) when it was founded in 1997. Using European film legislation as the model, Gabrea established funding for screenplays, production, and distribution. Some New Wave filmmakers are renowned enough to receive CNC funding almost automatically. (Says Apetri: "The second movie of Corneliu Porumboiu—funding from the government; Mitulescu—funding from the government.") It's a near replica of France's CNC, minus the box-office levy. "I think it was just copied," says Apetri. "It has the same name as in France, and the structure is very similar." The non-existent audience means little potential for financial return, but tax exemptions draw out some film investors. Still, the CNC is the primary funding source for Romanian cinema. "It's very low," Zenide says. "You can get €250–300,000. It's very hard to make a film only with Romanian money."

‡

Porumboiu is chain-smoking in his sparse upstairs office. Every morning he comes here to write ("the best period in the process"). There have been offers from France and the US, but he knows the danger of making movies in an unfamiliar culture. "That's why I want to continue here," he says. "I am used to it. Bucharest can be like a jungle; but it's okay. It's not my favorite town in the world. I love it and I hate it, but I meet a lot of interesting people here. It's a good place to be for an artist."

In 1994, when almost any profession was a more realistic choice than filmmaking in Romania, eighteen-year-old Porumboiu arrived in Bucharest from small-town Vaslui to study management, and promptly fell in love with movies. "I started to go often to the cinematheque. I finished the management school and applied to the cinema university [UNATC], and I got in." After his short film took second place at Cannes, he raised €200,000 privately, assembled cast and crew, and began making *12:08 East of Bucharest.* The movie reflects on events in one town during the upheaval that swept away Ceaușescu, asking: Was it or wasn't it a revolution? "In '89, I was thirteen years old, and all the time I heard this question," says Porumboiu. On the uprising's tenth anniversary, he watched a television show asking the same question. It stuck with him, and six years later he started to write the script. After the film premiered at Cannes, the audience roared for fifteen minutes. It sold in thirty-five countries. Porumboiu rejected the offers that followed. "I write my stories, and after that I shoot it, and after that I edit it, and after that I also produce it, so I'm independent."

What's it like, I ask him, to have your Romanian story celebrated everywhere except Romania? "It's frustrating, but on the other hand, in terms of audience, 13,000 is okay. And we—the directors—have to grow the audience."

‡

While Cristi Puiu enjoyed pirate movie screenings in the 1980s, his focus was on painting. His interest in film grew after his cinephile uncle lent him Jim Jarmusch's *Stranger Than Paradise* (1984). "It changed my point of view. It was visually so powerful, so very close to what I was thinking of painting. It was like a movie painting. So I started watching films from that moment." Years later, Puiu would direct *Un cartus de kent si un pachet de cafea* (*Cigarettes and Coffee*, 2004), an eleven-minute conversation between a father and son, titled in tribute to Jarmusch's *Coffee and Cigarettes* (2003).

Puiu studied painting in Geneva, but "after a year, I just said to myself, I want to switch to film." After graduating in 1996, he returned to Romania to make movies, and his first feature, *Stuff and Dough* (2001), played Cannes. In 2003, Puiu and other filmmakers were in a face-off with the CNC, voicing their anger at its unbalanced support for directors from the Ceauşescu era. "Not just me, all the younger directors, we were treated like shit." Puiu and co-writer Răzvan Rădulescu were working on *The Story of the Ambulance* (later renamed *The Death of Mr. Lazarescu*) when *Cigarettes and Coffee* was named best short at the Berlin Film Festival. Good reviews for *Stuff and Dough* hadn't meant access to CNC funding, but Puiu thought this award might open a door, so he submitted *Ambulance*. "They didn't give me the money. So I went to the ministry of culture to complain, because the CNC was a department of the ministry of culture." The ministry was impressed enough to fund it.

The plot of *The Death of Mr. Lazarescu* was taken from a story in the headlines. "At the end of the night a guy called the ambulance. It came and picked him up, and they tried to get him into six hospitals." Refused admittance everywhere, he was left in the street where he died. "Things like this are happening in Romania. We have a lot of problems at all levels." Puiu's movie told a similar story, focusing more on small moments than a dramatic climax. "What I'm interested in is to capture bits of life.". The film is a sober look at the anguished finale to an unremarkable man's life. "Lazarescu was not an angel. It is about human beings. And this is the thing I am in interested in."

Puiu's latest, *Aurora* (2010), is a deliberately paced, three-hour look at a bitter man's violent reaction to perceived slights. While Puiu's movies are his own, they also have a life of their own.

> I really want to make the film that I have in my mind, but at the same time I know that the film that I have in my mind tomorrow is not the same thing I had in my mind yesterday. It's changing little by little. In the end it's very organic because you are not just finishing the script and then shooting accordingly—you keep on proposing things to yourself and you accept changes from the actors, art director, the DP [director of photography], and the sound engineer. It is very dynamic and, in the end, even for you, the director, the film

is a sort of a surprise. You want to do your film and the film
wants to do something else.

‡

At the age of fourteen, Ruxandra Zenide moved from Romania to Geneva with her parents just before the revolution. After studying international relations at the University of Geneva, she took a short,
intensive filmmaking course at New York University, then enrolled
in Prague's FAMU film school. "I wanted to go back [to Romania]. It
was some kind of a call from my native country," she says. So though
she resides in Switzerland, she returned to shoot her short *Green Oaks*
(2003), about a Swiss family adopting a Romanian girl. "Maybe for the
little girl it will be better with this family, but what she left behind is
very emotional."

The early New Wave was as consumed with Ceauşescu's Romania
and the revolution as Italy's neorealists were with World War II. "You
have to talk about this in order to go on to something else," Zenide
says. "This is part of our personal history and our country's history so
it's normal to explore this topic." She returned again to Romania to
shoot her first feature, *Ryna* (2005), a reflection on life under Ceauşescu.
Young Ryna (Doroteea Petre) is disregarded by nearly everyone in her
village, especially by her dictatorial father, who is determined to define
her, but she ultimately defies all of the abuse and stupidity. "[Defiance]
is important for developing ourselves and our society, because otherwise it's some kind of regime where we are all doing what someone else
wants. Ryna has to first get rid of what her father obliged her to be, to
have this rebellion, and to leave if her soul wants to survive."

Like Zenide, *Ryna* is a Romanian-Swiss co-production. She had to
keep the film's producers in check. "They wanted it to be more like a
nice journey to the delta. I said, 'No, this is not the *National Geographic*.'
Because it's a low-budget film, I could do what I wanted." Zenide is one
independent with zero interest in going Hollywood studio. "It doesn't
appeal to me. It's like an industry. If you're not Kubrick, you get very
formatted. The producer tells you exactly what you have to do. And
this would be very frustrating. For me, what's important, and what is
really hard—and it's less and less visible on the screen—is how to use a
film to express something without compromise, not just to entertain,
but to reveal something bigger."

Along with her international inclinations ("I would like to make a

*Dorotheea Petre in a reflective mood in* Ryna. *Courtesy Ruxandra Zenide.*

film in New York"), Zenide considers herself a proud part of the new Romanian cinema. "My film was produced by Cătălin Mitulescu. I feel very connected with Corneliu Porumboiu, with all these people we are talking about, and we watch each other's movies."

For his part, Porumboiu is uncertain about the nature of the Romanian New Wave. "I don't know if we are like the French New Wave; we don't have something like a manifesto," he says. "When I am making a movie I invite them to see some of it." New Wave does not mean new uniformity, but there are similarities between their films: no-frills realism set in near-real time, minimalistic scores, a hand-held vérité look, naturalistic acting, strong dramatic sense, and long often silent shots. The film's protagonists are frequently isolated characters who have contempt for ridiculous authority figures, a world-weary bleakness combined with irascible irreverence. The filmmakers are writer-directors who shared the Ceaușescu experience and are determined to tell Romanian stories. "We have a lot of things in common," Porumboiu says. "We grew up with movies that present extraordinary characters in extraordinary situations, and I see that my generation has this very realistic touch. We don't make up history. In a way, we are the people of our time, and this gives us a certain taste. If you look back, all of us started to study something else, and at [around the age of] twenty-five, started to study cinema. When you change your life, this means that you really love cinema. We thought that cinema is something important."

Mr Lazarescu wasn't the only one struggling in the newly capitalist Romania in the early twenty-first century. Power struggles, fraudulent elections, and recurring economic crises left many wondering what had come of this revolution. The young anti-Communist rebels of 1989 Romania weren't—despite the delusions of conservative ideologues—fighting for global capitalism any more than the young Communist rebels of 1930s America were fighting for global dictatorship. They were heady young idealists confronting the injustice they were dealt. New Wave filmmakers are defiantly independent and anti-authoritarian, and what disparate politics they have are sometimes muddled—progressive on specific issues (abortion rights, corporate culture) and dismissive of those seen to be on the left. "If you lived through Communism," says Apetri, "you're a little bit reserved about the left as a whole." But, he adds, "I'm definitely not on the right." Says Porumboiu: "It's like a joke. My wife is French, and she said that I'm from the left, that it's obvious from my movies. But I think that I am from the right. I don't see my movies in a political way; I concentrate on characters."

Independent filmmakers in the West and Asia have often supported socialist causes, but the government of Ceaușescu had nothing in common with, for example, the left-wing alternatives envisioned in Paris '68 or Barcelona '36. Mike Leigh encountered post-Soviet Bloc Eastern European attitudes toward the left when he traveled to Poland in 1989 to screen his *High Hopes* (1988) with its sympathetic English socialist couple. "Socialism was a dirty word for many Poles," said Leigh, "and the political culture gap between our perspective and theirs is not one you can glibly argue across."[3] There are Romanian filmmakers, however, who know that life is not relegated to a choice between Nicolae Ceaușescu or one of the George Bushes. "I was always a socialist," says Zenide. "Yes, I'm on the left. But for me, Stalinism and Ceaușescu—they're not socialism." *Ryna* was the first film in a planned trilogy; her second installment, she tells me, will be about "someone who has a dream, which is confronted with materialist society, Western society, and it's very hard for her. Her dream disappears more and more."

‡

When foreign producers pioneered post-Ceaușescu Romania, they found it to be the Eastern Bloc-turned-Wild East, complete with corrupt officials, dated equipment, and non-unionized crews. Film-industry suits came to a Bucharest in which every carpenter willing to work for twenty dollars a day more than made up for the packs of wild dogs and pick-pockets roaming mean streets where people were afraid to leave their cars to go to a movie. "We were seen as an uncivilized country. The US crews would bring their own toilet paper," said Romanian producer Bogdan Moncea.[4] It may not be Burbank or Canada, but Romania had enough of an infrastructure to make movies that looked like movies at a fraction of the cost of filming in North America. Among the results: *Return of the Living Dead 4: Necropolis* (2005), *Gargoyle: Wings of Darkness* (2004), *Highlander: Endgame* (2000), *Van Wilder 2: The Rise of Taj* (2006), and *Return of the Living Dead 5: Rave to the Grave* (2005). Some of *Borat* (2006) was shot in Romania too, but the big arrival was Anthony Minghella's $80 million US Civil War melodrama *Cold Mountain* (2003). Once the luxury trailers, unavailable in Romania, were shipped in from the UK for Nicole Kidman, Renée Zellweger, and Jude Law, the shoot began, with rural Romania standing in for North Carolina. "Without the savings that Romania offered, *Cold Mountain* would absolutely not have gotten made," said producer Albert Berger, who estimated the savings on labor alone at $20 million.[5]

‡

The imposing old house on Dimitrie Racovita Street is working quarters for Saga Film, which started out servicing foreign productions. As permit fees and labor costs have edged upward, producers have increasingly turned to Ukraine and Bulgaria, so Saga has largely gone local. It produced *4, 3, 2*, which drew more than 300,000 admissions in France alone. Mungiu, having sold his *Outbound* script to Saga, saw Apetri's shorts and wanted him to direct. Apetri, still living in New York, rewrote much of it. The shoot was about to begin when I arrived in Romania, so I joined Apetri and company on a location scout. It's sweltering when we crowd into a mustard-colored Vauxhall Vivaro van with not very cool air conditioning and bounce our way out of the city, past block after block of Ceaușescu-era utilitarian drabness. *Outbound* is about, in part, the gap between city and countryside in Romania. "It has to be at a certain moment, this huge contrast," explains production designer Simona Paduretu. Onto the highway, we pass farmland, then turn into a suburban village called Brănesti. Its cramped, hilly cemetery is a mix of intricately designed headstones and impromptu wooden crosses, and

*Bogdan Apetri (second from right) on the set of* Outbound. *Courtesy Bogdan Apetri.*

we can check off one location on Apetri's list. "We have to find another house in another village, a mall, a train, and a school," he says.

Romania is an easily impressionable place: the country drew its name from Rome, and Bucharest is nicknamed "the small Paris." On this day, Bucharest is looking more like St. Petersburg with weather like Managua, when suddenly I see an L.A. palm tree. We continue the search at the Bucharest Mall, emblematic of the new Bucharest, which mixes glass-and-steel modernity with only slightly less aesthetic McDonald's-Starbucks architecture. The mall features Romania's first multiplex—the Hollywood Multiplex—which opened in 2000. In its first month, the Hollywood Multiplex sold more tickets than all other Bucharest theaters combined.

‡

By the end of the decade, the New Wave was focusing on the present in Radu Jude's *Cea mai fericita fata din lume* (*The Happiest Girl in the World*, 2009), a contemporary poke at the country's attraction to celebrity and filmmaking, or Marian Crisan's *Morgen* (2010), about two consuming issues in current cinema: borders and religion. Romania's old theaters sit waiting for innovative programmers to appropriate them, and there are Romanian filmmakers who haven't given up on local audiences.

*Ana Ularu on the run in* Outbound. *Courtesy Bogdan Apetri.*

After *4, 3, 2* debuted, Mungiu took his show on the road across Romania, screening it in gymnasiums and concert halls in towns without theaters. With so few cinemas remaining in Romania, he took the film directly to audiences in thirty cities. "We had fifty percent more admissions than *Ratatouille* (2007), which was the most popular American film at the time."[6]

But Puiu is unable to name a Romanian film he's enthusiastic about. "No, not even my films," he says. "I like bits of the films that I made; I like bits of the films that the others made. Cinema will change a lot in Romania, not because of us, but because of the way the young generation is getting attached to the whole world. We in Romania are making ten films per year, so it is very important to be a part of world cinema, but at the same time, I need to watch films in my language." A great movie in Romanian, however, speaks a cinematic language everyone understands.

Meanwhile, the future of Romanian cinema is uncertain. "I don't know this," says Porumboiu. "Maybe our movies will be very different in ten years. I will be here and I will be making movies. But you never know."

‡

Bogdan Apetri may not have returned to Romania to join any film scene, but his first feature, *Outbound* (2010), is a fine addition to the New Wave. Matilda (Ana Ularu) is given a prison pass to attend her mother's funeral, then makes a break for freedom. But "freedom" for Matilda means being weary and irascible and running headlong into everything Romania can throw at her. Despite the bleakness, she stubbornly keeps moving, reconnecting, and looking for open space. So tough is this movie that its most poignant moment is an eight-year-old smoking cigarettes with his mother.

Porumboiu walks me from his office to the street, where a cab waits. "Was that Corneliu?" the driver asks. He tells me he likes going to the movies, not necessarily Romanian ones, and recognized Porumboiu from television. We pass by a poster of Ben Stiller. "Pretty good," he says. "Pretty good." Still, there's something about Romanian movies that intrigues the cabbie. He's read about the New Wave in the newspapers, and thinks this young film scene could be good for the country. "Fifteen years ago, we had no movies," he says. "With this generation, we can have hope. Something good about Romania."

## CHAPTER FOURTEEN

## Canada: Goin' Down the US Road

SARAH POLLEY LOOKS INTO the audience, speaks her defiance, and the applause explodes in the Toronto theater.

"I brought up the idea of a quota system thinking everyone would laugh me off stage, because that was the sense I got from talking to people," she says, "and then everybody erupted into applause. It totally stunned me, which is why I said, 'Well, I really hope everyone who just clapped for that will actually fight for it.'"

Polley made her speech about the quota as she was named best actress at the 2004 Genies, the Canadian film awards. "I don't think the answer to making our films more accessible is to make dumber, more commercial movies," she told that audience. "I think it's to make sure people can see them and to ensure that a quota of our screens are dedicated to showing our films so that Canadians can have access to their own stories."[1]

‡

The quota hasn't always been an idea non grata in Canada. Over the years, filmmakers and even politicians have fought for it. Britain's quota of 1927 enforced screen time for films made in its Empire, handing producers in the then-British dominion of Canada sudden access to a ready-made international audience. Instead of leading to increased Canadian production, however, it led US producers north to make "quota quickies" for British theaters. This would not be the last time US productions would "run away" to Canada, nor was it the first.

In 1909, the US consul in Winnipeg noted: "In this new country where all forms of amusement are scarce, moving pictures are welcomed, and there is no reason why the manufacturers of the United States should not control the business."[2] Early made-in-Canada productions included, for instance, *The Cowpuncher's Wife* (1910) and *The War Pigeon* (1914). *Back to God's Country* (1919) was the best-known Canadian silent picture (or partially Canadian; some scenes were shot in Alberta, and it starred Victoria-born Nell Shipman), drawing crowds across the country. Years earlier, Shipman had moved to Hollywood, pioneering a tradition also being staked out by the better-known Mary

("America's Sweetheart") Pickford—Canadians packaged as Hollywood Americans.

A Canadian federal commission in 1931 concluded that American-owned Paramount's Famous Players theater chain had, by 1930, "in many important locations a monopoly of the moving picture business. In others, such a position as enables them to dominate the business, and this applies to practically all the towns and cities in Canada of 10,000 or more population."[3]

With studios dominating Canada's screens in the 1930s, the country was an intriguing test-tube for documentary filmmaker John Grierson. Credited with coining the term "documentary" and renowned for his work in the UK, in 1938 Grierson was invited by the Canadian government to report on the state of the country's filmmaking. Grierson concluded that Canada could not compete with Hollywood dominance of fiction features, so it should cede that territory and focus on documentaries. His report called for an agency to coordinate Canadian filmmaking, resulting in the creation of the National Film Board (NFB) with Grierson as commissioner. Grierson's preference for the documentary form had been influential but not dominant in England, with its dramatic fiction tradition, but in Canada his film ideology took hold. "Here was a new country, a clean slate," noted his collaborator Forsyth Hardy.[4] Grierson's single-minded focus left an outstanding NFB documentary filmography, but it also retarded the development of narrative Canadian cinema, resulting in a quarter century without English-language fiction features. In the postwar years, as inspired filmmaking emerged from Italy to England, Canada was left behind.

‡

Larry Kent had to make a Canadian feature to see one. In 1962, Kent was a theater student at Vancouver's University of British Columbia (UBC), brash enough to want to be a narrative filmmaker in a country that didn't have them. Kent created, for the first time anywhere in Canada, an independent body of work with the urgency and reality of the new auteur cinema emerging in Europe. His first feature, *Bitter Ash* (1963), was banished in British Columbia. "The characters say 'shit' and 'piss' and those sorts of things that now would be nothing. And there's a sex scene at the end. The minute we put it on at UBC, the shit hit the fan." The prudish moralism of the early 1960s wasn't confined to Canada and neither was the urge to overthrow it. For Kent, taboos

*Larry Kent. Courtesy Larry Kent.*

were waiting to be broken, and his trio of unruly no-budget independent features reflected the youthful rebellion that was brewing. Kent's Canada was filled with modern urban lives groping for glimpses of freedom—the young working-class tough who encounters Vancouver bohemia in *Bitter Ash*, the teenagers discovering their sexuality in *Sweet Substitute* (1964), or the woman desperate for escape from a stultifying marriage in *When Tomorrow Dies* (1965).

A red-diaper baby born in South Africa, in his youth Kent was a member of the Young Communist League, then turned to anarchism. "I was always very left, and I still am," he says. "My films deal with social situations more than they deal with overt political situations, but they have terrific sympathy for the feminist movement and working-class people." Kent enlisted an adventuresome ensemble of naturalistic actors, mostly from the UBC theater department, and workshopped *Sweet Substitute* with only a story outline. "We improvised every scene on audiotape. I went back, edited all the material, and rewrote it, keeping all of the rhythms."

When *Bitter Ash* was banned in much of Canada, Kent took it to L.A., where he was invited by University of Southern California film professor Arthur Knight to screen the film in a classroom filled with future filmmakers. (Years later, Donald Shebib, who would make the Canadian classic *Goin' Down the Road* [1970], told Kent he was at that screening.) Kent also screened the film for Sherpix, which operated a midnight circuit in theaters across the US. "A wonderful circuit," Kent says. "They would screen avant-garde movies. *Bitter Ash* played three places in Canada. But Sherpix sent us all around the US."

After making *When Tomorrow Dies*, Kent moved to Montreal, where Quebec censors didn't like his *High* (1967), about hippies on a crime spree, any more than BC censors had liked *Bitter Ash*. He followed that with *The Apprentice* (1971), the story of a well-meaning working-class kid (Steve Fiset) led astray by the system, with Susan Sarandon in her first starring role.

While Kent was the first of the English-speaking Canadian independents of the 1960s, he wasn't alone for long. Kent, along with Toronto's Dons (Shebib and Owen) and Davids (Secter and Cronenberg), and Vancouver's Jack Darcus and Morrie Ruvinsky, constituted a kind of scattered, barely visible English-Canadian ripple. A new narrative Canadian screen realism was emerging; some filmmakers, such as Kent, drew from Europe's New Waves, but others were more influenced by the NFB and Canadian Broadcasting Company's documentary sensibility. Don Owen shot *Nobody Waved Goodbye* (1964) under the NFB funding auspices of making a documentary, but instead made a coming-of-age comic drama about a young couple who reject the suburban materialism so popular in their parents' generation.

‡

Coming of age in Montreal in the 1950s meant, for Jean Pierre Lefebvre, that film was indeed a subversive art. From the beginning, film in Quebec faced church-inspired censorship. While studying literature at the University of Montreal, Lefebvre co-founded a campus film club. "It was the first opening to another [way of] filmmaking than the American way." Lefebvre and other young Quebecois cinephiles in the 1960s embraced Italian neorealism and the French New Wave, but also had a deepening interest in local culture and storytelling as part of the rising "Quiet Revolution" in Quebec that challenged every old convention. Film censorship was finally relaxed in 1967. ("Even a film like *Breathless* was forbidden in Quebec until 1967," says Lefebvre.)

There had been a spate of Quebec features in the 1940s and '50s. Quebec production started up with Fedor Ozep's family melodrama *Le père Chopin* (1945), but by the early 1950s the province's two studios, which had been struggling financially, closed—and Canadian feature filmmaking came to a close with them. The Cinema Direct documen-

*Jean Pierre Lefebvre (middle) shooting* The Last Betrothal. *Courtesy Jean Pierre Lefebvre.*

tary style, with filmmakers using hand-held cameras, percolated at NFB headquarters after it moved from Ottawa to Montreal in 1955, then developed into a new fiction cinema in the 1960s. Claude Jutra arrived with *À tout prendre* (1964), about an interracial relationship in Montreal, and Gilles Carle jumped-started NFB fiction when he got the go-ahead for his narrative comedy *La vie heureuse de Léopold Z* (*The Happy Life of Leopold Z,* 1965) by submitting it as a documentary about snow plowing in Montreal. Lefebvre's *Le révolutionnaire* (*The Revolutionary,* 1965) played six weeks at a Montreal art-house. "It went to Europe, it won a lot of prizes, was shown in Paris, and I sold it for $5,000 to television. With the $5,000, I started another film. So many films were made like that between 1960 and 1967, and that's why the federal government created what is now Telefilm Canada."

‡

Canadians drafting legislation to create a national film agency in 1964 met in New York with US studio representatives. The studios dismissed the notion of a Canadian cinema, and when the northern delegation broached the idea of France's eleven-percent solution, they were warned it would bring retaliation. Legislation was enacted in 1966 to create the

Canadian Film Development Corporation (CFDC). Canadian Secretary of State Judy LaMarsh said: "Many countries, in order to encourage the distribution of their own films, have applied quotas. We have chosen, however, not to introduce this kind of restriction in the bill at this time ... But in rejecting quotas we are counting on film distributors and cinema chains to give more than ordinary support to the aims of this program."[5] So was institutionalized the concept that theater own-ers' goodwill voluntarism would overcome self-interest when it came to screening Canadian movies, but the problem was (and still is) that the legislation didn't touch distribution or US control of Canadian screens.

In 1972 the CFDC proposed that the government establish a theater chain and negotiate with the provinces on a box-office levy and pos-sible quota. "We had been convinced that quotas and tax levies were the best means available to further our ambitions for homegrown Ca-nadian movies," CFDC director Michael Spencer later wrote. After ap-proaching each province, he noted: "Every one of them supported the principle of quotas."[6] In a March 1973 Gallup poll, a screen quota for Canadian films was supported by sixty-five percent of the public.[7]

The Canadian Motion Picture Distributors Association (CMPDA) worked closely with Jack Valenti's MPAA to stir a backlash. In a brief to the government, the CMPDA wrote: "A weak and willing govern-ment in support of special interest groups can install a quota system but this government cannot and will not compel the taxpayer to the box office."[8] Secretary of State Hugh Faulkner recalled: "People were telling me I should see Jack Valenti, and I said that's a total waste of my time and it's a waste of his time. He doesn't give a damn about Cana-dian film." But instead of legislation, Faulkner negotiated a voluntary quota with the Odeon and Famous Players chains for two weeks of screen time for Canadian films. Two years later, the voluntary quota, having proved ineffective, was shelved. The 7,000-member Council of Canadian Filmmakers criticized the government for its inaction. Before a parliamentary committee in 1974, the Council's Peter Pearson said: "The film financing system does not work ... The film distribution sys-tem does not work ... The film exhibition system does not work ... It is no wonder then that the Canadian Film Development Corporation cannot possibly work and neither can we."[9]

The Capital Cost Allowance (CCA) was enacted in 1975, allowing in-vestors to write off their entire contribution to a film—up to $100,000 a year. At its peak, the CCA annually poured about $200 million into film production, but it replaced the promise of the early independents with bottom-line made-for-Americans Canadian products. Most tax-shelter movies were awful (*Mondo Strip*, 1980), some bombed (*Mr. Patman*, 1980), a handful drew crowds (*Porky's*, 1982), a few were good (*Scanners*, 1981), and one (*Meatballs*, 1979), made for $1.6 million, grossed more than $40 million and delivered director Ivan Reitman to Hollywood. By 1982 the convoluted write-off system and its frequent failures—half of the CCA films were never released—resulted in investor indifference, and the tax-shelter era expired.

The CFDC was renamed Telefilm Canada in 1984, and the last substantial attempt at a change came three years later with proposed legislation that would have put restrictions on US distributors and defined Canada as a distinct film market. Canada is so American to the studios that its considered part of their domestic box-office. Valenti, President Ronald Reagan, and the CMPDA said the proposed bill undermined the Canada-US free-trade agreement then being pushed by Prime Minister Brian Mulroney. The legislation was killed.

‡

Atom Egoyan's Armenian parents named their son to commemorate the Atomic Age, but they settled in a place named for the Victorian Age, leaving Egypt when Atom was an infant to open a furniture store in Victoria, BC. After high school, he studied international relations and classical guitar at the University of Toronto, but was increasingly drawn to theater and movies and began collaborating on shorts with Bruce McDonald, Peter Mettler, and other young filmmakers at Ryerson Polytechnic Institute. The Toronto independent film scene was being born. Its first feature, Mettler's *Scissere*, arrived at the 1982 Toronto film festival, and Egoyan followed in 1984 with *Next of Kin*. The breakout came in 1987 with Patricia Rozema's *I've Heard the Mermaids Singing*, which won the Prix de la Jeunesse at Cannes. Then came McDonald's trio of rockin' road movies *Roadkill* (1989), *Highway 61* (1991), and *Hard Core Logo* (1996). Don McKellar, who wrote *Roadkill* and *Highway 61*, would move from scriptwriter to director with 1997's *Last Night*. Meanwhile, Egoyan was filmmaking at a prolific clip with *Family Viewing* (1988), *Speaking Parts* (1989), *The Adjuster* (1991), *Calendar* (1993), *Exotica* (1994), and *The Sweet Hereafter* (1997).

There had been individual Canadian filmmakers, but this was something new for the country: a community of resolute independents. Egoyan knew his independent antecedents, "especially the work of

*Mia Kirschner and Don McKellar in Atom Egoyan's* Exotica. © *Miramax Films /*
*Photofest.*

Jean Pierre Lefebvre. We were very aware of his films," he says, "and
we were aware he had been to Cannes at the Directors' Fortnight with
a lot of his work.

> Those were films that were made in a very artisanal way, and
> I found them very, very inspiring. There were certainly film-
> makers from the University of Toronto that I knew, but that
> was a much earlier generation, like David Secter. The one that
> really inspired me coming from BC was Phillip Borsos' *Grey
> Fox* [1982]. I thought that was just an amazing achievement,
> as were the shorts that he had made, like *Nails* [1979] and
> *Spartree* [1978]. Larry Kent was very important to me because
> 1984, the year my first feature was shown in Toronto, was
> also the first year of Perspective Canada [at Toronto's film
> festival], and they did a retrospective of his work. So that's
> where I first saw *Bitter Ash* and *High* and those early films of
> his, which were so ahead of their time.

Then there was David Cronenberg, "a mentor figure for all of us," says
Egoyan. At a glance, Cronenberg's early works were simply genre pictures, but his sci-fi often contained sexually charged, psychological

probings that foreshadowed the outstanding auteur filmmaking he was destined for. And they paid off at the box office. *Rabid* (1977), about an infectious vampire, was produced for $500,000 and made $7 million. He would go on to *The Fly* (1986), *Dead Ringers* (1988), *Crash* (1996), and *A History of Violence* (2005).

Don McKellar, from Toronto's North York area, quickly fell in with the emerging scene. "It was pretty great," he says, noting that it had none of the film-industry focus that's so pervasive at current film schools. "They're missing something, because they have these programs about how to fit into the industry. Fortunately that wasn't even a question for any of us; it really was about expressing our voice, and we consciously tried to do something uniquely Canadian. Those first films—*Roadkill* and *Highway 61*—were an attempt to mythologize the Canadian landscape like America had done so well." Besides writing the screenplay for *Roadkill*—Bruce McDonald's debut feature—McKellar co-starred as a congenial serial killer. The film combined the hip nonchalance of *Stranger Than Paradise* with an unrestrained Canadiana, introducing a generation to the intrigue of Northern Ontario and inspiring other filmmakers to wear their Canadian content on their sleeves.

‡

Sarah Polley *is* Canada to much of the world, having played the spirited Canadian Sara Stanley in the widely distributed *Road to Avonlea* (1990–96) TV series. Polley started out as a child actor in Toronto, moving between TV and US service-industry movies, but soon became aware of the Canadian independent cinema emerging around her and landed roles in Egoyan's *Exotica*, McKellar's *Last Night*, and Cronenberg's *eX istenZ* (1999).

Polley's childhood studio experience with Columbia's *The Adventures of Baron Munchausen* (1988) hadn't left her wanting more. "It was an epic disaster and riddled with studio politics at their absolute worst— just total chaos. Production was shut down for two weeks. David Puttnam, who was the executive in charge of the production, was fired during the promotion of the film, which meant they buried it. I got to see, at an extremely early age, how ridiculous the priorities became when you're making a studio film."

In 1991, in the midst of the Gulf War, when Polley was twelve years old, she wore a peace button to a children's award show. *Road to Avonlea* was a nominee; the series was co-produced by CBC and Disney, and personnel from the studio asked Polley to remove the button. She refused. At fifteen, she left the series. The following year, she lost two teeth to a riot squad billy club during a protest against the privatizing Conservative Ontario provincial government. She had just become "politically aware" and felt she had to also "be politically active. It's immoral to sit around and let this happen without dedicating most of my life to doing what I can. I was not interested in film; I was only interested in politics." Polley pulled out of acting to devote herself to socialism and social activism. In 2001, she was in the thick of the anti-globalization street protests at the Summit of the Americas in Quebec City.

But she found enough creative, independent filmmaking in Toronto to be drawn back to movies and was warmly welcomed. It was a community that had known Polley since childhood and deeply respected her uncompromising, principled character. "When I started to think about making my own short films, I spent a lot of time around Don McKellar and Patricia Rozema, and the city felt like a real community. I felt this sort of familial support and warmth from that community of filmmakers. And I was really affected by their sensibility."

After Polley co-starred in *The Sweet Hereafter*, she had offers to go south. Polley did take a lead in Doug Liman's *Go* (1999), a cult hit about a hipster drug deal gone awry, and the offers intensified. She appeared in the occasional US independent, such as Hal Hartley's *No Such Thing* (2001), but remained in Toronto determined to make her own films. "There was a lot of respect for the Toronto film community and there was a lot of respect for staying here and building an industry in Canada and making really specific films that were outside of the box," says Polley.

‡

While the independent scene was getting under way in the 1980s, so was Hollywood North, with provincial governments in a race to outdo each other—and every other place—in enacting fiscal enticements for American producers. The government largesse was abetted by an anemic dollar that bottomed out at sixty-two cents US. In the 1980s and '90s, "runaway production" meant Hollywood producers running off to Canada; Vancouver and Toronto, after L.A. and New York, became the continent's largest production centers. Some in the L.A. film community, still far and away the largest in North America, responded to the runaway production with an anti-Canadian campaign that included protest marches down Hollywood Boulevard. Who could blame them for being angry, after suddenly seeing longtime local jobs slip away to the lowest bidders? There were times, however, when cross-border sniping was misdirected at Canadian workers, rather than at the corporate ownership of film and its producer subsidiaries in both countries, who will go anywhere a cheap dollar leads them regardless of the impact on anyone. (By 2009, less than half as many studio features were being shot in California than in 2003.) When Canada's dollar rose in 2007, half the United Nations and US states had nouveau service industries concocting ways to give Hollywood North a run for its money.

In response, in 2006 unions in Vancouver agreed to an eighteen-percent wage cut on productions under $20 million—the vast majority of projects in Canada. Overtime was cut and seniority eliminated. "They [US producers] don't own a stick here," said Bruce Scott, of the Vancouver Teamsters local representing film workers. "That's the advantage they have. They come up here with a bag of money and they outline the terms, and if they're not suitable terms they tell us they're willing to shop around."[10] Quebec outdid itself in 2009, when its newest offerings to American producers, combined with federal concessions, added up to credits that could reach 41.2 percent of a production. (How long will it be before Canadians actually pay billionaire corporations to shoot their product in Canada?)

‡

"My favorite thing about this movie is it's so low-budget that nobody in here knows a movie's being shot except the people working on it," says Bruce Sweeney, setting up a shot with a small cast and crew for *Excited* (2009) at a Vancouver golf-course clubhouse. His previous movie, *American Venus* (2007), was an independent—with Rebecca DeMornay as a pistol-packing American following her runaway daughter to Canada—but with a budget large enough that Sweeney had to deal with the entire system of funding and distribution and producers. "To have to jump through all the hoops and get filtered through all the filters that you deem unnecessary ... is just so deadening." he says.

Sweeney wanted to get back to basics, so his next project was directing and producing a set-in-Vancouver story ("about sexual dysfunction and intimate relationships and unwanted familial intrusion") on bare-budget digital. He's seen too many good Canadian filmmakers frozen

*Bruce Sweeney on the set of* Crimes of Mike Recket *in 2011. Photographed by Noa Neuman, courtesy of Bruce Sweeney.*

at the fundraising stage. "And then the years roll past and nothing happens," he says. "If there's one rule it's that if you don't do it, it will not happen. There are a lot of reasons to *not* make films, but to me it's about creating the work itself. There's a feeling you get when you make a good scene, where the actors hit all the notes, and the cameraman's right on the money. You have these piercing, beautiful little moments."

Sweeney came out of the West Coast Wave that announced itself with John Pozer's *The Grocer's Wife* (1991). It was followed by Mina Shum's *Double Happiness* (1994), Sweeney's *Live Bait* (1995), and Lynne Stopkewich's *Kissed* (1996). The most prolific filmmaker of this scene, Sweeney grew up in small-town Ontario, then moved to the West Coast, where his daytime focus was the Simon Fraser University visual arts program, his evenings spent at art-house screenings. Sweeney enrolled in film studies at UBC, where classmate John Pozer was the most driven filmmaker to crash the university gates since Kent. Told the film program didn't produce features, Pozer set out to make one, finding clandestine ways to get his hands on campus equipment. The resulting *The Grocer's Wife* ignited the Vancouver independent scene, with eight future directors among its crew. "It was fantastic because there was a sense of community and there was the sense of possibility in the air," says Sweeney, the film's boom operator. "We all fed off so many films, like Jim

Jarmusch's, but also Guy Maddin's *Gimli Hospital* came out in '89 and that planted the seed in Pozer to shoot his film." Winnipeg's Maddin combines the absurdist sensibilities of the early silents with experimental filmmaking with Busby Berkeley musicals in such films as *Tales from the Gimli Hospital* (1989) and *The Saddest Music in the World* (2003).

*The Grocer's Wife* premiered at Toronto's Festival of Festivals (later renamed the Toronto International Film Festival) and then went to Cannes. "And then," says Sweeney, "I thought, 'I can make a feature too.'" Determined to tell Canadian stories, he set out to make *Live Bait*, a witty, sexy, semi-autobiographical feature drawn from a relationship he had with an older woman. While Sweeney worked on it, Mina Shum's *Double Happiness*—about a young Asian immigrant (Sandra Oh) torn between her parents' culture and her West Coast alternative sensibilities—was named best Canadian feature at the 1994 Toronto festival. The following year, *Live Bait* won the same award. "It was a Canadian break; it doesn't mean you rocket straight to the top," says *Live Bait* co-star Tom Scholte, "but we got the money to make *Dirty*."

*Dirty* (1998) was an ensemble piece set in the drug world of East Side Vancouver. Unlike the scripted *Live Bait*, Sweeney drew *Dirty* from a master's class with Mike Leigh at the 1991 Vancouver film festival. In his variation of Leigh's process, Sweeney workshopped *Dirty* with a forceful local cast, and the stunning result was acclaimed at Sundance and everywhere else it screened. Sweeney's next, *Last Wedding* (2001), an acerbic anti-romantic comedy about the intimacies of three interconnected Vancouver couples, was the first Western Canadian film chosen to open the Toronto festival.

With Vancouver filmmakers making their own waves, suddenly Toronto wasn't alone. "There was a point in the mid-'90s where it just seemed there was an incredible possibility," says Egoyan. "There was a tipping point. There were enough interesting films being made, and they were getting enough support critically and with distributors, that it felt like a tide was being turned." Egoyan's *The Sweet Hereafter,* about the traumatic aftermath of a deadly school bus accident, won three prizes at the 1997 Cannes festival and was nominated for two Oscars. It did considerable worldwide box office for a Canadian independent ($4.3 million) at a time when the critical and popular support for his previous film, *Exotica* ($5 million), had already made Egoyan a commodity of interest in Hollywood. At the time in Canada, though, Egoyan could easily find Telefilm funding and creative control. "People say, 'Why didn't you take advantage of the Academy Award nominations and go down [to L.A.]? Because I only got to make *The Sweet Hereafter* because it was made within this system. It was an American novel optioned by a US studio, which decided that they couldn't make it because it was too bleak or too ... you know." So Egoyan turned it into a signature Canadian film, drawing on local talent, and setting it in small-town BC.

A cross-country Canadian Wave seemed poised to break when the *Last Wedding* ensemble assembled to open the Toronto International Film Festival in September 2001. Instead, that event marked the end of an era; many of its promising filmmakers hit a wall after making a feature or two. "You get beaten down by the system," Scholte says. "The responses to your success are so lukewarm, that the responses to your failures are, *you're finished*. And it's gotten more conservative." Adds Sweeney: "For *Dirty*, they [the funders] were fine with local actors like Tom Scholte and Babz Chula. Flash forward ten years and distribution companies say, 'Look, you give me a film that has one of these people on the list, and you can make your movie. If you can't, then we're not making it.'" Canadian distributors forage the US TV series *Whatever Happened To ...?* for lead actors, as if any American who had a network show, circa 1984, means packed theaters in twenty-first century Canada. "People who are uncastable in the States get mentioned all the time in financing meetings for Canadian films," says Polley. "It was like, 'Oh my god, do you think you can get this person?' You want to say: 'Of course I can; they haven't worked in ten years.'"

‡

In 2000, the government set a five-year goal for Canadian film: five percent of box office (from about one percent that year). However, "they didn't do anything about distribution or exhibition," McKellar noted. "Unfortunately, that policy put all of the onus on the films as opposed to the system in which those films live, where people are not able to access their own movies. It's also a little bit misguided because they're saying, 'Okay, let's make movies that can compete with studio-system movies,' which we just simply cannot do. They have $100-million marketing budgets."

It only got worse the following year when Richard Stursberg took over Telefilm and then announced: "We are generally not prepared to invest more than $1 million in a film if it does not stand a reasonable chance of making more than $1 million at the box office."[11] To Polley,

Stursberg's vow to commercialize Canadian film was a declaration of cultural war. "I had come to awareness in this incredibly optimistic, creative environment, and when I was ready to start making my own films, I realized I was living in a world that didn't respect itself at all. 'Let's just toss out everything we've built and try to make films that look like they're American.' That was probably the first time in my life I really questioned my decision to stay in Canada. I thought, 'Well, if I wanted to make American films I would have gone to the States to do it.' I stayed here to make interesting Canadian films."

Quebec has the advantage of a de facto quota—the French language—that builds domestic audience. Since the 1990s, there has been a diverse parade of Quebec auteurs, including Jean-Claude Lauzon (*Léolo*, 1992), Robert Lepage (*Le confessional*, 1995), Léa Pool (*Emporte-moi/Set Me Free*, 1999), Louis Bélanger (*Gaz Bar Blues*, 2003), and Xavier Dolan (*Les amours imaginaires/Heartbeats*, 2010). In Lefebvre's films, Quebec is a star. ("The only stories I know, the only people I really know, are in Quebec," he says.) His *Les dernières fiançailles* (*The Last Betrothal*, 1973) chronicles the dying days of a long, rural-Quebec marriage. Through meticulous pacing, Lefebvre recreates a country life filled with Quebec routine; Rose and Armand know each other's every nuance, and the audience slowly learns and savours their ways. Denys Arcand has directed a string of noted features including *Le déclin de l'empire américain* (*The Decline of the American Empire*, 1986) and the Oscar-winning *Les invasions barbares* (*The Barbarian Invasions*, 2003). More recently, Denis Villeneuve has emerged with *Maelström* (2000), *Polytechnique* (2009), and *Incendies* (2010). "Quebec films are based on a culture that has been established much longer than the English-Canadian culture, which is not easy to define because all its influences are more vertical than horizontal," Lefebvre says. "All my friends in Vancouver were more influenced by Seattle and California than by the East Coast."

Most of Canada rarely watches the country's top grossing movies, which are made in Quebec. But Lefebvre is concerned that Quebec box-office is dependent on local versions of American genre movies such as the comic cop movies *Bon Cop, Bad Cop* (2006) and *De père en flic* (*Father and Guns*, 2009). "I've got nothing against the fact that a film like *Bon Cop, Bad Cop* is made," says Lefebvre. "But it's not cinema that interests me. My concern is that it's too much one way, too much the commercial way. There's a star system and distributors want *that* actor, *that* director."

As president of the L'Association des Réalisateurs et Réalisatrices du Québec (the Association of Directors of Quebec), Lefebvre made headlines in 2006 when, after Telefilm's Quebec office announced it would fund only five features that year, he called for a ten-percent levy on the province's box office, à la France. His proposal went nowhere. There is a systemic problem that won't be solved by simply replacing a commercially minded Telefilm executive with a well-meaning one. "It's because of the cowardice of all our governments," says Lefebvre, "especially the federal, that never wanted to enact laws to recuperate some of the money made by all the foreign films here. When you think of the billions of dollars profit that American movies are making in Canada, if only ten percent of that was used in production for Canadian film production—boom!"

In Quebec, there's enough cultural activism to stare down budget cuts, but English-Canadian filmmakers seldom unite to fight. The better ones are on the left, and Canada does have feisty politics—including the closest thing to a North American Paris '68 (with a near-general strike in Vancouver 1983) and more than 1,000 protestors arrested during the resistance to the G8 Summit in Toronto in 2010—but when it comes to Canadian film, weariness has set in because its advocates have been summarily dismissed by the government, exhibitors, and distributors for so long. "I've always felt like whenever I've said something political that there's a bit of, 'Oh, there she goes again,'" says Polley. "If I was in any other country, that would be expected. When I was talking to filmmakers in Spain about a quota system they went, 'Of course, we're all fighting for it together, aren't you?'"

Polley points to the MAPL (Canadian Music, Artist, Production, Lyrics) quota of 1971, requiring radio stations to devote twenty-five percent of air time to songs with Canadian content. "The music that we had to listen to at the beginning was not so great, but an industry got built upon it, and we ended up with a really vibrant, successful music scene." Adds Kent: "I think the need creates good stuff, and good stuff creates better. I don't believe Canadians don't want to see Canadian culture. There isn't a people in the world that doesn't want a mirror to see what they look like, but the mirror, to more and more Canadians, has become American. In cinema, we're a cultural colony. The studios are determined not to allow a Canadian cinema because they've always considered Canada as part of the American domestic market." Filmmakers who dare mention the quota in public have been dressed down by the film establishment. "I was definitely given some hints that the comments I made [at the Genies] could have negatively influenced how much my film was seen," Polley says. "I definitely felt that it had pissed people off." But Polley and other Canadian filmmakers continue to speak out. "I think the best idea is the quota system," says Sweeney. "It would work. It becomes institutionalized." McKellar mixes his support for incentives for exhibitors with the Q word, saying that they need "real financial incentives, or they need to be forced with some kind of quota, or maybe both." Adds Vancouver television producer Chris Haddock: "Some very radical moves could be productive—and the quota system in TV and movies is one of them. You'd get a better quality product. People would figure out a way to make the quality product to fill the quota." He has no doubt that a quota would be bitterly fought by US studios and their Canadian subsidiaries. "As they do with any good Canadian idea, including Medicare," he adds, "It would be vicious. It's not going to be easy."[12]

‡

There are nationalists who bang the drum for English-Canadian filmmaking—but theirs is a commercial Canadian filmmaking. Toronto actor-director Paul Gross's films try to do for English Canada what the local hit *Good Cop, Bon Cop* did for Quebec. His curling comedy *Men with Brooms* (2002) had a production budget of $7.5 million and a huge (for a Canadian film) advertising budget of $1.75 million. It opened in 207 Canadian theaters and made $4.2 million, losing only a few million, which somehow made it the success story of the year according to its producers. Gross's 2008 *Passchendaele* ($4.5 million) was another big-ticket film, but the stuff of 1950s' studio melodramas.

It is the auteur films such as Egoyan's *The Sweet Hereafter* and Polley's *Away from Her* (2006) that strike a chord internationally, and domestically when given half a chance. *Last Wedding* had a long run, even though it had virtually no marketing budget. A Canadian filmmaker can have a movie open strong after years of work, only to be pulled to make way for a US release. "It happens time and again," says McKellar. It happened with McKellar's *Last Night*, a smart, funny look at an extended ensemble (including Polley and Sandra Oh) spending their last night on planet earth. "When *Last Night* opened it was making lots of money," McKellar says, but it was pulled to make way for Universal's *Meet Joe Black* (1998).

There is a Canadian ritual of funding (in search of that elusive domestic hit) imitations of bad American movies like *Goin' the Distance* (2004)

*Director Sarah Polley. © Lions Gate / Photofest. Photograph by Chris Woods.*

(see *American Pie*, 1999) or *Intern Academy* (2004) (see *Police Academy*, 1984). Canada's auteurs are often lumped with foreign-language films and US independents as "the other" cinema. "I've recently heard certain people go on rants, saying, 'We have to get away from this kind of auteur model,'" Polley says. "I don't know what they're talking about; I have not felt for a long time that at any public funding agency you are required to do anything other than convince them your film will be a successful Hollywood-type film." So *Away from Her* became a "love story" in Polley's pitch. "I got a phone call before I got funding. 'You're saying it's a love story, but it's not ending the way a love story traditionally ends. So what genre is it?' I said, 'Why is this a question with an independent film—what genre it is? I don't know.' And she said, 'Can we say it's a movie about love, instead of a love story?' It's so weird that we have to fit into these categories when we're trying to do something that hopefully isn't in a category."

While Tom Scholte became a Canadian indie mainstay, he also found himself auditioning for unsatisfying work in Vancouver's US-based service industry. So he restructured his life—teaching acting at UBC, performing on stage and in Canadian films, and making his directorial debut with the Dogme-inspired *Crime* (2008), a bare-budgeted, bare-knuckle film made for under $30,000 from a UBC research fund. "I'm saying 'yes' to minor cinema. Let's be a minor cinema. I don't care if people say that's being backwards. Maybe if some day we get a quota system that will change, but for now it means making small films and getting them out in the world."[13]

The result of Sarah Polley's persistence, *Away from Her*, which she adapted from an Alice Munro story, showed that there is more audience for more subjects than Canadian funders might imagine. Awards and lineups were to be found everywhere—from Australia to Spain to Oscar night—for her feature directorial debut, about the altered lives of a woman (Julie Christie) with Alzheimer's, and her husband (Gordon Pinsent). As a young actress in the British New Wave's *Darling* (1965), Christie lit up the screen personifying the hipster women of the mid-1960s who disdained convention and its morality and were taking their first tentative steps toward freedom. In *Away from Her*, Christie is a Canadian version of the same woman, forty years older who, along with the despair of losing her memory, is now slowly finding a truth and freedom in nothing to lose. That this story was approached with such insight and empathy by a twenty-something director may be the most remarkable thing about this film. Like Polley and the best Canadian films, *Away from Her* speaks its mind. "We don't go to the movies much any more, do we Grant?" says Christie's character, Fiona. "All those multiplexes showing the same American garbage."

"I've always considered that my little films are part of a big puzzle," Lefebvre says.

They're important in my life, but as such their value is quite limited—unless they're linked with other films. And that's what changes a society. There are more and more people who are totally disgusted by the system. I did some acting recently for a second feature film for a young friend, with a crew of eight people. It was so wonderful. It's like food: Some people say, 'It's our twenty-fifth anniversary so we have to find the most expensive restaurant in Montreal, Ottawa, Toronto, Vancouver.' It costs $600 for dinner because they pay for the service and the decoration, but the food's no good. In all of those cities, you can say, 'I know a little restaurant where it's going to be extraordinary.' That's the film I believe in.

## CHAPTER FIFTEEN

## *America: Just Real*

SHE SITS ACROSS FROM ME in the lobby of Park City's Marriott hotel, having come in from the cold in her stocking feet—or rather, in socks pulled over her boots. She hangs up her cell phone. Ten minutes of our conversation later, a friend arrives to collect her.

"Have you seen her film?" her friend asks me as they leave. "It's the best in the festival."

"What's it called?"

"*Me*," she says, "*and You and Everyone We Know*."

‡

In a 1996 interview in *Sassy* magazine, *Me and You and Everyone We Know* (2005) director Miranda July, then twenty-one, explained her Big Miss Moviola female film-exchange/video chain letter. If a reader sent July a home-made film, she would send it to those who requested it. "This is for all girls, because if ten people see one girl's film, that's making it," July said in the article. "If these films circulate, they'll incite other girls to go 'I can do that!' and grab their parents' or school's camera to make the real *Sixteen Candles*—even though she may not get the guy and cake at the end … It doesn't have to be arty or punk, just real."[1]

A couple of days after meeting July at Sundance, I caught *Me and You and Everyone We Know* and agreed with July's friend. A few years after that, I spoke with July in her office in the Silver Lake district of Los Angeles. She grew up in Berkeley, where her parents operated an independent publishing house. Berkeley wasn't the only legendary locale of her childhood. Born Miranda Grossinger, she spent holidays at the famed Catskills' resort Grossingers. ("I went there every summer till I was twelve, till it went bankrupt.") While Berkeley is forever linked to the counterculture, July grew up in the '80s and '90s and, while still in high school, started writing plays and staging them at the punk club 924 Gilman Street.

July dropped out of UC Santa Cruz and followed a friend who had moved to Portland, Oregon, where alternative is mainstream. There she was drawn to the independent music scene. "In that do-it-yourself movement, every single thing was like a revolution. You felt like you were part of a movement. We really felt we were quite rebellious and changing the world. We started a recording studio in our basement. We had a music club."

Combining her enthusiasm for feminism ("In high school, I was quite the young feminist and liked causing trouble right and left and calling everyone on their behavior") with a growing interest in movie-making, she typed up the Big Miss Moviola manifesto, not knowing whether young female filmmakers even existed. "I gave it to bands like Bikini Kill that were touring. It was just the idea that girls should be making movies, that we were natural movie-makers, and that we should share them with each other. I got a few tapes in the mail but hundreds and hundreds of letters from all over the country saying, 'We want to see these movies made by other girls.' It had a huge effect on me." July was determined to pick up a camera herself. "I wanted some kind of context to think of myself as a filmmaker—but not film school, not Hollywood. All those things seemed so irrelevant to me." She took to the road screening her shorts and other Moviola films in high schools and living rooms. "It was right before the whole digital thing, so there was no other way to see movies like that. Over time, there were twelve or thirteen chain letters with ten movies in each. I still run into people who say, 'Oh, Big Miss Moviola was such a cool thing.'"

‡

The independents have won.
(Pause)
The independents are dead.

Studios and their media acolytes gushed at the triumph of independent cinema at the 2004 Oscars. So-called independent *Million Dollar Baby* won the best-picture award, but it was largely financed and released by Warner Bros. Meanwhile, a studio indie, Fox Searchlight's *Sideways*, was best film at the Independent Spirit Awards. The following year, four of the five best-picture nominations were captured by "independents," financed by the likes of Universal's Focus Features and Warner Independent Pictures, adding to the growing conviction in some quarters that studio and independent had become indistinguishable. The studios had bought out the mini-majors (Disney with Miramax) or made them satellite contractors (Warners with Orion); Wall Street happily invested in slates of studio films, including their independent divisions, figuring the overall profit would outweigh the occasional loss; independent film festivals, TV channels, and award shows were all helping to institution-alize the studio-independent brand. So virtually the entire film world was becoming "independent"—and if everything is independent, noth-ing is independent. But everything isn't independent—studio-financed movies, including their "independents," have instant wide release (Fox Searchlight's *The Banger Sisters* [2002], for example, opened on 2,738 screens); actual independents hope for a screening at the Cedar Rapids film festival.

Cracks had started to form in Hollywood, Inc., and by the mid-2000s, DVDs and film libraries were depreciating due to piracy and online movies. Fox stopped production on the big-budget Jim Carrey-Ben Stiller vehicle *Used Guys*. In 2006, Disney's movie division eliminated 650 jobs. The average studio indie cost $74.9 million to produce and re-lease in 2007.[2] These "indies" were increasingly under the thumb of the parent studios, whose expensive specialty slates meant they would pur-chase fewer actual independent movies for distribution. Their bidding wars over finished product had re-cast film festivals as show-biz marts, but at Cannes 2008, several high-profile features, including Steven So-derbergh's *Che*, couldn't find buyers. When the "financial crisis" hit that same year, Wall Street withdrew from Hollywood and some studios abandoned their independents. After all, these movies were relatively unprofitable and troublesome and, unlike blockbusters, had no ancil-lary windfalls when they bombed at the box office. In May 2008, Time Warner closed Picturehouse and Warner Independent Pictures. In June, Paramount Vantage vanished into its corporate owner. Mini-majors were downsizing, and producer Mark Gill told the L.A. Film Festival's financing conference that the "sky is falling" for independent film. "If you decide to make a movie budgeted under $10 million on your own tomorrow, you have a 99.9 percent chance of failure."[3] Gill's solution was to make fewer but better movies, budgeted in that "sweet spot" between $15 and $50 million. (He had worked for Warner Independent Pictures, so for him $15 million is roughing it.) While his emphasis on quality was a step up from most producers, he was essentially deliver-ing the studio independent's "state of the union"—independent film will cease to exist if Warner Bros. won't finance them anymore. Some studios were so convinced of their ownership of the movies that they believed they even controlled independent film—but the template for independent cinema isn't *Juno* (2007), which Gill lauded in his speech, but *Shadows* (1959), which was made for $40,000.

‡

Actual independents, on the other hand, have continued to do what they've always done; by the early 2000s, the sheer critical mass of American independents made it impossible for the studios to define them out of existence. Independents, old and new, include Miranda July, John Sayles, Charles Burnett, Henry Jaglom, Susan Seidelman, Todd Haynes, Stephen Soderbergh, Richard Linklater, Jim Jarmusch, Mike Mills, Hal Hartley, Woody Allen, David Lynch, John Waters, Tom DiCillo, Alex Cox, Cory McAbee, Gus Van Sant, Kelly Reichardt, Harmony Korine, Rebecca Miller, Nicole Holofcener, Catherine Hardwicke, Gregg Araki, Charles Kaufman, Tanya Hamilton, Todd Field, Rian Johnson, Darren Aronofsky, and the Mumblecore filmmakers.

Some of these filmmakers move between independent and studio work, a survival mechanism since Cassavetes. But it's getting harder. In 2009, for example, as established a director as Soderbergh was fired from the baseball movie *Moneyball* (2011) three days before shooting was to begin because Sony was unhappy with his unconventional vision. Richard Linklater found out how enduring a commercial producer's (in this case, Participation Productions) backing can be when he turned the nonfiction best-seller *Fast Food Nation* (2006) into a fictionalized movie about coming to terms with the unhealthy consequences of the fast-food industry. "It was down-and-dirty filmmaking where we were stealing locations everywhere," says Linklater. "After Cannes, I got a call from legal saying we had to lose the Wal-Mart scene. [The scene remained with the "Wal" digitally erased.] They said insurance wouldn't cover the film. I tried to rally the producers but these people who had been so behind the movie just caved."[4]

Besides dominating the rest of the world's screens, the studios leave little room for American independents in US theaters. As with local films in Korea or Canada, popular American independent films, such as Haile Gerima's *Sankofa* (1993), have been pulled from US screens to make way for studio films. "It was taking up space," says Charles Burnett, "and it was an embarrassment to the studios. You have a film that costs virtually pennies, comparatively speaking, showing up your $100 million movie. They'll tell you independent films don't do well, but they wanted his film out [of the theaters] when it was making more money than any other film in the multiplex."

Single screens are closing and, like multiplexes, independent theaters have reduced screen runs. "Even if the reviews are good, there's going to be another eight big movies opening the next week," says John Sayles. "Our distributor for *Silver City* [2004] dropped the movie on Saturday night—he didn't even wait for Sunday. He just stopped doing any work for it and then went so far as to not submit it to the Academy because he didn't want his name associated with it. The reviews weren't good in New York. He didn't think he was going to make any money on it and wanted to disassociate himself from it, and not spend more money."

In Tom DiCillo's *Delirious* (2006), a photographer (Steve Buscemi) walks that fine line between losing it and being heroic, as if *Taxi Driver's* Travis Bickle had been a paparazzi instead of a taxi driver. It's DiCillo and Buscemi at their best, but the film was caught in a damaged distribution system. "We showed it at Sundance, and we won three awards at San Sebastian, then it disappeared pretty much off the face of the earth, after five years of work," DiCillo says. "Most people don't even know that I made that movie. The people who do know it never played, and that's all they know about it. That's so painful, you can't even comprehend; you feel, on the darkest days, that you have no place in this environment." But DiCillo keeps shooting, and was back with *When You're Strange* in 2009.

Whenever Gus Van Sant's disillusionment with studio work set in, he remembered the independent *Mala Noche* shoot. "I was always trying to go back there. I mean, it's better." In 2002, he finally did return, shooting *Gerry*, a largely improvised movie about the interaction between two men named Gerry (Matt Damon and Casey Affleck) wandering the desert. Next up was the scantily budgeted *Elephant* (2003), a Columbine-influenced piece of fiction that won the 2003 Palme d'Or. That was quickly followed by *Last Days* (2005), based, in part, on the life and death of Kurt Cobain, then the shot-in-Portland teen tragedy *Paranoid Park* in 2007. The sober, unsettling *Paranoid Park* shatters the studio-indie formula Van Sant found so frustrating—no redemption, no stars. Returning to pure independence has been an exhilarating experience for Van Sant. "Eventually we got to a good pattern when we did *Last Days*. We found a set which was perfect the way it was—we didn't have to move anything. On *Elephant,* we were shooting with a few lights, but on *Last Days* we promised ourselves that we wouldn't use lights. And that made it go; we were making these films in seventeen days."

Van Sant returned to a larger budget for *Milk* (2008), the biography of gay activist Harvey Milk set in a vivid recreation of San Francisco's Castro district. He is, however, the antithesis of those directors who use indie work as a calling card, having chosen to make independents even though he could do nothing but make bigger-budget movies. "You can get the control and the ability to do what you want by fighting or you can get it by just saying I'll do it for cheap. Just let me do exactly what I want—and I don't even know what I want. I paid for the first one, *Gerry*, myself."

The studios' ideal director will make product that looks hip while challenging nothing. Alexander Payne's *Citizen Ruth* (1996), made for Miramax-Disney, gives the impression of brave filmmaking. It's about a woman who considers abortion at a time when filmmakers were running scared from the very word, but it carefully paints pro-choice advocates with the same shrill brush as the religious right (unlike the independent films *Vera Drake* and *4 Months, 3 Weeks, and 2 Days*). Similarly, Jason Reitman (*Juno*, 2007; *Up In the Air*, 2009) is a sure hand at avoiding anything remotely resembling a point of view. "I make very specific films tonally, films that kind of walk a tightrope," he says. "I'm the opposite of Michael Moore. His movies are all about, 'This is the answer, this is the way to think, and those guys are [expletive] idiots.' Whereas I say, 'I'm not going to give you any answers, and let's be a bit more opening-minded about everything.'"[5] Open-minded or empty-headed? This filmmaker, who prides himself on standing for nothing, does represent something: studio-indie formula, with its caution and near-nothing to say. "It's a hard struggle once you get into Hollywood, so I don't expect too much but formula from anyone who does, unless they've established themselves and know who they are before they get in," Charles Burnett says. "You get out of college and you make a film and then you immediately go into the studio system. There is no more development after that in terms of who you are as a person or as a filmmaker. You're just a paid employee, this gun for hire. I think you have to be in a position to really experiment and find out who you are."

Actors face similar choices about commercial versus independent work. Catherine Keener, for example, works consistently with Tom DiCillo, Charlie Kaufman, Nicole Holofcener, and other independents, although she could have taken a route that includes more studio jobs. "I told her that," says Holofcener. "'You could have been Catherine Keener-Jones!' She just laughs. I don't think she regrets anything, and she is doing the kind of material she wants, she is picking and choosing."

‡

The French New Wave was Paris. Jarmusch and friends were New York.

True to the digital age, the latest independent wave in the US is scattered—Andrew Bujalski in Austin, Aaron Katz in Portland, Joe Swanberg in Chicago, Lynn Shelton in Seattle, Mark Duplass in L.A., and Ry Russo-Young in New York. They act in each other's movies, write together, and have loosely formed a low-budget, non-organized, organic movement known as Mumblecore (they didn't choose the handle). The core of Mumblecore met at Austin's South by Southwest (SXSW) film festival, arriving with their films as the studios were redefining the "independent" movement as something that required a multi-million budget and a star. "Independent film was really dormant," says Lili Taylor. "Mumblecore was, for me, the first glimmerings of seeing it happening again. I'm very excited by that movement."

Bujalski arrived first with *Funny Ha Ha* (2002), dialogue-driven with multiple relationships, its characters struggling for words and lives in the great post-graduate unknown. Like anything original, the first Mumblecore movie was of its time. The interest it attracted came slowly. "We won a couple of awards and got some good reviews. Every time I thought that the film had run its course, something else would come along to pump a little bit more life into it," Bujalski says. Finally, having drawn enough investment to self-distribute, he took it on the road. "That film had a very protracted life span, and by the time it had its official release, I had already made the second film." *Mutual Appreciation* (2005) brings New York anti-romantic comedy into the new century; a musician arrives in the city and crashes with a friend, resulting in challenges to friendship, loyalty, and sexual attraction. "I was promoting two films at once. I would go to festivals with *Mutual* and then go out on the road with *Funny Ha Ha*. We went city by city." Bujalski was surprised that his work was seen as anything larger than himself, but most every film wave has wondered what the rest of the world sees in it. Some of the Mumblecore films are improv-driven, others follow a script—but they're all low-budget. Many are digital, though Bujalski uses 16mm—and they're all character-driven, often following the lives of college students or recent grads with indefinite futures. "With all of these films, the similarities are the least interesting thing about them," Bujalski says. "Take something like Swanberg's *Nights and Weekends* [2008], which probably didn't get the love and attention it deserved out in the world, and try to compare it to *Puffy Chair* [2005]."

‡

*Kate Dollenmayer in* Funny Ha Ha. *Photograph by Matthias Grunsky. Courtesy of Andrew Bujalski.*

During the making of Joe Swanberg's first feature, *Kissing on the Mouth* (2005), he tossed away his skeleton script and got down to the business of digital improv filmmaking. His impromptu *Hannah Takes the Stairs* (2007) is insightful and witty and the consummate Mumblecore movie. Its title character is played by Mumblecore mainstay Greta Gerwig, and the cast includes Bujalski, Russo-Young, and Mark Duplass. Swanberg's *Uncle Kent* starred at Sundance in 2011. Katz's *Cold Weather* (2010) starts out with the usual post-2000, post-college confusion, but just as its audience is getting comfortable with a Mumblecore movie, expectations are unsettled as it abruptly turns criminal noir. Mark and Jay Duplass's *The Puffy Chair* (2005) is the poor man's studio indie, as the brothers set out to prove that every film wave, no matter how independent, has one (or two) directors shooting for the stars (and studio jobs); the brothers Duplass followed with Fox Searchlight's *Cyrus* (2010). Others in the group are also attracting outside interest. Gerwig co-starred in Noah Baumbach's studio-indie *Greenberg* (2010), and other gainful employment followed. "I'll be curious to see what comes of that for her, but it's very exciting," says Bujalski, "and certainly no surprise to any of us who have worked with her."

Like Mumblecore, Bujalski isn't about one city. *Funny Ha Ha* was shot in New England, where he grew up. He moved on to New York for *Mutual Appreciation* (2005), and shot his next film, *Beeswax* (2009), in

Austin, where he now lives. "There's been a sense that if you want to have a career, you go to New York or L.A." he says. "In the professional world, that's still the case. But I had a sense that this model—you go there and you start on the bottom rung and maybe someday you get to make the movie you want—wasn't working. Maybe that worked for some people, and maybe this is just a generation of impatient people, but it seemed like most people who were going to go out and hustle in those cities were just going to spend their lives hustling and not necessarily getting anywhere. The machine has gotten too big; there's really no reason to be in New York or L.A."

‡

Nicole Holofcener's movie-making started with the opening bank robbery scene in Woody Allen's *Take the Money and Run* (1969). "He runs by two kids—that's my sister and me. I was eight. My sister, who was ten, really stood in my light, and you can see her a lot better. She took the limelight. Welcome to my world." Holofcener is not the only filmmaker to start with Allen. When he delivered *Annie Hall* (1977) and *Manhattan* (1979) within two years of each other, he changed the American cinematic landscape: the anti-romantic comedy genre was now a staple; intellectual conversation was suddenly desirable; the city was a cast member; and a Gershwin soundtrack meant New York as much as the Beach Boys meant L.A. It wasn't long before movie critics were crowning nouveau Woody Allens at a rate rivaling new Bob Dylans or new Marlon Brandos. There was a black Woody (Spike Lee), a British Woody (Mike Leigh), a Latin Woody (Daniel Burman), a Canadian Woody (Bruce Sweeney), and a pair of West Coast Woodys (Albert Brooks, Henry Jaglom). So a female Woody (Nicole Holofcener) came as no surprise. Like most of these filmmakers, Holofcener did not pursue or relish this title, but she does acknowledge Allen's influence ("massive, yeah").

Unlike the other new Woodys, Holofcener (her stepfather, Charles Joffe, produced Allen's movies) grew up near his sets. She lived in Manhattan, then L.A., but after high school headed east again to attend NYU and then Columbia. While she began with Allen, she soon moved on to Jarmusch, DiCillo, and Seidelman, attending NYU not long after they had graduated. "*Stranger than Paradise, Mystery Train* [1989]—those two movies were amazing, and they made me feel like I could do this. I was completely inspired; they were telling stories they wanted to tell.

*Repeat collaborators Catherine Keener and Nicole Holofcener. Photograph by Alison Rosa. Courtesy of Nicole Holofcener.*

I tried to get a job as a PA on *Desperately Seeking Susan*. When Susan Seidelman started to make that movie, there weren't too many women filmmakers. It just seemed so cool, and I wanted to be part of it."

Despite all the talk about independents in the early '90s, it took Holofcener six years to turn her script for *Walking and Talking* into a movie. This New York story of best friends at pains to understand their love lives screened at Sundance in 1996 and was bought by Miramax. Her *Lovely and Amazing* (2001) is a raw and funny look inside a family of L.A. women (including Catherine Keener and Emily Mortimer), with depths of character an actress waits a lifetime for. Holofcener provided more good roles in *Friends with Money* (2006) and *Please Give* (2010). Again, the action is so dialogue-driven that those films have the look of workshopping, but they're scripted. "Let's say that ninety percent of it is a script, although there are things all over my movies that actors came up with and I said, 'Oh, great, say that again.' It's a collaborative process, especially with Catherine, because she has been in all of my films. She has written so many things, I don't remember what she made up and what I made up."

Holofcener has a great gift for reaching into her characters—especially female ones—and finding strikingly real fears and foibles. "I want to make movies that are emotional and about things that are important to me—issues about the world and our culture. I'm writing about things that will keep me interested—relationships and characters." She's developing her first murder mystery, but Holofcener is far more interested in the people she's creating than she is in the genre. "I'm looking forward to doing scenes with those characters."

‡

Catherine Hardwicke would go on to direct, but in 1989 she was an architect-just-turned-production designer when she saw *sex, lies, and videotape* at Sundance. "My eyeballs were just popping out of their sockets. I had never seen a film like that; I loved it so much, I ran up to [Steven Soderbergh] afterward and said, 'Listen, if you come to L.A. and you need anyone to drive you around or answer phones for you, I'll volunteer for anything.' I said, 'Even right now, if you want me to lie down so you can walk across this ice patch, I'll do it.' And he was kind of shocked. But I had just caught fire; here was a whole new world that I didn't even know existed."

Small-town McAllen, Texas, where Hardwicke grew up, was more Friday night football than Friday night art-house cinema. After graduating with a University of Texas architecture degree, she moved to L.A. in the mid-1980s to attend UCLA film school. "I realized that, as an architect, people don't want you to experiment too much. They are very conservative with their money. They want you to repeat traditional-looking homes or buildings. I mistakenly thought that the film business would encourage creativity and innovation." Her architectural background led to work in production design on films such as Richard Linklater's *SubUrbia* (1996) and Lisa Cholodenko's *Laurel Canyon* (2002), but she continued directing shorts and writing. "I was trying to get my movies made; finally, I wrote the film *Thirteen* with Nikki Reed [her thirteen-year-old neighbor, who also acted in it], and it was so low budget that they couldn't stop me." *Thirteen* (2003) captures that precarious borderline age when some are still children, others sudden adults, uncontrollable with wild abandon. "It was boiling up inside me while I was doing *Laurel Canyon*. Nikki had all these problems, and I was trying to help her and her mom out. We wrote it in six days over the Christmas holidays; we just sat down and did it, and then she went back to eighth grade. I waited one day, then read it again and thought, 'Fuck, this is going to be something, this is going to have some power. I'm shooting this film this summer no matter what.' From the day I started writing it till the day it was at Sundance was one year exactly."

Now it was time for Steven Soderbergh's eyes to pop open. Hardwicke was named best director at Sundance and the film was a sensation on the art-house circuit. Like Stewart Stern, Hardwicke approaches adolescent angst without judgment or cliché. Her followup, *Lords of Dogtown* (2005), was a look inside the teen skateboarding scene which, like Hollywood, started in L.A. but wanted the world. Hardwicke's *Twilight* (2008) would gross nearly $400 million. In that film, she brought the youthful anxiety of *Thirteen* to teen vampires and wrapped the adolescent female curiosity about the supernatural in a broader cultural context. Once *Twilight* was finished there were other projects to consider, such as *Monkey Wrench Gang*, an adaptation of Edward Abbey's eco-activist novel, and *Swerve*, which Hardwicke wrote "after reading *No Logo* and that kind of literature. The film is set in the marketing world, the teenage world."

The *Twilight* sequel *New Moon* in 2009 was again huge box office, but it was a more conventional vampire movie, minus the first movie's grasp of teen sensibilities—and minus Hardwicke. She had walked away from the movie and its big paydays reportedly because of Summit Entertainment's rush to production to cash in on the original's popularity. *Entertainment Weekly* quoted studio "insiders" aghast at Hardwicke's choice. Said one: "You'd have to have a very high standard for art, hate the movie business, and hate money to walk off this sequel."[6]

‡

*Me and You and Everyone We Know* won numerous awards at Sundance and Cannes, then went worldwide, making more than $8 million.

July had written a draft for the script and in 2003 was accepted into the Sundance Screenwriters Lab, where she reworked it with well-traveled advisors. (Among that year's advisors: Stewart Stern and Walter Bernstein.) She had toured the continent with her unique short films and performance art and had no reverence for cultural convention, be it studio or indie or studio-indie. "I didn't have any training; I'm coming at it from this perspective of having taught myself all these other forms, like performing live and then writing short stories and making experimental movies. At the Sundance Lab, people asked me, 'Are you even aware of what a three-act structure is?'"

She pitched the script to the Independent Film Channel and Britain's Film4, and they both signed on. "When I was pitching, I didn't have an agent. Looking back, I see that was also a benefit. That agent would

*Miranda July and John Hawkes in* Me and You and Everyone We Know. © *IFC Films / Photofest.*

have made me question whether I can really do this, because you're not supposed to be able to do it very easily," July says. "Everything I didn't know really was a benefit, because that's the area where you're going to do something different than anyone else. For example, in casting, I didn't even know what a big deal the star thing was; I thought it was just an aesthetic decision. There was a phone call from IFC that was like, 'There's one role where we think you could get Sigourney Weaver or someone in there.' And I said, 'Oh, no—that would be a bad idea.' It wasn't a negotiation like you're supposed to have with the people who are funding." By the end of the shoot, July knew why filmmaking conventions exist but also understood that the only real rule is whether something works, and that so many movies with "everything" don't connect with anyone.

The interest from studios after Sundance wasn't something July had ever aspired to. "I knew that the last thing I wanted to do was strike while the iron was hot because it was never a career path. I never thought, 'Oh, I'll I go to film school and then I'll move into the industry.' I did Big Miss Moviola for ten years, so I wrote a lot about how this could be enough—this audience and this way of making movies—and there's something wrong with thinking that making it means getting to Hollywood. And it's pretty much all collapsing now anyway, the way the music industry fell apart."

So July turned from filmmaking and finished her book of short stories, *No One Belongs Here More Than You*. "The hope is that I can continue in these different mediums that support each other." A filmmaker in L.A., no matter how independent, is also surrounded by an enticing, omnipresent "industry" that wants to make anyone who has never felt the glow of their own Sunset billboard feel like a loser. "I'm not some kind of saintly person who's not lured," July says. "If I hear someone wants a meeting, I'll think, 'Well, maybe I should do that.' So, it's better to just not even know." Her second feature, *The Future*, is a surreal romance that opened at Sundance in 2011. But July hasn't discarded the young woman who invented Big Miss Moviola.

I understand, now that I'm here [in L.A.], more than ever why that kind of thing is important. I mean, this industry is awful. You really have to act in opposition to it to maintain your creative self. I'm in full support of any kind of alternative systems people have for making movies and getting them shown and creating a kind of community for themselves, because this really is not the answer. It's kind of a no-brainer that you try and find a way to get around [the industry] if you want to keep on doing this.

I would love to change the system. In the long term, I'd love to have some kind of impact on it, but for the most part, I'm just going to keep making my work according to my own expectations. Over a lifetime, if you keep making things exactly the way you want to make them, hopefully you've created a little bit more space, especially for other women to do the same. When I was pitching my movie, any movie that didn't have stars suddenly became really valuable for me to point to when people said 'it never works.' We're all making space for each other.

The ingredients for *Me and You and Everyone We Know* came to Miranda July on a Chicago "L" Train: start with a fearless female cab driver/video artist (played by herself), add a single-dad shoe salesman (John Hawkes), mix in smart children who speak like smart children, and spice with innocence and wit and sexuality and originality. Unlike generic romantic films, its focus is on more than one couple. Everyone here is involved with someone—from teens engaged in sexual discovery to strangers exchanging online messages—and they're all groping for human interaction. All the fragility of life is captured in one scene with a goldfish trapped on the roof of a moving vehicle. As America's screens fill with boring predictability, July invents ways of looking at things you don't expect or never thought of—things you never dreamed before.

Tom DiCillo is considering the popularity of "utter meaninglessness" in modern America. "I think Sarah Palin is an exact mirror of where the film business is today. Why is she even allowed to open her mouth? She speaks gibberish, she knows nothing, and yet she is up there. That's where this country is at." As is its "independent" filmmaking, he says, noting that *Juno* screenwriter Diablo Cody wore bangs, tattoos, and a vintage-looking dress to the Oscars. "That is the state of American independent film right there—bangs, tattoos, and a vintage-looking dress," he says.

The film business has got this cool-hip factor to it—'indie cred.' What's his name? Chistopher Nolan. All the reviews for *Batman* go, 'Wow, you can really see his indie cred.' And I'm sorry, don't fucking confuse the two. Do not tell me that a commercial blockbuster film like *Batman* has indie cred. Just call it what it is. 'Wow, he combines the two. That's really smart.' You have to be smart in order to survive, you have to play the game, you have to work it. So the smart ones are the ones that adapt and do the Hollywood films. '*Batman*— yeah, arty, arty.' Fuck it. If it's truly independent and truly Hollywood, they should cancel each other out. They should poison each other.

## CHAPTER SIXTEEN

## *Hollywood Ending*

PARAMOUNT HAD JUST DITCHED its "low-budget" specialty division when in 2009 the digital *Paranormal Activity* became a word-of-mouth sensation and turned a $15,000 budget into nearly $200 million in box office receipts. In 2010, Paramount established Insurge Pictures, with a mandate to produce ten $100,000 digital features, throw them against the screen, and see if any stuck around to make $100 million. It was like going back to the '70s, when the studios were dazed and confused and willing to sign on with young filmmakers they didn't understand or even like.

"Aren't you tired of being fed the same movies wrapped in different paper?" wonders Insurge's website. "We want to find and distribute crazy, unpredictable, and hopefully awesome movies—movies that make you want to line up to see at your local theater with all your friends (and us). Movies that a big studio would never release because they're too risky, too silly, and they don't star Sandra Bullock. Insurge Pictures is devoted to the distribution of micro-budget movies and we're the little crew running it. We want to try something different and deconstruct the Hollywood system."[1] But Paramount is interested in the genre no-budget of *Paranormal Activity*, not the art no-budget of Mumblecore. "If they don't have a *Paranormal Activity* in the bunch, that'll probably be the end of that experiment," says Andrew Bujalski.

‡

The studios were always one box-office-smashing independent film away from picking up their specialty divisions where they dumped them and they continue to keep a hand, albeit a smaller one, in lower-budget filmmaking. (After a short break for the "financial crisis," buying resumed at Sundance in 2011.) Any status quo is stubborn. The technology now exists for new, liberating forms of film production and distribution, but the studios and their megaplexes and their marketing machine remain entrenched. Their emphasis is on making a global product, and this makes it almost impossible to find funding for a good movie in Hollywood and, in a way, everywhere else. Film financiers from England to Mexico demand a "commercial" product, as formulaic as a studio blockbuster or a studio independent—British or Mexican versions of Fox Searchlight's *Little Miss Sunshine* (2006) with its dysfunctional family on a road trip to a happy ending. "And of course the grandfather smokes pot and blah, blah, blah," says Eva Truffaut. "All the films end up looking the same, and that's supposedly indie." Sarah Polley notes: "That's what's scary—the idea of what an independent can look like to be successful. 'How do we make it look like *Garden State* or how do we make it like *Juno*?' They're independent in name, but in spirit there's something actually quite commercial about them." The Romanian New Wave's Renate Zenide thinks "it's like clothes—you now have a section for 'grunge' where you can buy destroyed jeans for $200; it's fashionable. This, to me, is not independent. If you want to express something which is not commercial, *that's* independent."

Commercialization challenges any authentic cultural alternative. Says Mary Harron: "It does have a very definite effect—it becomes more mainstream, more homogenized; punk became New Wave." Adds Jello Biafra: "Any subculture and counterculture is going to be co-opted and dumbed down and sold back to the originators at twice the price … With bands, and maybe you'll say with filmmakers too, sometimes their most interesting work is before they get enough of a grip to make things come out the way they want them to."

‡

The studios watched as their corporate brethren in the recording industry became devastated by digital. Suddenly, downloading meant someone didn't have to spend twenty dollars for the one song they liked on an album. By 2000 Napster had 20 million users per month. The labels believed in their old model—record stores, radio hits, and lawyers—so instead of buying into the Internet, they took Napster to court and raided downloaders' homes. But no matter how many times they won in a courtroom, there were more Napsters by other names. Record stores closed, radio audiences dropped, payola dried up and, most important of all, in the offices of the Big Four record labels, expense accounts shriveled.

The labels' response, or lack of it, might have been a lesson to the studios. But the MPAA formed MovieLabs to develop anti-piracy techniques and announced arrests across the US for viewers who camcorded *Transformers* (2007). Lawsuits of *FOMDB.com*, *MovieRumor.com*, and *RealNetworks.com* followed. Meanwhile, the studios drafted plans for theaters to go digital and 3D. "We have to adapt, or we'll become dinosaurs," said Warner Bros.' Barry Meyer.[2] The major studios appeared to be weathering new technology far better than the major labels. Said MPAA CEO Dan Glickman: "From the threat and eventual reality of a writers' strike to the global impact of film theft to concerns over the economy, the film industry faced significant challenges in 2007. But, ultimately, we got our Hollywood ending."[3]

Box-office numbers—bolstered by inroads into Russia, China, and Latin America—didn't tell the entire story. DVD revenues were disappearing, along with broadcast sales, as Netflix and illegal subscription services made films readily available. In 2010 the number of tickets sold in North America was the lowest since 1996. And studios were increasingly less important to the corporations that own them "While we enjoy thinking about the film business, the reality is that film doesn't matter nearly as much to the stocks of media conglomerates as it previously had," said a 2010 report by Barclays Capital. The report estimated that Warner Bros. (a subsidiary of Time Warner), Paramount (Viacom), Disney (the Walt Disney Company), and 20th Century Fox (the News Corporation) amounted to just ten percent of the value of their parent companies. Another report, in Global Media Intelligence, noted that Universal Studios was of little consequence in Comcast's decision to take over the studio's parent, NBC Universal.[4] In January 2010, the sale of MGM drew offers that were less than half of the $5 billion its consortium ownership paid for it in 2004.

‡

Along with the commercial online challenges to the studios, digital has meant alternatives from outside the system. Film is "on demand," whenever, wherever—laptops, iPods, home theaters, digitized movie theaters. Digital can mean distributing directly to an independent theater and bypassing costly prints and distributors, an appealing prospect for independents who have been burned by the established process. Julie Dash tells me that she loves the digital upheaval "because it puts the studios on notice; the gatekeepers are already dinosaurs, even if they're twenty-five years old."

At first digital was used for special effects, but as the technology quickly developed, it was adopted by every kind of independent, from Peter Greenaway's boundary-breaking *The Tulse Luper Suitcases* (2003) (which includes three features, a TV series, ninety-two DVDs, a website, and gallery exhibitions); to Steven Soderbergh's *Bubble* (2005), which shattered the window between theatrical and online release; to Alexandr Sokurov's *Russian Ark* (2002), which realized the potential of the single, sustained long shot. And digital technology is readily accessible. "If you're in Africa and there's no lab, you can still make a feature film," John Sayles says. "I've always been a real film lover," says Bruce Sweeney, "but with the advent of the RED camera, you end up with exactly what you had before, but you get there at a third of the price." After a negligible Canadian theatrical run, Sweeney's *American Venus* went to the New York-based Independent Film Channel where 20,000 viewers paid to see it. "The numbers are low, and it's niche-audience stuff, but I'm still excited that I can find a home for what I'm doing now in the States because if you don't have recognizable names you're not going to get theatrical." Distributing a movie online, however, doesn't necessarily mean it will be more popular than it would have been before the new technology. When everyone's got a digital camera—there were 10,000 submissions to Sundance in 2011—it's easy to get lost in the massive shuffle, and there are unresolved issues. "There is a side to digital that is pure, which is great, but you want to be able to pay your actors. How do you get anything back from it? There are some problems; it's still developing," Sayles notes.

Still, the home-viewing pioneered in Romania may soon become the way audiences watch movies everywhere. "I think that's the future of cinema—that theaters and cinemas will eventually disappear, and screening will take place at home," Catherine Breillat says. "We've seen the success of specialty TV channels around the world. I think that's the possible salvation for independent cinema. We'll reach an audience; it'll be a specialty audience, but an audience that can see our films whenever they choose to."

‡

While some independents explore online distribution, others remain committed to freeing up the screens. Like the Spanish peasants demanding immediate freedom in his *Land and Freedom*, Ken Loach takes no half measures when it comes to movie theaters. "We shouldn't lose sight of the main objective, which is that cinemas—a valid and, I think, permanent medium—should be able to show a diverse range of films from all across the world," Loach says. "My feeling is that people like you and me, people who are interested in the future of cinema, shouldn't be satisfied with minimum demands because they've been shown not to work. I think the only thing that will really work is a change in ownership in the cinemas." He points to Norway, where 149 municipalities own and operate local theaters, and to a resolution calling for the nationalization of theaters that Britain's film workers' union passed in the 1970s. To Loach, a movie theater should be a public place, like a park or library. "It doesn't have to lose money," he says. "It can be commercially viable. And it doesn't mean that American films would never be shown, it just means that others would, and [US movies] wouldn't be allowed to dominate. If a library only had American airport novels, you'd think it wasn't a very good library. Or if an art gallery only showed one or two mainstream American painters, you'd think it was a bit limited. We should have a vision of cinema that has the breadth of a good library, and this will not happen unless the cinemas are owned and controlled and programmed by the community."

Axelle Ropert and Tom DiCillo aren't about to give up on theaters either. The French New Wave was born in a cinematheque, and Ropert celebrates the "passion" for cinema that comes with watching a great movie in a crowded theater. "Downloading doesn't accomplish the same thing." Says DiCillo:

> It would be detrimental to be coming from the point of view, "Oh, those were the good old days." I'm just saying that, from the beginning, theater, music, opera, and film were communal experiences, and that's where the power was. To me, it is the only real church that there is, the only religion I am interested in: you get a group of people in a dark room and they watch [the movie] together. They experience it and each of them goes somewhere. It is so disappointing to see the screen of visibility for films constantly shrinking. The only things guaranteed to get onto that big screen are these pieces of shit that are like someone cuts open the top of your head and removes your brain. It's extremely frustrating for a filmmaker.

Not only do Canadians, for example, not get to see their own country's films in theaters, they're seeing less of other countries' films. In the 1960s, European auteurs would have long runs in North American theaters, but now foreign films, with rare exceptions, are ghettoized to film festivals.[5] Would anyone other than festival devotees have heard of

*Director Francisco Vargas (left) during the making of* The Violin. *Courtesy Francisco Vargas, Cámara Carnal Films.*

Truffaut or Kurosawa had they arrived today? Some discerning movie-goers get their annual "hit" during their local festival and then don't go to a theater for another year. ("I don't know what the festivals do for someone now that you can get your film seen online," Larry Kent says. "I mean, festivals don't pay you, and you get far more eyeballs by putting it on the Internet. We keep hearing about independent films being bought at festivals, but those usually have very well-known actors in them.")

No battle for the screens is complete without mention of the quota. When Mexico repealed its quota after entering NAFTA in the 1990s, its film industry collapsed overnight from 100 features a year to five. "The sad condition of the Mexican film industry will continue if our film legislation is not changed," Francisco Vargas says. "If the Mexican state does not implement measures to protect our cinema, there will never be an industry ... France, Spain, Brazil, Argentina, etc., have done this; their film industries are in a much better situation." In South Korea, the quota meant more domestic production, but without provisions supporting non-commercial films—a quota within a quota—it mostly benefits local versions of US producers. "Theater owners want to show commercial, successful films—based on money logic, not cultural logic," says Seo Won-tae. "So the quota should protect various films, including commercial film, independent film, experimental film."

Catherine Breillat notes that American distributors rarely allow foreign films in US theaters, while flooding foreign screens with studio films. "I think that in Africa, Europe, and Asia, the same laws that America applies to the rest of the world should be applied to American films," she says. "We should apply quotas on how many American films can be bought. We should also apply laws that regulate how much Americans can spend on marketing their films so that they don't make it impossible for national films to achieve any recognition."

⸸

"I remember traveling down Highway 61, and we were thinking about making *Highway 61*," Don McKellar says. The Canadian filmmaker hadn't seen the American towns he was passing by before but had watched their facsimiles mythologized onscreen a million times. "And when I saw them I thought, 'These are really no more interesting than Sudbury.'" Sudbury is a mining town in Northern Ontario that, to McKellar, "looked like the moon because it was devastated by the steel industry and pollution—not so great for living purposes but sort of an amazing, striking place." McKellar and his friends were determined to make a Canadian film ("just out of perversity and things"), so his script for *Highway 61* begins in Sudbury.

In opposition to globalization, which does to local culture what industry did to Sudbury, is internationalism, which is the interaction of local cultures—the local as universal. It's François Truffaut making the whole world fall in love with Paris; it's Mike Leigh's London, Susan Seidelman's New York, or Cristian Mungiu's Bucharest. It's the working woman in the British New Wave's *Room at the Top* who can see the "top of the world" from her rooftop above hard-scrabble North of England streets. It's Dolores del Rio returning home to act in the quintessential Mexican story, *María Candelaria*. It's Im Kwon-taek meticulously recreating lost Korean culture in *Seopyeonje*, or Cristi Puiu ripping a story from Bucharest newspapers and making it into a film that launches the Romanian New Wave, or new waves of auteurs, from Jean-Paul Civeyrac to Axelle Ropert, continuing to tell consummate French stories.

Corneliu Porumboiu is not about to follow the money out of Romania. "I can't speak for others, but I am not thinking to work abroad. I can't say that I will stay here forever, but now I want to make my movies here. I love to write my stories and to shoot them." Tom Scholte's been conjuring ways to shoot Canadian while thinking internationally since co-starring in Larry Kent's *Hamster Cage* (2005), a film about incest, murder, and worse inside a typical family of dysfunctional Canadian intellectuals. "It played a film festival in Scandinavia and got runner-up for the People's Choice Award. It was a huge wakeup call for me. Those awards in North American festivals go to soft, feel-good movies. As long as there isn't a quota system, thinking you're just going to win over Canadian audiences is a dead end. Now I think it's about finding a way to make the film you want to make and sending it out into the world—any city you go to, any country you go to, you find that underground." But Scholte's stories will be Canadian. "It's beyond even some kind of ideological position. Anything that I make that isn't about where I'm actually from or people that I actually know or isn't set in locations that I understand would be so full of shit."

Sally Potter is curious about new definitions of "local" communities of interest being created online. "I've always been interested in exploring the identity of exiles, migrants, and those that don't fit in with whatever culture they're supposed to be part of. So it's traveling local. But the pressures of the globalized marketplace are to make something that appeals to everybody. One of the things that's interesting about the Internet is that people make their own localities or find a niche within this enormous plethora of information; it suggests a different way of defining what local is. Communities can gather internationally around something that interests them, rather than geographically around something that's just where they happen to be." In film, the specific or local as universal can mean more than a particular place. Just as a city—François Truffaut's Paris or Woody Allen's New York—can seem universal, a story about a specific race (*Killer of Sheep*) or gender (*Orlando*) or sexual orientation (*Milk*) can also be universal and enjoyed by far-flung audiences.

As the studio system narrows, those specifics are afforded the same disrespect it gives local culture. "There are a lot of good independent female directors, but in the studio system, more and more films are geared toward special effects and action and comic-book heroes, and women don't get asked to do those kinds of movies," Susan Seidelman says. "As more of those kinds of movies are getting made by the corporate powers that be, it decreases the opportunities for female directors." Potter isn't impressed with talk about advances for women in the film industry. "A lot of that is very superficial," she says.

> A lot of what I encountered when I was starting out doesn't
> happen anymore. Then, people didn't mind at all saying
> things like, 'Women don't make movies, dear.' Now people
> know what is acceptable to say, but the facts speak more
> loudly about the actual proportion of women who really
> make it through and manage to make films. They [cost] large
> sums of money, even on the very low-budget end of things,
> and therefore it's much more difficult for women to be
> considered the ones who can tell the story, hold the money,
> be captain of the ship. It's an enormously difficult barrier to
> break through. There are quite a few women who have made
> one or maybe two feature films, and then they just disappear.

‡

So the future of cinema will be in theaters *and* online. There is no end
to creative solutions, including quotas, online distribution, nationalization, Big Miss Moviola, local storytelling, self-distribution, a box-office
levy, and independent digitized theaters. Tom Scholte imagines a new
kind of vertically integrated studio system—all digital with filmmaker-
owned-and-operated theaters. ("My idea is that it happens on a really
local level.") Alex Cox thinks that "maybe we should try to create films
for a regional audience rather than a national one, which tends to favor
[films that are] very fast moving, fast editing, made in English, lots of
music—you know, that kind of Hollywood storytelling, and that kind
of value system as well." John Cassavetes' appeal for contributions on
late-night radio is now called "crowd funding," and it's done via *indi-
egogo.com, cinereach.org,* and *kickstarter.com.* "I could definitely see doing
movies outside the whole system," Miranda July tells me. "You can't
make an indie movie right now without having those conversations."

New models are everywhere, but some things about the movies
haven't changed. "I don't believe, 'Oh, I'm going to make a low-budget
movie because I have a camera,'" says Susan Seidelman. "To me, the
genesis is always the story I want to tell and the best way to tell it."
The Mumblecore filmmakers have access to different technology than
she had when she made *Smithereens* in 1982, "but they're telling stories
about their lives," says Seidelman. "You sense these stories are their
stories."

*Susan Seidelman behind the camera. Courtesy Susan Seidelman.*

For Andrew Bujalski, the focus is on the film itself, not on where it may take his career.

> I always thought that my greatest weapon was that I wasn't putting the sustainability of a career first. For most people, with a certain amount of wisdom and sense, that usually is top priority. You go into a film thinking, how am I going to make this film so that it can make its money back, or make enough of a splash that I'll be able to do the next one, and then the next one? I'll go bigger, bigger, bigger until I'll have a good career—whether you're dreaming of being Steven Spielberg or Gus Van Sant. Most people shoot for that, but I always thought that I would be better off if I made sustainability my last priority, that it opened up a lot more options for the film. I make as much effort as I can to get the film to bring money in, but I always put that off until the film is done, and this lets me make the film that other people aren't going to make.

As we wrap, Bujalski adds, "It's never *not* been difficult. You can always say that everybody had it so great thirty or forty years ago, but you name the greatest filmmakers who ever lived and all of them strug-

*Andrew Bujalski (left) brings anti-romantic New York comedy into the 21st century with* Mutual Appreciation. *Photograph by Ethan Vogl. Courtesy of Andrew Bujalski.*

gled, all of them were up against a commercial culture that didn't make it easy for them. So in that sense, nothing's changed. The struggle goes on and, every once in awhile, great films come out of the muck."

Henry Jaglom, in his way, has been making Mumblecore movies since his first film in 1971. He has stayed outside the studio system, maintaining the creative autonomy he had on *A Safe Place*, at his best when crossing narrative and documentary in movies such as *Eating* (1990), "a very serious comedy about women and food," or exploring relationships improv-style in *Venice/Venice* (1992), which follows an indie filmmaker from the Venice (Italy) Film Festival to his home in Venice (California). "I've just been insistent—no matter what else I do or what else I have to give up, it'll be my film. It is not ninety-nine percent important to me, it is 100 percent important. You love it or you hate it—every frame of the film is mine. Would you ask a painter to let somebody else choose the colors in a painting? To me, it's just completely incomprehensible."

‡

A half century after the blacklist, Walter Bernstein hasn't stopped writing scripts or espousing socialism. "I believe there are the people who run the world and there are the people who make the world run. And you choose between which of those you want to be part of or support." Adds Sally Potter: "I think that everywhere, everything has become a product with a price in a market, and therefore everything has a price and nothing has a value." And having witnessed the privatization of Mexican cinema, Francisco Vargas isn't buying into free-market platitudes either.

> The large film monopolies sustain and defend the idea that the laws of the market are the ones that determine the situation of world cinema, the notorious supply and demand theory. It is a stupid and false truth, and we must go against it. Nowhere in the laws of the market do we find good intentions or just causes or social benefits or identity, or the cultural benefits that are created when a country has its own cinema. Who said that cinema has to be ruled only by the laws of the market, and why do we have to respect something that only benefits a few and has a negative impact on so many? It is absurd.

‡

Years ago, a filmmaker told me that one film can't change the world. "But one film can change a few people's whole world," Sarah Polley says. And collectively, it's one part of a long cultural assault on consciousness, by film and art and music and literature that, over time, has changed how you and me and everyone we know sees everything from race to sexuality. Look hard enough and you can see a new world being born in the clenched fists of Ken Loach's Spanish Civil War volunteers and in Mike Leigh's improvved politics of everyday life. Look closely at *Shadows*' Lelia Goldoni and thousands more marching down Hollywood Boulevard for striking writers in 2007, and you'll see defiant pickets surrounding Warner Bros. in 1945. Just as Alfonso Cuarón, Gus Van Sant, and Susan Seidelman carry with them the memory of their first independent shoots as a reminder of what can be, good ideas don't die; they move from country to country, scene to scene, film lover to film lover. Whether it's called Mumblecore or Romanian New Wave or nothing at all, new forms of community are forming, and in the early years of the twenty-first century, it's as if the French New Wave is everywhere.

So it's a fine time to be a filmmaker. And to challenge studio power. The struggle for independents can seem unending. "But on the other hand," says Mike Leigh, "the tectonic plates are shifting at a deeper level because there is no question that in the future people are going to make films and show films and see films in different ways. I like to think—as much as I love big screens and celluloid and all the rest of it—that the Hollywood dinosaur will actually become extinct."

You and your friends, however, will be left standing. And shooting.

# Endnotes

INTRODUCTION

1. Dave McNary, "Scribes chase blurb bonanza: Product placement perturbs," *Variety*, November 13, 2005.
2. Stephen Galloway, "Dialogue: Alfonso Cuaron," *The Hollywood Reporter*, March 12, 2007.
3. Alan Lomax, *Folk Song Style and Culture* (New Brunswick, NJ: Transaction Books, 1968), 4.
4. Denise Mann, *Hollywood Independents: The Postwar Talent Takeover* (Minneapolis: University of Minnesota Press, 2008), 237.
5. John Trumpbour, *Selling Hollywood to the World* (New York: Cambridge University Press, 2002), 244.
6. "The Independents," Indie Diehards, *Variety*, September 8, 2004.

CHAPTER ONE

1. "Film Strike Riot Ended by Police," *Los Angeles Times*, October 5, 1945.
2. Gerald Horne, *Class Struggle in Hollywood* (Austin: University of Texas Press, 2001), 182.
3. Revier Films ad, *The Moving Picture Word*, January 7, 1911.
4. Douglas Gomery, *The Hollywood Studio System* (London: BFI Publishing, 2005), 14.
5. Ibid., 47.
6. John Drinkwater, *The Life and Adventures of Carl Laemmle* (New York: Amo Press, 1978), 70.
7. Gomery, *The Hollywood Studio System*, 19.
8. Trumpbour, *Selling Hollywood*, 227.
9. Jill Hills, *The Struggle for Control of Global Communication* (Urbana: University of Illinois Press, 2002), 249.
10. Kerry Segrave, *American Films Abroad: Hollywood's Domination of the World's Movie Screens from the 1890s to the Present* (Jefferson, NC: McFarland, 1997), 45.
11. Robert Murphy, ed., *The British Cinema Book* (London: British Film Institute, 2009), 195.
12. Trumpbour, *Selling Hollywood*, 66.
13. Ibid., 63.
14. John Izod, *Hollywood and the Box Office, 1895–1986* (New York: Columbia University Press, 1989), 69.
15. Michael Asimow and Shannon Mader, *Law and Popular Culture* (New York: Peter Lang, 2004), 22.

16. Tom Sito, *Drawing the Line: The Untold Story of the Animation Unions from Bosko to Bart Simpson* (Lexington: University Press of Kentucky, 2006), 139.
17. William Young and Nancy Young, *Great Depression in America: A Cultural Encyclopedia* (Westport, CT: Greenwood Press, 2007), 285.
18. Steven J. Ross, *Working-class Hollywood: Silent Film and the Shaping of Class in America* (Princeton, NJ: Princeton University Press, 1999), 62.
19. Louis B. Perry and Richard S. Perry, *A History of the Los Angeles Labor Movement* (Berkeley: University of California Press, 1963), 324.
20. Horne, *Class Struggle,* 39.
21. Sito, *Drawing the Line,* 63.
22. Steven J. Ross, *Movies and American Society* (Oxford: Blackwell Publishing, 2002), 61.
23. Gomery, *The Hollywood Studio System,* 185.
24. Sito, *Drawing the Line,* 63.
25. Ibid., 122.
26. Ibid., 138.
27. "L.A. Then and Now: Mobsters Muscled Into Film Industry," *Los Angeles Times*, January 2, 2000.
28. "Stars, Directors, Writers in Move to End Film Strike," *Hollywood Citizen-News*, March 13, 1945.
29. Horne, *Class Struggle*, 53.
30. Ibid., 162.
31. "Studio Strikers Defy A.F.L. Head," *Los Angeles Times*, March 17, 1945.
32. "Strike Stands Made Plain," *Los Angeles Examiner*, March 17, 1945.
33. Conference of Studio Unions, *To Our Fellow Workers* (n.p.: 1945).
34. "High I.A.T.S.E. Chiefs Defied by Members," *Los Angeles Times*, March 28, 1945.
35. Horne, *Class Struggle,*168.
36. Ibid.
37. "Studio Rioting Shifts to Republic," *Los Angeles Times*, October 4, 1946.
38. "New Violence at Studios," *Los Angeles Examiner*, October 15, 1945.
39. "2 More Studios, RKI-Pathe and Columbia, Close," *Los Angeles Times*, October 13, 1945.
40. "Bowron, Biscailuz Berated by Union," *Los Angeles Herald Express,* October 11, 1945.
41. "Studios Order 936 Off Lots in Union Row," *Los Angeles Times*, September 24, 1946.

42. "Conspiracy Charge Jails Sorrell," *Los Angeles Times*, December 19, 1946.

43. "Kidnapped Sorrell back; says 'I know who paid them off'," *Los Angeles Daily News*, March 6, 1947.

44. Horne, *Class Struggle,* 41.

45. "IATSE Praises Mayor's Action in Movie Strike," *Hollywood Citizen-News,* October 15, 1946.

CHAPTER TWO

1. Will Irwin, *The House That Shadows Built* (Garden City, NY: Double-day, 1928), 280.

2. Yannis Tziourmakis, *American Independent Cinema* (Edinburgh: Edinburgh University Press, 2006), 28.

3. Clinton Heylin, *Despite the System: Orson Welles versus the Hollywood Studios* (Chicago: A Cappella Books, 2005), 152.

4. Horne, *Class Struggle,* 57.

5. Victor S. Navasky, *Naming Names* (New York: Penguin, 1991), 79.

6. Trumpbour, *Selling Hollywood,* 76.

7. Steven MIntz and Randy Roberts, eds., *Hollywood's America: Twentieth-Century America Through Film* (Malden, MA: Wiley-Blackwell, 2010), 172.

8. Stephen Vaughn, *Ronald Reagan in Hollywood: Movies and Politics* (New York: Cambridge University Press, 1994), 159.

9. Horne, *Class Struggle,* 136.

10. Saverio Giovacchini, *Hollywood Modernism* (Philadelphia: Temple University Press, 2001), 175.

11. Trumpbour, *Selling Hollywood,* 92.

12. John Kenneth White, *Still Seeing Red* (Boulder, CO: Westview Press, 1998), 32.

13. J.A. Aberdeen, *Hollywood Renegades* (Los Angeles: Cobblestone Entertainment, 2000), 179.

14. Welles, Orson, "Orson Welles Writing about Orson Welles," *Stage,* February, 1941, 35.

15. "Welles—The Man and His Art," *Cahiers du Cinema in English* (1966) 5.

16. Welles, Orson, "The Third Audience," *Sight & Sound,* January–March, 1954.

17. "Films Fight for Life—Byrnes," *The Hollywood Reporter,* February 12, 1948.

18. "Indies Hail High Court for 'Breaking Backbone of Trust,'" *Variety* May 5, 1948.

CHAPTER THREE
1. Patrick McGilligan and Paul Buhle, *Tender Comrades* (New York: St. Martin's Press, 1997), 220.
2. Trumpbour, *Selling Hollywood*, 267.
3. Irwin M. Wall, *The United States and the Making of Postwar France 1945–54* (New York: Cambridge University Press, 1991), 118.
4. Paul Swann, *The Hollywood Feature in Postwar Britain* (Routledge, 1987), 90.
5. Swann, *Hollywood Feature*, 101.
6. Kerry Segrave, *American Films Abroad: Hollywood's Domination of the World's Movie Screens from the 1890s to the Present* (Jefferson, NC: McFarland, 1997), 179.
7. Connie Bruck, *When Hollywood Had a King* (New York: Random House, 2003), 113.
8. Aberdeen, *Hollywood Renegades*, 187.
9. Ibid., 185.
10. Segrave, *American Films Abroad*, 316.
11. Trumpbour, *Selling Hollywood*, 105.
12. John Huston, *An Open Book* (New York: Knopf, 1980), 353.
13. David Zurawik, *The Jews of Prime Time* (Hanover, NH: University Press of New England, 2003), 45.

CHAPTER FOUR
1. David Spaner, "Hoffman Holds Court," *Vancouver Province*, October 20, 2000.
2. David Dalton, *James Dean: The Mutant King* (San Francisco: Straight Arrow Books, 1974), 198.

CHAPTER FIVE
1. "Cooperative," *New York Times*, January 20, 1957.
2. Ann Charters, *Beat Down to Your Soul* (New York: Penguin Books, 2001), xxix.
3. Denise Mann, *Hollywood Independents* (Minneapolis: University of Minnesota Press, 2008), 53.
4. Ibid., 58.
5. Ibid., 62.
6. Cecil Smith, "Actor Directs No-Script Film," *Los Angeles Times*, January 31, 1960.
7. Jonas Mekas, "The Film-makers Cooperative: A Brief History." http://www.film-makerscoop.com/history.htm

8. Patricia Bosworth, "Cassavetes: Why Do Marriages Go Sour?" *New York Times,* December 1, 1968.
9. "Cineastes de notre temps." Interview with John Cassavetes, in *Faces*. DVD. Directed by John Cassavetes (New York: The Criterion Collection, 2004).

CHAPTER SIX

1. Domenic Priore, *Riot on Sunset Strip* (London: Jawbone Press, 2007), 248.
2. Ibid., 251.
3. Abbie Hoffman, *Woodstock Nation* (New York: Vintage Books, 1969), 156.
4. "Easy Rider: Shaking the Cage," in *America Lost and Found*. DVD. Directed by Charles Kiselyak (New York: The Criterion Collection, 2010).
5. Peter Watkins, "Punishment Park" in "Films." Peter Watkins website. http://pwatkins.mnsi.net/punishment.htm.

CHAPTER SEVEN

1. Thomas Colbath and Steven Blush, "Jim Jarmusch: Interview," *Seconds Magazine* 37, 1996.
2. Nick Zedd, "Cinema of Transgression Manifesto," at the Official Nick Zedd website. http://www.nickzedd.com/

CHAPTER EIGHT

1. Peter Biskind, *Down and Dirty Pictures* (New York: Simon & Schuster, 2004), 335.
2. "Remembering DIY Queen Sarah Jacobson, 1971–2004." *indieWIRE,* February 18, 2004.
3. Jack Valenti "The 'Foreign Service' of the Motion Picture Association of America," *Journal of the Producers Guild of America*, March 10, 1968.
4. Gomery, *The Hollywood Studio System*, 295.
5. David Spaner, *Dreaming in the Rain: How Vancouver Became Hollywood North by Northwest* (Vancouver: Arsenal Pulp Press, 2003), 202.

CHAPTER NINE

1. Rémi Fournier Lanzoni, *French Cinema: From Its Beginnings to the Present* (New York: Contimuum, 2005), 38.
2. Naomi Greene, *The French New Wave: A New Look* (London: Wallflower Press, 2007), 27.

3. Greene, *The French New Wave*, 5.

4. Michel Marie and Richard John Neupert, *The French New Wave: An Artistic School* (Malden, MA: Blackwell Publishing, 2003), 87.

5. Greene, *The French New Wave*, 63.

6. Murray Bookchin, *Post-Scarcity Anarchism* (Palo Alto, CA: Ramparts Press, 1971), 262.

7. *Stolen Kisses*. DVD. Directed by François Truffaut. Special Feature: Newsreel footage from Cannes 1968 (New York: The Criterion Collection, 2003).

8. Richard Eder, "Truffaut and the Enigmatic Woman," *New York Times*, October 11, 1981.

9. Walter S. Ross, "Splicing Together Jean-Luc Godard," *Esquire*, July 1969.

10. "Grim, Shocking, Didactic, a New New Wave Rolls In," *New York Times*, November 22, 1998; "La nouvelle Nouvelle Vague," *Variety*, May 11, 2003.

11. Bruce Alderman, "Lang Defends Art Policies," *Variety*, March 30, 1992.

12. Michael Williams and Chris Fuller, "France Adamant on GATT," *Variety*, October 18, 1993.

13. Alan Citron, "GATT: Wasserman Wins, Valenti Loses," *Los Angeles Times*, December 17, 1993.

14. Wheeler Winston Dixon, *Visions of the Apocalypse: Spectacles of Destruction in American Cinema* (London: Wallflower Press, 2003), 112.

15. Etan Vlessing, "Violent femmes," *Hollywood Reporter*, September 19–25, 2000.

## CHAPTER TEN

1. "*if...*" Directed by Lindsay Anderson. DVD. Special Feature: Interviews with Stephen Frears and Ian Rakoff (The Criterion Collection, 2007).

2. Neil Sinyard, "The Sporting Life: The Lonely Heart," *Current*, January 21, 2008.

3. Murphy, *The British Cinema Book*, 40.

4. Sue Harper and Vincent Porter, *British Cinema of the 1950s: The Decline of Deference* (Oxford: Oxford University Press, 2003), 190.

5. "*if...*" DVD. Special Feature: Interview with Malcom McDowell.

6. Tony Shaw, *British Cinema and the Cold War: The State, Propaganda and Consensus* (London: I.B. Tauris, 2006), 198.

7. Wade Major, "The Passionate Populist," *Entertainment Today*, March 29–April 4, 1996.

8. Amy Raphael, ed., *Mike Leigh on Mike Leigh* (London: Faber and Faber, 2008), 46.

9. Kenneth Turan, "The Case for Mike Leigh," *Los Angeles Times*, September 22, 1996.

10. Raphael, *Mike Leigh on Mike Leigh*, 207.

11. UK Film Council, *2010 Statistical Yearbook* (London: UK Film Council, 2010), 14. http://www.ukfilmcouncil.org.uk/media/pdf/e/q/Statistical_Yearbook_2010.pdf

12. *2010 Statistical Yearbook*, 13.

13. Murphy, *The British Cinema Book*, 383.

14. Potter, Sally, "Money?" http://www.sallypotter.com/money

## CHAPTER ELEVEN

1. Heejin Koo, "South Korean Actor, Star of 'Old Boy,' Returns Medal to Gov't," *Bloomberg.com*, February 7, 2006.

2. Paolo Bertolin, "Koreans, French Fight Hollywood Domination," *Korea Times*, May 5, 2006.

3. Tom Vick, *Asian Cinema: A Field Guide* (New York: HarperCollins, 2007), 151.

4. Ibid., 153.

5. Frank Segers, "Korea Battles Pay Off For U.S. Pix," *Variety*, February 15, 1990.

6. Lorenza Munoz and Josh Friedman, "Coming Attractions," *Los Angeles Times*, November 5, 1976.

7. Patrick Fraser, "Korea fights Hollywood," *Screen International*, September 8, 2000.

8. Patrick Fraser, "Q&A: Yang Gihwan," *Screen International*, August 10, 2001.

9. Hanna Lee, "S. Korean Quotas Split Gov't, Pick Biz," *Variety*, August 17, 1998.

10. Ibid.

11. Mark Schilling, "MPA Rejects Korean Aim to Please," *Screen International*, August 20, 1999.

12. Mark Schilling, "Korea's Spring," *Screen International*, November 5, 1999.

13. Dana Harris, "Valenti Offers S. Korea Film 'Renaissance' Plan," *The Hollywood Reporter*, March 29, 1999.

14. Christopher Alford, "Goliath Balks at David's Quotas," *Variety*, August 9–15, 1999.

15. Mark Russell, "Homegrown Pics Top Korea," *The Hollywood Reporter*, January 2, 2007.
16. Darcy Paquet, "Koreans Cut Pic Quotas," *Variety*, January 30, 2006.
17. Barbara Demick, "US, South Korea in a Cinema War," *Los Angeles Times*, October 31, 2005.
18. Fraser, "Q & A: Yang Gihwan."
19. *Woman Is the Future of Man*. DVD. Directed by Hong Sangsoo. Special Feature: Interview with Sung Hyunah (New York: New Yorker Video, 2007).
20. Fraser, "Q&A: Yang Gihwan."

CHAPTER TWELVE
1. Andrea Noble, *Mexican National Cinema* (Oxon. England: Routledge: 2005), 49.
2. Michael O'Boyle, "Mexican Business on Notice," *Variety*, February 24, 2007.
3. Noble, *Mexican National Cinema*, 31.
4. Ibid., 87.
5. Sergio de la Mora, *Cinemachismo: Masculinities and Sexuality in Mexican Film* (Austin: University of Texas Press, 2006), 175.
6. O'Boyle, "Mexican Business."
7. Elisàbeth Malkin, "Mexican Film: High Art, Low Budget," *New York Times*, July 15, 2003.
8. O'Boyle, "Mexican Business."
9. Anna Marie de la Fuente, "Mexican Industry Anger at Valenti," *Screen International*, February 21, 2003.
10. Ken Bensinger, "Mexican Filmmakers Denounce Gov't Plan," *Variety*, November 12, 2003.
11. Ken Bensinger, "Mexico May Nix Pix," *Variety*, November 10, 2003.
12. Chris Kraul and Lorenza Munoz, "Mexico Says It's a Wrap," *Los Angeles Times*, November 12, 2003.
13. Ed Morales, "Pulp Nonfiction," *Village Voice*, April 3, 2001.
14. Lorenza Munoz, "Cuaron: Outspoken Director," *Los Angeles Times*, April, 2002.
15. Lorenza Munoz, "A New Mexican Revolution," *Los Angeles Times*, March 10, 2002.
16. Sheila Johnston, "The Arriba Has Arrived," *The Times of London*, April 11, 2002.

17. John Powers, "Great Expectations," *LA Weekly*, March 14, 2002.
18. Lorenza Munoz and Reed Johnson, "Mexico's Creative Brain Drain," *Los Angeles Times*, February 24, 2007.
19. Powers, "Great Expectations."
20. Reed Johnson, "A Bond Beyond Borders," *Los Angeles Times*, October 1, 2006.
21. Ginger Thompson, "Gael Garcia Bernal: Just Another Homeless Young Star," *New York Times*, September 19, 2004.

CHAPTER THIRTEEN
1. Mihai Viteazul, "Michael the Brave." In *The Cinema of the Balkans*, edited by Dina Iordanova (London: Wallflower Press, 2006), 79.
2. Katja Hofmann, "Romanian Cinema on the Rise," *Variety*, June 22, 2007.
3. Raphael, *Mike Leigh on Mike Leigh*, 194.
4. John Horn, "Filmmakers Are Swept Away by Romania," *Los Angeles Times*, October 2, 2005.
5. Ibid.
6. Dennis Lim, "Romanian Cinema Seizes the Spotlight," *Los Angeles Times*, January 31, 2008.

CHAPTER FOURTEEN
1. "*Barbarian Invasions* Wins Six Genie awards," *CTV News*, May 2, 2004. http://www.ctv.ca/CTVNews/Entertainment/20040502/genie_awards_040501/)
2. Kirwan Cox, "The Majors and the Mandarins: Through the Years," *Cinema Canada* 22, October, 1975.
3. Ian Jarvie, *Hollywood's Overseas Campaign: The North Atlantic Movie Trade, 1920–1950* (Port Hope, ON: Cambridge University Press, 1992), 35.
4. George Melnyk, *One Hundred Years of Canadian Cinema* (Toronto: University of Toronto Press, 2004), 67.
5. Manjunath Pendakur, *Canadian Dreams and American Control: The Political Economy of the Canadian Film Industry* (Detroit: Wayne State University Press, 1990), 150.
6. Michael Spencer and Suzan Ayscough, *Hollywood North: Creating the Canadian Motion Picture Industry* (Montreal: Cantos International Publishing, 2003), 111–12.
7. "Canadian Film News," *Cinema Canada*, June/July, 1973.
8. Spencer and Ayscough, 129.

9. Cox, "The Majors and the Mandarins."
10. David Spaner, "Film Workers: How Low Do You Go?" *Vancouver Province*, April 8, 2007.
11. Richard Stursberg, "The ABC of Audience Building in Canada: Film: Can We Do It?" Keynote Address to the Academy of Canadian Cinema & Television, Vancouver, BC, November 13, 2002. http://www.telefilm.gc.ca/upload/flash/Stursberg-Film-speech.pdf.
12. David Spaner, "Will a Canadian Film Scene Step Up to the Plate?" *Vancouver Province*, April 8, 2007.
13. David Spaner, "Indie Mainstay Moves On," *Vancouver Province*, April 8, 2007.

## CHAPTER FIFTEEN
1. "She's Way Sassy," *Sassy*, April 1996.
2. Pamela McClintock, "MPAA: Specialty Films See Rising Costs," *Variety*, March 5, 2008.
3. Thompson, Anne, "Los Angeles Film Festival: Mark Gill on Indie Film Crisis." *Variety*, June 21, 2008.
4. Tim Robey, "The Best Years in the Life of Richard Linklater," *Sight & Sound*, April 2007.
5. Johanna Schneller, "Jason Reitman: An Independent Mind Making Independent Films," *The Globe and Mail*, December 4, 2009.
6. Nicole Sperling, "Twilight Director Pulls Up Stakes. Who'll Take Over Now?" *Entertainment Weekly*, December 19, 2008.

## CHAPTER SIXTEEN
1. David Denby, "Big Pictures," *The New Yorker*, January 8, 2007.
2. Michael Cieply and Brooks Barnes, "In Hollywood, Grappling With Studios' Lost Clout," *New York Times*, January 17, 2010.
3. Ibid.
4. "Americans Are Seeing Fewer and Fewer Foreign Films," *Philadelphia Inquirer*, May 9, 2010.

## Selected References

Aberdeen, J.A. *Hollywood Renegades*. Los Angeles: Cobblestone Entertainment, 2000.

Asimow, Michael and Shannon Mader. *Law and Popular Culture*. New York: Peter Lang, 2004.

Barrow, Sarah and John White. *Fifty Key British Films*. London: Routledge, 2008.

Barzman, Norma. *The Red and the Blacklist*. New York: Nation Books, 2003.

Behlmer, Rudy, ed. *Inside Warner Bros. (1935–1951)*. New York: Viking, 1985.

Bernstein, Walter. *Inside Out*. Cambridge, MA: Da Capo Press, 2000.

Biskind, Peter. *Down and Dirty Pictures*. New York: Simon & Schuster, 2004.

Biskind Peter. *Easy Riders, Raging Bulls*. New York: Touchstone, 1999.

Bookchin, Murray. *Post-Scarcity Anarchism*. Palo Alto, CA: Ramparts Press, 1971.

Bowyer, Justin, ed. *The Cinema of Japan and Korea*. London: Wallflower Press, 2004.

Bruck, Connie. *When Hollywood Had a King*. New York: Random House, 2003.

Buhle, Paul and Dave Wagner. *Blacklisted*. New York: Palgrave MacMillan, 2003.

Buhle, Paul and Dave Wagner. *Radical Hollywood*. New York: New Press, 2002.

Buhle, Paul and Patrick McGilligan. *Tender Comrades*. New York: St. Martin's Griffin, 1999.

Cassavetes, John. "Interview with John Cassavetes," excerpt from "Cinéastes de notre temps." *Faces*. DVD. Directed by John Cassavetes. New York: The Criterion Collection, 2004.

Ceplair, Larry and Steven Englund. *The Inquisition in Hollywood*. Berkeley: University of California Press, 1983.

Charters, Ann. *Beat Down to Your Soul*. New York: Penguin Books, 2001.

Conference of Studio Unions. *To Our Fellow Workers*. n.p.: Conference of Studio Unions, 1945.

Cox, Alex. *X Films: True Confessions of a Radical Filmmaker*. Berkeley: Soft Skull Press, 2008.

Dalton, David. *James Dean: The Mutant King*. San Francisco: Straight Arrow Books, 1974.

Martine Danan. "French Cinema in the Era of Media Capitalism." In *Europe-Russia Conference Series*. London: Sage Productions 2000. Reproduced from *Media, Culture & Society* 22 (2000): 355–64

Davis, Mike. *City of Quartz*. New York: Vintage, 1992.

Dixon, Wheeler Winston. *Visions of the Apocalypse: Spectacles of Destruction in American Cinema*. London: Wallflower Press, 2003.

Drinkwater, John. *The Life and Adventures of Carl Laemmle*. New York: Amo Press, 1978.

"Easy Rider: Shaking the Cage." *America Lost and Found*. DVD. Directed by Charles Kiselyak. New York: The Criterion Collection, 2010.

Frears, Stephen and Ian Rakoff. "Interview with Stephen Frears and Ian Rakoff." *if...* DVD. Directed by Lindsay Anderson. New York: The Criterion Collection, 2007.

Gabler, Neal. *An Empire of Their Own*. New York: Crown, 1988.

Giovacchini, Saverio. *Hollywood Modernism*. Philadelphia: Temple University Press, 2001.

Gomery, Douglas. *The Hollywood Studio System*. London: British Film Institute, 2005.

Greene, Naomi. *The French New Wave: A New Look*. London: Wallflower Press, 2007.

Harper, Sue and Vincent Porter. *British Cinema of the 1950s: The Decline of Deference*. Oxford: Oxford University Press, 2003.

Hays, Matthew. *The View from Here*. Vancouver: Arsenal Pulp Press, 2007.

Heylin, Clinton. *Despite the System: Orson Welles versus the Hollywood Studios*. Chicago: A Cappella Books, 2005.

Higham, Charles. *Brando*. New York: New American Library, 1987.

Hills, Jill. *The Struggle for Control of Global Communication*. Urbana: University of Illinois Press, 2002.

Hoffman, Abbie. *Woodstock Nation*. New York: Vintage Books, 1969.

Horne, Gerald. *Class Struggle in Hollywood*. Austin: University of Texas Press, 2001.

Huston, John. *An Open Book*. New York: Knopf, 1980.

Irwin, Will. *The House That Shadows Built*. Garden City, NY: Doubleday, 1928.

Izod, John. *Hollywood and the Box Office, 1895–1986*. New York: Columbia University Press, 1989.

Jarvie, Ian. *Hollywood's Overseas Campaign: The North Atlantic Movie Trade, 1920–1950*. Port Hope, ON: Cambridge University Press, 1992.

Johnson, Reed. "A Bond Beyond Borders." *Los Angeles Times,* October 1, 2006.

Johnston, Sheila. "The Arriba Has Arrived." *The Times London,* April 11, 2002.

Knopper, Steve. *Appetite for Self-Destruction*. New York: Free Press, 2009.

Lanzoni, Rémi Fournier. *French Cinema: From Its Beginnings to the Present.* New York: Continuum, 2005.

Lax, Eric. *Conversations with Woody Allen.* New York: Alfred A Knopf, 2009.

Leggott, James. *Contemporary British Cinema.* London: Wallflower, 2008.

Litvak, Joseph. *The Un-Americans.* Durham, NC: Duke University Press, 2009.

Lomax, Alan. *Folk Song Style and Culture.* New Brunswick, NJ: Transaction Books, 1968.

Mann, Denise. *Hollywood Independents: The Postwar Talent Takeover.* Minnesota: University of Minnesota Press, 2008.

Marie, Michel and Richard John Neupert. *The French New Wave: An Artistic School.* Malden, MA: Blackwell Publishing, 2003.

McDowell, Malcolm. "Interview with Malcolm McDowell." *if...* DVD. Directed by Lindsay Anderson. New York: The Criterion Collection, 2007.

McGilligan, Patrick and Paul Buhle. *Tender Comrades.* New York: St. Martin's Press, 1997.

Mekas, Jonas. "The Film-makers Cooperative: A Brief History." http://www.film-makerscoop.com/history.htm.

Melnyk, George. *One Hundred Years of Canadian Cinema.* Toronto: University of Toronto Press, 2004.

de la Mora, Sergio. *Cinemachismo: Masculinities and Sexuality in Mexican film.* Austin: University of Texas Press, 2006.

Miller, Toby, Nitin Govil, John McMurria, Richard Maxwell, and Ting Wang. *Global Hollywood 2.* London: British Film Institute, 2005.

Mintz, Steven and Randy Roberts, eds. *Hollywood's America: Twentieth-Century America Through Film.* Malden, MA: Wiley-Blackwell, 2010.

Mottram, James. *The Sundance Kids.* London: Faber and Faber, 2006.

Mundy, John. *The British Musical Film.* Manchester, UK: Manchester University Press, 2007.

Murphy, Robert, ed. *The British Cinema Book.* 3rd ed. London: Palgrave Macmillan, 2009.

Navasky, Victor S. *Naming Names.* New York: Penguin, 1991.

"Newsreel Footage from Cannes 1968." *Stolen Kisses.* DVD. Directed by François Truffaut. New York: The Criterion Collection, 2003.

Noble, Andrea. *Mexican National Cinema.* Oxon, England: Routledge: 2005.

Pendakur, Manjunath. *Canadian Dreams and American Control: The Political Economy of the Canadian Film Industry.* Detroit: Wayne State

University Press, 1990.

Perry, Louis B. and Richard S. Perry. *A History of the Los Angeles Labor Movement*. Berkeley: University of California Press, 1963.

Pollan, Michael. *The Omnivore's Dilemma: A Natural History of Four Meals*. New York: Penguin, 2006.

Porton, Richard, ed. *Arena I: Anarchist Film and Video*. Hastings, East Sussex, UK: ChristieBooks, 2009.

Potter, Sally. "Money?" http://www.sallypotter.com/money

Priore, Domenic. *Riot on Sunset Strip*. London: Jawbone Press, 2007.

Raphael, Amy, ed. *Mike Leigh on Mike Leigh*. London: Faber and Faber, 2008.

Revier Films, advertisement. *The Moving Picture World*. January 7, 1911.

Rhode, Eric. *A History of the Cinema*. New York: Da Capo Press, 1976.

Ross, Steven J. *Movies and American Society*. Oxford: Blackwell Publishing, 2002.

Ross, Steven J. *Working-Class Hollywood: Silent Film and the Shaping of Class in America*. Princeton, NJ: Princeton University Press, 1999.

Segrave, Kerry. *American Films Abroad: Hollywood's Domination of the World's Movie Screens from the 1890s to the Present*. Jefferson, NC: McFarland, 1997.

Shaw, Tony. British *Cinema and the Cold War: The State, Propaganda and Consensus*. London: I.B. Tauris, 2006.

Sito, Tom. *Drawing the Line: The Untold Story of the Animation Unions from Bosko to Bart Simpson*. Lexington: University Press of Kentucky, 2006.

Sklar, Robert. *City Boys*. Princeton, NJ: Princeton University Press, 2001.

Sklar, Robert. *Movie-Made America*. New York. Vintage, 1975.

Spaner, David. *Dreaming in the Rain: How Vancouver Became Hollywood North by Northwest*. Vancouver: Arsenal Pulp Press, 2003.

Spencer, Michael and Suzan Ayscough. *Hollywood North: Creating the Canadian Motion Picture Industry*. Montreal: Cantos International Publishing, 2003.

Sperling, Cass Warner and Cork Millner. *Hollywood Be Thy Name*. Lexington: University Press of Kentucky, 1998.

Stursberg, Richard. "The ABC of Audience Building in Canada: Film: Can We do It?" Keynote Address to the Academy of Canadian Cinema & Television, Vancouver, BC, November 13, 2002. http://www.telefilm.gc.ca/upload/flash/Stursberg-Film-speech.pdf.

Sung Hyunah. "Interview with Sung Hyunah." *Woman Is the Future of Man*. DVD. Directed by Hong Sangsoo. New York: New Yorker Video, 2007.

Swann, Paul. *The Hollywood Feature in Postwar Britain*. London: Routledge, 1987.

Swindell, Larry. *Body and Soul: The John Garfield Story*. New York: William Morrow, 1975.

Trumpbour, John. *Selling Hollywood to the World*. New York: Cambridge University Press, 2002.

Tzioumakis, Yannis. *American Independent Cinema*. New Brunswick, NJ: Rutgers University Press, 2006.

UK Film Council. *2010 Statistical Yearbook*. London: UK Film Council, 2010. http://www.ukfilmcouncil.org.uk/media/pdf/e/q/Statistical_Yearbook_2010.pdf

Vaughn, Stephen. *Ronald Reagan in Hollywood: Movies and Politics*. New York: Cambridge University Press, 1994.

Vick, Tom. *Asian Cinema: A Field Guide*. New York: HarperCollins, 2007.

Viteazul, Mihai. "Michael the Brave." In *The Cinema of the Balkans,* edited by Dina Iordanova, 79. London: Wallflower Press, 2006.

Vogel, Amos. *Film as a Subversive Art*. New York: Random House, 1974.

Wall, Irwin M. *The United States and the Making of Postwar France 1945–54*. New York: Cambridge University Press, 1991.

Wallace, David. *Exiles in Hollywood*. Pompton Plains, NJ: Limelight Editions, 2006.

Watkins, Peter. "Punishment Park" in "Films." http://pwatkins.mnsi.net/punishment.htm.

Willis, Holly. *New Digital Cinema*. London: Wallflower Press, 2008.

Wise, Windham, ed. *Take One's Essential Guide to Canadian Film*. Toronto: University of Toronto Press, 2001.

White, John Kenneth. *Still Seeing Red*. Boulder, CO: Westview Press, 1998.

Winter, Jessica. *The Rough Guide to American Independent Film*. London: Rough Guides, 2006.

Young, William, and Nancy Young. *Great Depression in America: A Cultural Encyclopedia*. Westport, CT: Greenwood Press, 2007.

Zedd, Nick. "Cinema of Transgression Manifesto." http://www.nickzedd.com/.

Zurawik, David. *The Jews of Prime Time*. Hanover, NH: University Press of New England, 2003.

PERIODICALS

*American Cinematographer*

*Cahiers du Cinéma*

*Canadian Journal of Communication*
*Cineaste Magazine*
*Cinema Canada*
*Current*
*Entertainment Today*
*Entertainment Weekly*
*Esquire*
*Europe-Russia Conference Series*
*Fade In*
*Film Comment*
*Filmmaker: The Magazine of Independent Film*
*The Globe and Mail*
*The Guardian*
*Hollywood Citizen-News*
*The Hollywood Reporter*
*Indie Slate*
*The Independent*
*Journal of the Producers Guild of America*
*The Korea Times*
*L.A. Weekly*
*Los Angeles Daily News*
*Los Angeles Examiner*
*Los Angeles Herald-Express*
*Los Angeles Times*
*MovieMaker Magazine*
*Moving Picture World*
*Moving Pictures*
*The New York Times*
*The New Yorker*
*The Philadelphia Inquirer*
*Sassy*
*Screen International*
*Seconds Magazine*
*Sight & Sound*
*STAGE*
*Take One Magazine*
*TimeOut New York*
*The Times London*
*Variety*
*Venice*
*The Village Voice*

# INDEX

Note: page numbers in **bold** indicate photos.